Facing Up to the Risks

FACING UP TO THE RISKS

How Financial Institutions Can Survive and Prosper

Dominic Casserley

McKinsey & Company, Inc.

JOHN WILEY & SONS, INC.

New York • Chichester • Brisbane • Toronto • Singapore

In recognition of the importance of preserving what has been written, it is a
policy of John Wiley & Sons, Inc., to have books of enduring value printed on
acid-free paper, and we exert our best efforts to that end.

Copyright © 1991, 1993 by McKinsey & Company, Inc.
Published by John Wiley & Sons, Inc.

This publication is designed to provide accurate and authoritative information
in regard to the subject matter covered. It is sold with the understanding that
the publisher is not engaged in rendering legal, accounting, or other
professional service. If legal advice or other expert assistance is required, the
services of a competent professional person should be sought. From a
*Declaration of Principles jointly adopted by a Committee of the American Bar
Association and a Committee of Publishers.*

Library of Congress Cataloging-in-Publication Data:

Casserley, Dominic, 1957–
    Facing up to the risks : how financial institutions can survive
and prosper / Dominic Casserley.
        p.   cm.
    Originally published: New York, NY : HarperBusiness, © 1991.
    Includes index.
    ISBN 0-471-59219-6
    1. Financial institutions—United States—Management.
2. Financial institutions—Management.   3. Financial services
industry—Management.   I. Title.
[HG181.C38 1993]
332.1'0973—dc20   92-40871

Printed in the United States of America

10 9 8 7 6 5 4 3 2 1

This book is dedicated
to my mother and father

Acknowledgments

In many respects this book is a team effort; I had the pleasant task of turning team ideas into a book. The teamwork all began back in 1989, when five of us at McKinsey—Paul Allen, Arnab Gupta, Clarence Hahn, Zosia Mucha, and I—ran a project, involving many other colleagues, to examine risk and reward management in financial institutions. Out of that original work came many of the ideas outlined in this book.

Arnab Gupta, Clarence Hahn, another colleague, Steve Rehmus, and I continued working in this area. This book could not have been written without the support and new thinking that Arnab, Clarence, and Steve provided. In addition, Steve and Hut Holahan gave crucial help to me in documenting and checking the facts and references in the text. Further, Will Allman, Joan Kapfer, and Tom Seeman provided me with help on certain sections of the book.

The support provided to me by many of my fellow partners was crucial. In particular, Lowell Bryan's continued encouragement and advice was an essential guide, as it has been throughout my career at McKinsey. Mike Bulkin's and Don Waite's support and assistance were crucial to letting me complete the work. Pete Walker helped me navigate the difficult shoals of the insurance world with a sure touch. Finally, Fred Gluck provided constant encouragement throughout the process.

Many of my fellow partners reviewed portions of this book for clarity and accuracy. They include Carter Bales, Joel Bleeke, Tom Copeland, Peter Flaherty, Gil Marmol, Ted Hall, Robert Kaplan, Jon Katzenbach, Roger Kline, Mike Pritula, Tino Puri, Tom Steiner, and Doug Woodham. I thank them for their wise advice.

Bill Matassoni and Brook Manville had a very direct role in the book. They encouraged me to write it in the first place, and were key supporters throughout the process.

Very special thanks must go to Stuart Flack. Stuart had the unenviable task of editing this book with me as I wrote, and engaging in tactful but lengthy debates about each chapter and the overall flow of the argument. For both his editorial skills and patience I thank him. My publisher at John Wiley, Karl Weber, was also a constant supporter and help throughout the whole process.

The true award for patience, however, must go to my administrative assistant Paula O'Grady. She had to suffer my raw word-processed drafts, reconstruct them, and then process and check iteration after iteration. Many, many thanks, especially for the polite conversions of English spelling.

Finally, this book could not have been written without the support and advice of my wife, Nancy, and the patience of our sons, Edward and Henry. I can never give back the many lost weekends, holidays, and evenings, but I will cherish their love, patience, and advice that run through every page.

Acknowledging all this help, and all that I have overlooked, it still remains true that none of these individuals is responsible for what follows. They provided excellent advice and counsel; all the flaws and errors that may be contained herein are mine alone. Specifically, although McKinsey & Company sponsored the research upon which this book is based, the opinions expressed are my own and do not necessarily reflect those of McKinsey as a whole, my colleagues, or our clients. Of course, the examples used in the text are either drawn from public information, or if drawn from my professional experiences have been disguised to protect client confidentiality.

Contents

Facing Up to the Risks

1

The Financial Firm of the Future: Three Propositions

Not very long ago, the world's financial markets were much cozier than they are today. Interest and foreign exchange rates were pegged, stockbroking commission rates were fixed. Communications were still by memo and letter, with the help of the occasional telephone call. In this environment, banks stuck to collecting deposits and making loans, and made a good living. Insurance companies took in premiums, invested them safely in bonds, and easily took care of the claims from policyholders. Stockbrokers bought and sold shares for their clients, and did some underwriting and merger and acquisition work as well. Skills and performance varied, but everyone knew who his or her competitor was and what was required to make money.

From the mid-1970s onward, however, a combination of deregulation of interest and foreign exchange rates; the tearing down of some boundaries between banking, stockbroking, and insurance; and the introduction of new information and communication technologies has vastly changed this world. More volatile markets and new competitive opportunities introduced a period of great excitement in financial markets. Some competitors expanded activities, and some new industrial competitors such as GE, GM, AT&T, and Sears Roebuck entered markets, attracted by the new freedom of the financial world. New products like swaps, futures, and options appeared, creating new risks and opportunities for competitors.

During the first half of the 1980s, it seemed as if all this change would create a new bonanza for financial firms. Symbolic of this prosperity was the fact that in 1987 Nomura Securities, a stockbroker and investment bank, was Japan's most profitable company. Then the ripples from the October 1987 stock market break, and the impact of the slowdown of growth on real estate markets around the world, created crisis after crisis. The U.S. government had to rescue the savings and loan industry at a cost of over $150 billion, and recapitalize the Bank Insurance Fund. In 1990, nearly $3 billion was needed to recapitalize investment banks like First Boston, Kidder Peabody, Prudential Bache, and Shearson Lehman. The situation in Europe was no better, with even some Swiss banks struggling under the weight of bad loans and trading losses. The costs of such risks as pollution and hurricanes threatened to bring down the venerable Lloyds of London insurance market. Midland Bank of the United Kingdom, weakened by years of losses and low profits, was bought by Hong Kong and Shanghai Bank. In Japan, Nomura had fallen from its perch: in 1991 both the firm's chairman and president resigned over the scandal that the firm had covered some large clients' trading losses, and in 1992 earnings fell to levels far, far below those of 1987 as trading volumes and prices sank in Japan.

Volatile market prices, periods of boom and bust, the opportunities and threats from new technologies, and new, aggressive market entrants—against this background, financial firms wonder what is the recipe for success. What will the financial firm of the future look like? This book describes a foundation for winning firms of the future. Throughout the turbulent 1980s and 1990s, there have been patterns of success and failure that provide guidance for managers of financial firms. Specifically, the book sets out three propositions that can underpin success for financial firms in the future. These propositions apply to all types of financial firms—banks, securities firms, insurance companies, and investment firms alike. In sum, the three propositions require us first to rethink why financial firms exist at all, and then to use this base to determine how they can survive and prosper.

The first proposition, reviewed in Chapters two and three, is that financial firms will win only if they remember that they are fundamentally different from other businesses.

The difference revolves around the fact that risk and reward management is the core skill required for success by financial firms, whereas that is not the case for other types of companies. Of course, most businesses take risk of one form or another. An oil exploration company runs the risk that it will drill only dry holes; a computer or soft drinks company, that nobody will buy its products. But for these consumer and industrial companies, the core skill required for success in their businesses is not managing risk for reward—it is respectively geological knowledge, computer design and marketing, and drink concoction and marketing. Consumer and industrial companies try to focus on these key skills, and pass on their financial risks to others so that they can concentrate on making and selling their products. For financial firms, however, managing risk for reward *is* their core skill for success. Designing products and marketing are very important for financial firms, but they are not the *core* skills required for success. Financial firms must seek out risk and wring profits from it, whereas consumer and industrial companies try to minimize risk and focus on mastering different skills to earn profits. Financial firms can only prosper in their businesses by being able to separate well-priced from badly priced risks. By avoiding all risk, however, they cease to be financial firms at all and will wither away.

This fundamental reason for their existence should permeate the way financial firms are managed every day. Financial firms, whether banks, securities firms, insurance companies, or investment firms, attack risks in one of three ways. They *absorb* the risk in return for payments, as insurers do when they write coverage against an earthquake, flood, or fire, or as bankers do when they lend money for interest in the hope that it will be repaid. They *intermediate* risk in return for payment, as deposit gatherers do when selecting investments for our deposits and as insurance agents do when pooling our risks for insurance carriers. They *advise* about risk in return for payment, as merger and acquisition firms do during a deal or as an investment counselor does when helping us select stocks and bonds.

In order to attack risk effectively in these three ways, financial firms of all types can develop three key skills or attributes that, for brevity's sake, will be referred to simply as *skills*. *Valuation* skills help these firms discern risk and then select only attractively priced risks. This skill is based on garnering information about risks, analyzing this information to judge whether the risk is worth taking for the payment on offer, and creating options or escape routes should the firm be wrong or should the risk go sour. *Flexibility* skills are required to capture risk opportunities before others do. These organizational skills encompass moving quickly to grab an opportunity and being adaptable to new situations. *Resilience* skills are required to survive and fight back after the inevitable losses and disappointments that characterize the financial world. Resilience encompasses more than just having a strong capital base; it includes developing an organization that can weather a loss and still have the courage to take risks for profit.

By using these three skills, financial firms will be able to select markets and transactions where they have a valuation advantage and then act to win attractive business, earning the highest reward possible for the risk. This first proposition requires managers to develop strategies and create organizations around the risk and reward advantages that their companies possess or can develop. Management of risk and reward will differentiate the winners from the losers.

The second proposition of this book is argued in Chapters four to nine. It is that there are five main risk and reward strategies that matter for financial firms. When you analyze how financial firms compete and win, these five strategies are the ones that count. If managers can master these strategies, then they can hope to profit in the financial markets of the future. Importantly, each of the five strategies is built around unique ways of making profits from risks. Traditional strategic thinking focuses on winning market share, controlling costs, or providing superior customer service as some of the keys to success. While not discounting these factors, the five strategies for financial firms are different because financial firms are different. Financial firms do much more than manage the risk and reward balance, but risk permeates everything they do. The underpinning of all five strategies, therefore, is a unique way to manage risk and reward.

The *segmentation strategy* takes large amounts of data about risks and uses computer analysis to separate the attractive risks from the unattractive ones. This strategy is found in mass retail markets like credit cards, life insurance, and automobile insurance, and in wholesale markets like equity brokerage to large institutions and foreign exchange sales to corporations.

The *insider strategy* does not refer to illegal stock trading, but instead to the need to get "inside" some risks legally in order to understand them. It is focused on markets where unique risks exist and judgments are required to separate the acceptable from the unacceptable ones. Selecting a company for a lever-aged buyout, insuring an oil rig, or making a loan to a corporation require getting inside the risk and then making judgments about it.

The next two strategies are found in the world's trading and investing markets. The *technical strategy* takes large amounts of historic price information about trading and uses computer analysis to find patterns in those prices that can be used to predict prices in the future. Index arbitrage and much of the trading in the world's swap, futures, and options markets are based on the technical strategy. The *inference strategy* applies research and judgments about forces in the external world to predict future securities prices. When you or I select a stock because we think the company's profits and dividends will go up, we are basically inferring the future price of the stock from our research. The inference strategy is used by financial firms as they make interest rate bets, use research to invest in stocks, or to select one currency over another.

The *scale strategy* relies upon sheer size to bring success. In many financial markets, large periodic losses are to be expected, and even a player with excellent skills at selecting risks can be undone by these losses. In other markets, cross-subsidization from one activity to another can squeeze out those players who do not have the opportunity to cross-subsidize.

These five strategies cover the bulk of what financial firms of all types do. They are all based on risk as the key differentiater among financial firms, and so describe unique ways to win in risky markets. These markets evolve, of course, so that which of the five strategies is appropriate for any market may change over time. Companies have to watch how markets evolve and be able to move from, for instance, an insider to a segmentation strategy.

The third proposition is covered in Chapters ten to twelve and relates to the day-to-day management of financial firms. Even after risk is mastered by the use of the three skills (valuation, flexibility, and resilience) in one of the five strategies (segmentation, insider, technical, inference, and scale), managers of financial firms still have to turn to the nuts and bolts of running the company. Risk may be their primary focus, but they cannot forget the disciplines other companies face. Nevertheless, the methods financial firms use to tackle the organizational, information technology, pricing, cost, and capital management challenges they face should still be driven by the risk and reward strategies they choose to pursue. For instance, management of these issues is different within the segmentation strategy than it is within the insider strategy. Financial firms cannot forget their differences from other companies even when they are facing apparently common problems such as cost control or setting prices.

Financial firms are central to all our daily lives. Without them, the world would be a more uncertain and inconvenient place. If banks, securities firms, insurance companies, and investment companies did not exist, we would soon invent them. These firms, after two decades of dramatic change, are in trauma around the world, but it is in all our interests to see them prosper. This book sets out a way for them to strengthen themselves while still serving us by dealing with our risks. Risk is their opportunity and salvation.

PROPOSITION I

RISK/REWARD SKILLS WILL DIVIDE WINNERS FROM LOSERS

2

Risk Is an Opportunity

During the 1970s and 1980s, financial institutions—banks, stockbrokers, insurance companies and investment firms—came out of the regulatory cocoon they had lived in for much of the twentieth century. Prices that had once been controlled were set freely, and boundaries between businesses were pulled down. This trend toward deregulation was most marked in the United States but also was alive and well in the United Kingdom, major European markets, Japan, and Australia.

Bankers, brokers, and insurers felt a little less aloof from the normal concerns of other businesses than they had in the past. No longer able to earn profits from artificially raised prices or protected customer markets, financial institutions now had the same strategic concerns as industrial and consumer products companies around the world. Basic strategy development became central to survival. Bankers asked what their company did that would create a sustainable competitive advantage. Under pressure from stockholders, who still demanded large profits and rising dividends, regardless of the competitive and regulatory environments, the managers of these firms were forced to analyze customer needs, and to compare and contrast their strengths and weaknesses with those of the competition. They had to worry about costs far more seriously than had ever been necessary in the past and to ration capital for those ventures that looked most promising

Such basic strategic work was normal for industrial and consumer products companies that had not been protected by regulation. Recognizing this, the top managers of financial firms started to look outside their normal milieu to attract managers with broader strategic and marketing experience than they could find in-house. Banks like Citibank in the United States raided companies like Procter & Gamble to find managers with the skills associated with selling toothpaste and detergent. Bankers, brokers, and insurance managers were to be found talking about "product-market segments" and what was required to win in each segment they had decided to target. They invested heavily in market research to understand better what their customers wanted and how they could adjust their product offerings to win business.

Most important, these managers started to think dispassionately about the products and services that they were selling, treating them as profit centers. The romantic attachments they once had to a particular group of activities they offered to the market vanished. Products and services were disposable. They would be dropped if they were unprofitable or altered beyond recognition to make them profitable. New ways of delivering these services became acceptable—ATMs and telephone information services in the retail markets, on-line computer information services like Reuters in the corporate markets.

As these deregulated financial markets matured, they showed all the signs of being no different from other business markets. Specialist firms emerged and became excellent at one activity, driving the old-style, broad-based competitors out of their markets. These new entrants had entirely new ways of doing business that revolutionized some markets, as the discount stockbrokers did in retail stockbrokerage in the United States. Long-term customer relationships from the past became irrelevant if firms were unable to adapt. Just as in the industrial and consumer products markets, if financial products and services were uncompetitive, market share would move swiftly to competitors that offered customers the best cost and service packages. Corporate heroes emerged from the financial markets. Once derided as the homes of the most boring businesspeople one could imagine, financial firms became the glamor sector, and newspapers and magazines were filled with profiles of companies or managers admired as dynamic leaders. Financial institutions, emerging from a great slumber, had come of age. Years of pent-up business opportunities were unleashed.

Then it all went wrong. By the end of the 1980s, all one could see were dying banks overcome by loan losses or unprofitable new businesses. The U.S. government was forced first to bail out the savings and loan industry and then to seek new financing for the insurance fund underpinning the banking industry. Japanese banks, once the terror of nearly all markets, were retreating as their balance sheets creaked because of the declining value of many of their loans and investments. British and even Swiss banks were finding the going tough, with the benefits of the new opportunities hard to decipher.

Meanwhile, brokerage companies and securities firms were no better off. In the United States in 1990, major firms had to be rescued as a result of severe losses, while the high flyer of the 1980s, Drexel Burnham Lambert, collapsed under the weight of depreciating junk bonds and government inquiries. U.K. brokerage houses fared no better, losing hundreds of millions of pounds in share dealing in the newly deregulated markets; many folded under the strain. Across Europe the story was little better. Even in regulated Japan, the brokers reeled as the Nikkei index collapsed and trading volumes shrank in sympathy.

Insurers fared little better, seeing many of their investment portfolios collapse in value, while the pricing on both the basic property and casualty, health and life insurance products was often unappealing. The ultimate reinsurance market, Lloyds of London, was under such competitive pressure and losing so much money that many asked whether it could survive to the next century.

What had happened? Why had the great promise of just a few years earlier evaporated? At the heart of many of these problems were structural failures in the competitive environments of these industries. The U.S. banking crisis at the end of the 1980s was fueled fundamentally by the collision of a series of old, inefficient regulations that limited banks' profitability and liberal use of federal guarantees to fund these institutions. As they gambled in commercial real estate and highly leveraged transaction lending to find profits where regulation and overcapacity denied them returns, bankers were able to fund themselves with federally guaranteed deposits. This was an uneven equation, and disaster followed. The earlier savings and loan crisis had been a much more extreme version of the same set of circumstances: fundamentally disadvantaged competitors gambling for profits with federally insured funding. Similarly in the securities world, overcapacity in many of the trading markets was at the root of the losses incurred. In some markets, this collapse had been predicted by the simple act of dividing available revenues by the number of new competitors and their costs. For instance, even before one stock or bond was traded in the newly deregulated London markets after Big Bang, smart bankers and traders knew that the industry was heading for massive losses. Finally, in the insurance world, especially in the American property and casualty markets, relatively low entry barriers to the reinsurance markets meant that pricing was cyclical, leading to periods of large losses.

So, across the financial market disasters of the late 1980s and early 1990s, a common theme is that fundamental competitive imbalances or illogical regulations led directly to some of the most spectacular losses. But there was something else at play here: a key factor that divides the experience of these firms from that of the industrial and consumer products companies they were trying to mirror. Success for financial firms indeed now hinged on many of the same approaches that other businesses had adopted for years; financial firms were no longer off in some protected world that made them special and unique, insulated from the need to market, provide good services and products, and control costs. Yet, the experiences of the late 1980s confirmed that financial firms *were and are* different from other businesses. The difference was and is that financial firms sell a fundamentally different product or service than other firms: They absorb, intermediate, and advise on *risk*. It is this core risk element that differentiates them from other businesses and explains why the way they make money will always be different from that of other types of companies. What characterized many of the disasters of this period was that many financial competitors forgot this difference. As a result, they failed to invest in truly differentiated skills in the selection and management of risk to make money.

The risks that financial firms face are many, but they can most easily be thought of as falling into five broad classes: credit risks, market risks, operational risks, environmental risks, and behavioral risks.

Credit risks are the traditional ones of banking—the risks that a borrower will be unable first to pay interest and then to repay the borrowed amount and so defaults. Loan losses follow, and if they are extensive, as they were in the cases of U.S. banks with real estate exposure in Texas and New England in the 1980s, then the whole institution can be brought down. Credit risks, however, run well beyond this simple (but very dangerous) example. Credit risks exist whenever a financial firm extends credit on the basis that it will be repaid at some future time. In the world's trading markets, where one firm sells securities to another, it takes the risk that when it has bought the securities to sell on to the other party (or counterparty), the latter will be unable to pay. As trading transactions have become increasingly complex over the years and have involved more and more parties in each transaction, often in different time zones, this counterparty credit risk has become increasingly serious. The extraordinary increases in intraday trading volumes in some markets mean that tracking this risk became a major challenge for the leading trading firms.

Credit risk is also to be found in the operational services provided by financial firms. When a firm agrees to clear the security transactions of a trading firm, it assumes that it will not be left in the middle with a defaulting trading client and others refusing to cover its positions. Credit analysis and control, therefore, extends well beyond making sure that borrowers can repay interest and principal; it affects trading and operating activities as well. Insurance companies too find that credit analysis is becoming more and more important to them. Under pressure to increase the returns they offered to life insurance investors or stockholders, U.S. insurance companies were forced to diversify their investment portfolios beyond the usual low-risk bonds. They had to consider credit risk much more directly than in the past. Those that overinvested in high-yield junk bonds, like First Executive, paid the price for lack of attention to credit risk.

Market risk comes in many flavors. The most basic form is the risk that the value of a security or a market position will decline from the price paid for it, causing a loss. For instance, if a company buys U.S. Treasury bonds at 100, and then sees interest rates rise and the price of the bonds decline to the point where they are worth only 95, then the firm has lost out to market risk, in this case interest rate risk. Alternatively, a Japanese firm could buy Treasury bonds. The firm is investing its money to make future payments in yen, so it is interested in the yen-denominated return it receives. The price of the bonds stays stable at 100, but the yen appreciates from 135 to 125 yen to the dollar. The Japanese investor has lost nearly 7.5 percent of the original yen investment, this time because of another market risk: foreign exchange risk. Moving beyond interest and foreign exchange risk, there is, of course, performance risk in equity securities. This is the risk that the future profits of a company, which underpin the value of its shares today, may turn out to be below everyone's projections, causing a rapid decline in the price of the shares. Then there is liquidity risk—the risk that when a firm wants to sell a position in, for instance, bonds or stocks, it cannot find any buyers, or can find buyers only at a large discount to the quoted market price. Lack of liquidity is a problem in the high-yield junk bond market and in many penny-stock markets.

But as investors and traders have become more sophisticated, and as new securities have been invented, a whole new raft of market risks has emerged to haunt the financial firms. Prepayment risk has become more important as securities backed by pools of mortgages and other loans have become more popular. Bondholders count on having a specified level of interest for a certain period of time. The risk here is that the cash to provide that level of interest may not be available because the mortgages behind the bonds are prepaid if interest rates decline. Because the bonds are then prepaid, the interest will stop long before the investor hoped. The price of the securities subject to this risk will vary from day to day as the prepayment risk waxes and wanes, and those who do not follow the price carefully can be left with large losses. Moving further into the trading world there is basis risk, which occurs when a trusted relationship between the prices of two securities turns out to be more volatile than was once thought. If an investor has been offsetting or hedging one investment with another and the offsetting relationship turns out to be false, then large losses can result if the investment positions are significant.

Operating risks are a little more tangible but no less difficult to manage. These are the risks that the basic operating mechanisms of markets or of a financial firm will fail or be disturbed, exposing the market or firm to financial loss. Computers that malfunction, providing incorrect information to traders or lenders, can cause havoc. Fires in operations centers can take a player out of a market at a crucial time, perhaps blinding it and exposing it to new credit or market risks because it is not able to operate swiftly. The competitive pressure to keep down costs limits the constant checks and rechecks that an operations function can provide and exacerbates operating risk.

Environmental risks are reasonably obvious, although they extend beyond what the layman might understand as environmental issues. The *environment* here means the whole natural, legal, regulatory, political, and social environment in which financial firms operate. Natural environmental risks are both direct and derivative for financial firms. Most obviously, insurance companies face direct environmental risk when they underwrite risks to property or to business continuation from hurricanes or fires, and have incurred large losses as a result. Lenders mainly face derivative environmental risks; for instance, they will suffer if a borrower is unable to operate because of a natural disaster or a new environmental development. Lenders to companies involved with asbestos found this out, to their cost, as once secure borrowers saw their finances imperiled because of increases in awareness of the dangers of asbestos. In the United States, there is the risk that banks will be subject to environmental fines if property on which they have foreclosed turns out to be polluted.

Moving beyond natural environmental risk, legal and regulatory changes can have major effects on financial firms. Japanese stockbrokers have had to change fundamentally the way they make money as the old regulations that protected prices on stock trades have been changed, and we have already seen how regulatory changes have reduced profitability in the major trading markets in London. But the most stunning regulatory change for banks in Britain involved interest rate swap agreements they had made with local or municipal authorities. During the mid-1980s, many local authorities engaged in significant swap positions. Many did this prudently, to control their exposure to interest rate movements by exchanging floating-rate debt for fixed-rate debt with a bank. Others, however, tried to create profits from this maneuver, and in the process dabbled in a complex world they knew little about. One, the London borough of Hammersmith and Fulham, lost nearly £200 million. This prompted several court cases that finally reached the House of Lords, the nation's highest appeals court. In 1991 the House of Lords effectively nullified all interest rate swap contracts involving local authorities as being outside their legitimate operations. Many banks faced major losses because of this legislative action.

Tax changes can, of course, have a direct impact on financial firms' profitability through taxes on their profits or on turnover, but they can also have an indirect effect by their impact on clients or on the feasibility of doing certain kinds of transactions. Reduction of the tax advantages previously provided to real estate development hastened the reversal in real estate markets that proved so costly in the United States in the late 1980s for so many financial firms. Finally, major changes in society can create significant risks for financial firms. Banks that have large investments in branch networks in cities with declining populations can find themselves with declining deposits, loan balances, and earnings.

Finally, behavioral risk is either the risk that, with the best will in the world, staff will make mistakes that cost money; or the risk that staff within a financial firm, or between two or more financial firms, will deliberately engage in fraud. Again, as transactions have become more complex, the opportunities for both types of risk to cause major losses have increased. While especially dramatic and unnerving, the risk of fraud is probably much the lesser of the two. Even with the possibilities created by computers, basic operational controls and checks can take care of many such opportunities. The U.S. savings and loan disaster and the BCCI scandal, however, showed that, even if eventually detected, fraud can be very expensive if left to fester. More dangerous and difficult to monitor are mistakes made in good faith by staff members. This problem is particularly acute in large organizations like commercial banks and insurance companies. In such firms, the key economic decisions are often made by hundreds of loan officers, underwriters, and claims administrators who are several levels below senior management and who are probably personally unknown to them. Managers must thus determine not only how to avoid colossal mistakes, but also how to make sure that these decision makers are not making a series of slightly suboptimal decisions that in aggregate, perhaps several years later, will cause serious problems. Behavioral risk, therefore, lies at the heart of the management challenge facing the top executives of large financial institutions and is as serious as the day-to-day credit, market, operating, and environmental risks that are so much more visible.

These five types of risk—credit, market, operating, environmental, and behavioral—are becoming more closely connected as deregulation of financial markets has allowed financial firms to devise ways of linking markets—and thereby their risks. If a German investment and trading company considers investing in U.S. stocks and bonds, all five risks are at work. Obviously, it is exposed to market risk; the bonds and stocks could go down in value. Further, the dollar could depreciate against the deutsche mark, further lowering returns. In addition, the firm must monitor credit risks; for instance, which U.S. trading firms will it work with, and how certain is it that these firms will not run into problems and suddenly be unable to fulfill their side of a transaction? Then there are operating risks. Investing across borders creates a whole series of steps in the settlement and clearing process that could go wrong and cause loss of value, funding of positions prior to delivery of the securities, or an inability to satisfy clients. Environmental risks are very serious. Cash-strapped governments may try to discourage cross-border investment by attaching a new tax to such activity. Alternatively, the vision of a newly united Germany and its potential could cause fundamental shifts in the way investors value deutsche mark investments, at the expense of dollar-denominated invest-ments. Finally, there is behavioral risk. The complexity of the transactions opens up opportunities for fraud and increases the likelihood that traders may simply make mistakes.

Not only are the risks often linked in a simple transaction or investment, they are also merging or becoming entwined. This means that a financial firm that believes that it is taking one type of risk may actually find itself taking quite a different type. For example, middle market lenders to small companies may believe they are taking credit risk, only to find that if a borrower defaults, they are exposed to a market risk—specifically, the value of the real estate they took as collateral. Real estate lenders in Texas found that they were taking not just credit risk but were also exposed to a market risk—the price of oil—which would determine if anyone could afford to lease the properties they were funding.

So, financial firms are hemmed in by risks. The late 1980s and early 1990s illustrated how severe these five types of risk could be as the financial fabric of major nations was weakened by waves of losses. But this is only half the story. Risk is in fact not just the danger of loss. When you look at any change in a market, the real risk is not knowing the future. Even if a market goes down, if one knows this in advance, one can prepare for the event or even profit from it. Therefore, *risk is the volatility of potential outcomes.* Markets can go up as well as down, credits can recover as well as go sour, operations can work better than everyone else's as well as fail, environmental forces can help as well as hinder, and staff can outperform as well as make mistakes. Just as it is risks that differentiate financial firms from other types of companies, so it is risks that set them apart when they *make* money. What is special about financial firms is this great paradox: To make attractive returns, they have to seek out risk. Manufacturing and consumer products companies avoid risk or try to pass it on to another party. Financial firms, in contrast, must go straight for risk, seek it under every rock they can find, and expose it. That is what they get paid for.

Financial firms attack risk in three major ways. They absorb it, intermediate it, and advise on it. Risk absorbers accept risks from customers; there is an actual transfer of risk to the financial institution in return for payment. Risk intermediaries diversify risks as a central clearing house and make it easier for everyone to operate in the knowledge that they will not be hit by one large loss but will only face some residual risk. Risk advisers do not absorb any risk, but their advice helps others to navigate through treacherous waters. The major functions of financial firms can be thought of in one of these three ways, illustrating how risk is at the heart of a financial firm—and, indeed, why societies require financial firms in the first place. It is because societies need institutions to manage or absorb their risks that they first created and now put up with financial firms at all—and so, it is only through the successful absorption, intermediation, or advisory work on these risks that financial firms can expect to be rewarded. It is because there is risk in the world that financial firms exist, and so these firms must seek out risk if they are to grow and prosper. So, whenever and wherever there is risk, for the best financial firms there will be opportunity. For the weaker players, however, there will be losses.

The first of the three risk roles, risk absorption, is central to many of the functions financial firms know so well and use day by day. Most obviously, it is the core of the lending done by banks, mortgage companies, and savings institutions. At first, this may seem a little incongruous; surely the borrower, whether an individual or a company, has no risks he wants to pass on to the lending financial firm. In fact, however, there is a significant credit risk transfer, the risk that the loan or mortgage will not be repaid in full or on time. If the bank, for example, did not exist, the borrower would have to seek out an individual or another corporation prepared to lend the money. Undoubtedly, the interest rate and repayment terms negotiated with the lender would be far worse than those offered by the bank, because the lone lender would be so exposed to the credit risk of this one borrower. To justify the risk, the individual lender would have to charge very high rates on tight terms. The bank, on the other hand, makes a large number of loans and benefits from the diversification of risk that results, as well as from the experience gained from making so many loans. These two factors mean that the bank is able to absorb the credit risk of the borrower at much lower cost than the individual lender. It is by absorbing and diversifying many risks that banks, mortgage companies, and insurance companies are able to offer borrowers the best terms and the lowest rates. Lenders' role in society, therefore, is to lower the cost of capital for industry and the cost of debt for individuals by absorbing and diversifying individual credit risks. To make money, then, lenders must seek out risks and work out ways to control them and get paid for absorbing them.

Sophisticated borrowers have found ways to bypass financial

firms and head straight for the pools of investment funds available in the capital markets of the world. So, large corporations issue commercial paper to fund short-term working capital needs, and turn to the bond and equity markets for longer-term financing. But even these companies face major risks that they will not get the financing they want, when they need it, at the right price, and on the right terms. Will enough investors buy the issue a company is offering, or will it be embarrassed by a shortfall in funds and have to seek alternative (more expensive) sources? Will it receive the needed money for its securities at the hoped-for price, or will volatile markets go down at the last moment and leave the issuer paying more than was budgeted? To cover these risks, securities underwriters—the investment and commercial banks of the world—absorb these market risks by agreeing to buy the issuer's securities at a certain price should the markets fail or fall. The central role securities underwriters play in society, therefore, is to absorb this market risk for issuers and thereby lower their cost of capital. The underwriters are able to diversify the risks of a large number of underwritings over the year, apply their detailed knowledge of the markets, and thereby absorb these market risks at a real saving to the issuers. To profit from this role, however, these underwriters must constantly seek out new risks to underwrite or new types of securities aimed at new investors. If they settle for the same risks all the time, they will soon add little value that others cannot replicate, and they will wither away through lack of reward for their services. On the other hand, if they try to underwrite too many risks, or risks they do not understand, they will suffer large losses and may fail completely.

Securities firms provide risk absorption services in some of their trading activities as well as their underwriting services. A good deal of securities trading is still done in an auction market, where the broker is really just a middleman and absorbs little risk. But in more and more trading markets, the broker is also a market maker who takes the market volatility risk. In over-the-counter equity markets, such as that run by NASDAQ in the United States, the brokers set prices and must be able to step in and buy or sell at those prices—even if there is no other party to whom to pass on the stock immediately. The brokers take significant market risk. Their inventories of stock increase if all the investors are sellers and decline if all the investors are buyers. By acting as central clearing houses and offering to use their balance sheets to smooth out market flows, over-the-counter brokers and traders absorb significant risk that otherwise would fall on the investor. Because of market makers, the investor has some hope of finding liquidity in the market, and therefore is more prone to invest in the first place. Through this increased confidence in the market the cost of raising capital for industry and commerce is reduced, and thereby the brokers and traders in the middle, making markets, offer a crucial service to society.

Market-making roles are not limited to the over-the-counter equity markets. Most bonds around the world are traded this way, as are foreign exchange currency contracts, interest rate and currency swap agreements, and many new derivative futures and options contracts. These markets embody the bulk of capital formation and trading activity around the world. In all of them, the market maker offers the crucial liquidity and price determination role that bring confidence and money to these markets. To succeed, market makers must seek out risks and offer to absorb them. Should they be successful, the rewards can be very large. But should they get on the wrong side of the flow and be unable to hedge or cover their inventories of long or short positions, the losses can be large.

If both banks and securities companies play an obvious but crucial risk absorption role in society, so too do life, health, and property and casualty insurers. Clearly, life insurers are in the business of absorbing risk—in this case, the risk of financial disaster for the bereaved. Health insurers cover the costs of doctor and hospital services for individuals or groups of employees when no such coverage is provided by the state. Property and casualty insurers play a critical risk absorption role. The insurance of individuals' homes, automobiles, possessions, and liabilities, as well as corporations' property and liabilities, are obvious risk absorption services for society. Again, through superior expertise and diversification of risk, these insurers provide better terms than would be available in a series of one-on-one deals. To make money, however, the insurers must constantly hone their risk management skills to avoid excess losses and yet absorb risks that others cannot.

So, banks through lending, securities firms through underwriting and market making, and insurance companies through insuring our lives, health costs, and property and possessions all play risk absorption roles in society. But, in fact, this risk absorption goes beyond these core functions. For instance, banks do not just lend money; they are also at the center of the payment systems between individuals and between corporations. We use this network when we write a check that will eventually lead to money being transferred from our account to someone else's, or when we charge a purchase to a credit card company that first pays the shop before then collecting the money from us. Corporations use these payment services every time they transfer funds to or from other companies, or when they are on the other end of our checks or credit card payments. The shop that accepts our check or credit card payment faces the risk that we are in fact insolvent or a late payer (credit risk), simply make mistakes when paying bills (operational risk), or in fact are not who we purport to be (behavioral fraud risk). The bank or credit card company absorbs these risks when it stands in the middle of the transaction. Without the assurance provided by a safe, error-free payments system, many modern economies would be unable to function.

This payments role extends to all the institutional services that banks offer to corporations and investors—cash management, securities clearance, and trustee and custody services. For instance, major funds managers need to keep the constantly changing flows in their portfolios under control and in safe hands. So they turn to the trustee and custody services offered by major banks as a way to pass on this risk. These trust and custody specialists develop detailed knowledge about clearing and settlement procedures, as well as the computer programs to monitor and report all the investment flows, and get paid for the safety and up-to-date information they provide. Without these services, the volumes and types of investments that asset managers could pursue would be severely constrained. The banks offering these services, however, have to seek out more and more complex risks to absorb and report on if they are to be paid; should they fail to control these risks properly, however, they will suffer large losses.

The second way financial firms attack risk is through risk intermediation and diversification. In these situations, the financial firm is serving as a clearing house for risk without itself absorbing significant risk. It acts as the focal point to provide liquidity or to diversify risk, but in fact it does not absorb all the risks should something go wrong. The most significant example of this is the basic deposit-gathering role provided by banks, savings institutions, and money market mutual funds. In the advanced world of sophisticated savings products, of ATMs offering cash on practically every street corner, of direct deposits of wages and salaries in bank accounts, it is easy to forget that one role of banking and savings institutions is to offer a safe place to keep excess cash. Savings institutions and banks offer basic custodian services every time we deposit money; we take as a given that our money will be safe and accessible when we need it. This is primarily a risk absorption role, absorbing the risk of theft, but the risk intermediation role goes further. First, through diversification and collection of large numbers of deposits, banks and savings firms are able to ensure liquidity— the availability of our money when we want and need it. But savings institutions also offer interest. Obviously, individuals, corporations, or institutions could earn interest on their excess cash by depositing it directly with each other, but they would be taking very large credit risks when they did so. By absorbing these risks through diversifying the assets that produce the interest, banks, savings institutions, and mutual fund companies play a valuable risk role for investors and savers. However, it is not a full risk absorption role; they do not guarantee the returns. Should they experience losses on their portfolio of assets, these losses are often passed on to investors through lower deposit yields or lower money market mutual fund returns. They are diversifying risk, not absorbing it in full. To be successful, however, the best banks and mutual fund companies must seek out the highest-yielding assets that fit the requirements of depositors and savers, and then learn to manage the risks to provide stable, safe returns. Should they fail, these risk-adverse customers will quickly flee elsewhere. On the other hand, should they avoid risk and offer low yields or too few deposit products they will win little business.

Just as some banking activities move from risk absorption to more of a risk intermediation and diversification role, so do some activities of securities firms. We saw how the market-making role of many securities markets absorbs risk and provides liquidity. In some auction markets, however, like the New York Stock Exchange market and the new electronic stock trading markets such as Instinet, the brokerage houses and securities firms function mainly as clearing houses for bids and offers for stocks from their customers and take little principal risk. This risk is absorbed by a smaller group of specialists on the floor of the exchange, and the brokers are the conduits through which the trades are collected. If you or I had to go directly to these specialists traders we would suffer at their hands as complete novices at how to trade with them. Also, we would always be bringing in very small orders to be executed, which would be extremely expensive. By bringing experience and a concentrated flow of orders to the floor, the intermediary broker plays a key role in diversifying away the risk of being picked off by the market makers on the floor of the exchange. At the same time, the confidence this service provides for investors increases interest in the market, raising liquidity and lowering bid-offer price spreads. These brokers do not absorb any of the market risk directly. But to win as brokers in this way, they have to get the best prices, which means understanding the way the market works and bringing enough volume to the market to be able to influence the way the market makers deal with them. Should the intermediary forget that these risks are real for investors and offer bad prices, it will not be in business for long; on the other hand, should it move too aggressively and start to absorb risk in what is essentially still an auction market, it will expose itself to a whole new series of risks.

Risk intermediation roles also exist in the insurance business, in the services offered by insurance brokers and agents. These middlemen do not absorb any risk directly, but individual corporations would be lost in the market without their ability to pool needs and bring them to the final underwriting insurance companies. Acting alone, corporations or individuals would face the severe risks of choosing a weak underwriter or of getting bad prices because of small volumes. Like all risk intermediaries and diversifiers, insurance agents and brokers use the advantages of pooling and large numbers to reduce risks for their customers, without absorbing any risk themselves. Like everyone in this role, however, they must constantly seek out new ways of adding value through pooling more buyers to reduce purchasing risks further, or by bringing new insurance offerings to a wide enough purchasing public to make the offering viable. Should they simply maintain a low-risk approach, the final underwriters will slowly and surely find a way around them. On the other hand, should they take on too many products, they will incur costs without being able to find large enough pools of customers to add any value, in terms of volume discounts to either side.

The third risk role that financial firms play in the economy, the risk advisory role, often blends into the prior two. It is seen very clearly in the corporate banking markets, where, as well as providing loans and deposit services, bankers work with their clients to help them restructure their finances to achieve the best financial balance and the lowest possible cost of capital. Bankers cannot simply react to a need already identified by the client. Instead, they have to seek out the risks their clients may face and find ways to redesign their finances. They must be more than just product providers. This advisory role is also seen at the top end of the individual banking markets, where private bankers play as much an advisory role as a product provider role to their customers; indeed, the only way these banks can sell their products is by offering this advisory function. Some institutions have been able to turn this advisory role into a stand-alone service; most often, however, it is linked to a risk absorption (e.g., lending) or risk intermediation (e.g., deposit-gathering) service. Nonetheless, it is real, and if a bank does not understand and structure the most advanced risk opportunities for its clients, it will see little other business. On the other hand, if it moves too far and offers unsound advice, it will soon lose not only credibility as an adviser but the linked risk absorption and intermediation businesses as well.

Perhaps the most visible risk advisory role in the corporate banking world is the role played by mergers and acquisition advisers. A merger or acquisition often happens to a top manager of a company only once or twice in a lifetime. Faced with career-creating or -destroying decisions, these managers are often vulnerable and concerned about a variety of risks. Is the target acquisition the right company for the business need they are trying to fulfill? Is the offering price too high? Is the transaction as tax efficient as possible? What should be done if another company bids for the target? These are all crucial questions, and often they have to be answered under the glare of publicity. The mergers and acquisition teams play a crucial role in advising on how to manage these risks. They absorb no risk themselves (when they do, as the U.S. investment banks did in their late 1980s forays into merchant banking, they are entering a new business), but they play a crucial role for their clients. By structuring transactions correctly, they can create enormous value. To win in this business, however, the advisers have to understand the most aggressive risk options for their clients; otherwise, the competing team will outfox them. On the other hand, should they be too aggressive and urge their clients to overbid for companies or to adopt too aggressive financing or tax structures, they will soon get a poor reputation in the business.

The risk advisory role is important in the asset management and more complex savings environments, and often exists as a viable stand-alone service. Once investors move beyond the most basic money market mutual fund and deposit savings products, many of them become overwhelmed by the range of options available for their savings and need advice. This applies as much to individuals as to major corporations. So, for example, individuals turn to stockbrokers for help in researching and selecting stocks. The stockbrokers do not warrant their performance or diversify risk away. But the advice they offer is seen as the key value by the investor. These investors face the risk that the information they have about a company is incomplete or out-of-date, so they look to the brokers, with their large news collection and research capabilities, to reduce this risk, while accepting that they, as the investors, bear the ultimate risk of the investment. To win and retain customers, therefore, brokers must reduce these information and research risks for investors. This applies in the mutual fund business too, where purchasers of these funds are seeking out skills in selecting investments of a level they would never be able to achieve alone. Similarly, in the corporate fund management business, when a major company turns over its employees' pension fund savings to a professional fund manager, it knows it is not purchasing risk absorption services. The company, or its employees, still bear the investment risks. They hope, however, that the advice the asset manager provides will lead to better investment performance. They are seeking advice about risks, and they will reward those who provide good advice and avoid those who do not. A risk adviser cannot afford, however, to play it safe. Advisers are judged against a whole series of market indices, and if they select only the lowest-risk investments, then they will find that their performance falls behind those averages. The risk adviser must constantly seek the right balance between risk and reward.

Finally, in the insurance world, the risk-consulting role certainly exists and in fact is known under that name. Insurance companies offer loss control consulting services to help companies understand the risks they face and reduce them. The insurance company is not absorbing any risk when it offers these services (in fact, it may be controlling its own exposure by eliminating the risk of major unforeseen losses), but it is offering a risk service that is valued by customers and is often linked to the purchase of traditional risk absorption services. Insurance brokers offer similar services and hope to win more risk intermediation business by so doing. Both insurance companies and insurance brokers have to recognize, however, that to win in this risk advisory role, they must find a balance between being too conservative, and reducing their clients' business opportunities too much, and being too liberal and leading their clients to incur significant unforeseen losses.

Risk absorption, risk intermediation, and risk advisory. These are the core roles that financial institutions play in society— why, indeed, these firms exist at all and are tolerated by the rest of us. So, even though, during the 1970s and 1980s, banks, securities firms, and insurance companies around the world were being released from the controls of regulation and were being allowed to compete, as industrial and consumer products companies had done for years, this essential difference between them and all other companies survived. While other companies do not on purpose target risk, financial firms, to succeed, must seek out risk. If they can find risk, master it, and price it correctly, they will be winners. If they either avoid risk or find it but are mastered by it, they will lose.

To earn attractive returns as a financial firm, of course, it is necessary to match costs to revenues, to be responsive to customers' needs, to develop the best products, and to have a highly tailored service organization. Further, it is obvious that in all financial businesses, basic processing errors have to be kept to a minimum. But while financial firms do much more than manage the balance between risk and reward, risk and reward permeate everything they do. It is their management of risk opportunities that is a key determinant of success or failure, and given that financial firms are fundamentally risk absorbers, intermediaries, or advisers, this should come as no surprise.

The problem faced by financial firms is that the processes of a competitive marketplace have made the risk skills required for success more specialized every year. In theory, in any single market where a financial firm is paid for absorbing, intermediating, or advising about risk, the rewards will go to those who understand where the line between accepting too little or too much risk for the available price lies. Those who do not know where this line falls will be at a severe disadvantage in one of two ways. First, and more spectacularly, they will think that the risks are less severe than they are in reality, and will either accept more risk than the offered price is worth or will bid down the price for a certain risk. Losses will result from this miscalculation, and the firm will either fail or have to withdraw much shaken. Second, and no less troubling, is the firm that thinks the risks are worse than they really are and avoids them. Although this firm will not lose money in one short period of loan losses, securities write-downs, or excessive insurance claims, it will nevertheless suffer the slow death of declining market share, demoralized staff, and disaffected investors. Takeover by another firm or liquidation of the firm could result if the economics of this approach are especially weak. In either case, that of the too aggressive or too conservative risk taker, the central problem is not knowing where the risk/reward line lies in that particular market and therefore being unable to compete effectively. Even if such firms had the most sophisticated marketing plans, the lowest costs possible, and the will to win, they could not do so. For they would lack the central skill required to compete in financial markets—the ability to determine where the risk/reward line lies and to price and market accordingly.

The challenge for financial firms is continually intensifying. Due to the natural forces of competition, the bands around the risk/reward lines in each financial market are becoming tighter and tighter. In a particular market, as competitors become more skilled and can determine the nature of the risks more accurately, the pricing around the risks narrows. This trend is copied in market after market, so that the skills that work in one market may be irrelevant in another because the margin for error is so low. For instance, as competitors become more experienced in a particular lending market and understand how the risks work through business cycles, they become able to predict losses more accurately. As a result, they price each loan more and more finely, to earn enough to cover their operating costs and expected losses from a portfolio of such loans and to earn a reasonable profit. But competitive pressure will ensure that this price is kept as low as possible. New entrants to such a market, who perhaps may believe that success in an adjacent market is the basis for competing here, will find themselves at a severe disadvantage. They will either think that the loan rates are ridiculously low (if they believe that the risks are more severe than more experienced competitors know them to be) or that the rates are high and offer an opportunity for them to win at lower rates (if they believe that the risks are much less severe than more experienced competitors have found them to be). The specialization of lending, securities underwriting, insurance, deposit gathering, and risk advisory markets around the world, through increased competition, has produced a situation where, to win in a market, competitors must have an intimate understanding of the risk/reward line for that market. What works in one market may lead to disaster in another.

The focus on risk is what distinguishes financial firms from all others; understanding exactly where the risk/reward line lies in each of its chosen markets will differentiate the successful financial firm from the less successful. Competitive advantage in financial markets comes ultimately from this risk/reward determination. The challenge financial firms face, therefore, is to understand the risks they intend to get paid for absorbing, intermediating, or advising about. These firms must be prepared to develop specialized skills, and to upgrade them constantly to remain ahead of the competition. At the same time, these firms need to recognize where they do not have the best skills in the market, and be prepared either to improve these skills or to withdraw from the market.

3

Risk/Reward Skills: The Building Blocks for a Strategy

Risk is the opportunity in financial markets—and the problem. Throughout financial industries you find that whenever some are suffering losses, others in the same environment are thriving. Only where there is fundamental distortion of the competitive situation because of unbalanced regulation is this not the case—and even in markets where regulation undermines the economics for all, some firms are still surviving much better than others.

The reason for differences in performance is obviously that some competitors are more skilled than others. As we have seen, in a financial market, this means they see the risk/reward line more clearly than others. In practice, this means that risks in a particular market do not look the same to all competitors. Some overestimate risks, price too high, and win little business; others dramatically underprice risks and initially win significant market share before the sins of the past catch up with them, their balance sheets are undermined, and their new clients desert them. Differences in pricing and performance indicate fundamentally different perceptions of the risks inherent in a market; competitors perceive the risks differently, behave differently, and so perform differently.

To many who grew up in the business world in the 1970s and 1980s, this may seem at first a little incongruous. It became fashionable to talk about "efficient" markets, where all publicly available information was built into the price of a security or an opportunity. It was thought to be impossible to beat the average performance consistently, since the prices of risk were already set at the correct level and reflected the best thinking of a large number of competitors. This theory became particularly popular in equity investing as institutional investors consistently failed on average to beat the market indices, and even those that did found that their chances of doing so continuously were very low. When performance was measured net of costs, the best portfolio managers could not consistently beat a "passively" managed portfolio of stocks (that is, a portfolio invested in a basket of stocks mirroring an index like the S&P 500) because markets were believed to be so efficient. The theory argues that before you move to buy what you think is an underpriced stock, the market price already reflects most of the potential price appreciation. Your chances of repeatedly catching stock after stock before the market reflects the latest information is close to zero; therefore, you do not beat the market because you cannot do so. The question is, if the efficient market theory applies, how do some financial firms consistently outperform others? Why do not all firms perform at about the same level?

The answer, of course, is that markets vary considerably in their efficiency. In theory, to produce no differentiation in performance, markets would have to be *perfectly* efficient, or perfect. In reality, few come close to being able to be called perfect. The canniest investors claim that the analysis of even the most efficient equity markets in the world, those in the United States, vastly overestimates the thoroughness and speed with which information is disseminated, leaving ample opportunities for superior investors to beat the market over time. For instance, Warren Buffet, the Chief Executive Officer of an extraordinarily successful investment and insurance company, Berkshire Hathaway, made a pertinent if caustic observation on this score in the 1985 Berkshire Hathaway *Annual Report:*

> Most institutional investors in the early 1970s ... regarded business value as of only minor relevance when they were deciding the prices at which they would buy or sell. This now seems hard to believe. However, these institutions were then under the spell of academics at prestigious business schools who were preaching a newly-fashioned theory: the stock market was totally efficient, and therefore calculations of business value—and even thought, itself— were of no importance in investment activities. (We are enormously indebted to those academics: what could be more advantageous in an intellectual contest—whether it be bridge, chess, or stock valuation—than to have opponents who have been taught that thinking is a waste of energy?)

Buffett had superior long-term performance to back up his bravado. Largely due to superb investment results within the investment portfolio of Berkshire Hathaway, the stock price of the firm showed a compound annual growth rate of over 31.7 percent from 1980 to 1990, against the still impressive 9.3 percent rate achieved by the S&P 500 index of stocks during that same 10-year period.

With this level of performance, it is easy to see why Buffett has retained so much confidence in the ability of good risk/reward skills to beat the averages. In fact, however, examination of the criteria for a perfect market shows that very few markets can come close to meeting them. There are still plenty of opportunities for those prepared to step up to the risks and apply their skills. To be regarded as perfect, a market has to fulfill three key criteria. First, it must be frictionless. This means that the costs of switching into or out of a position (transaction costs) must be close to zero, the product for sale or trade must be homogeneous and easy to divide into units that all can swallow, and there must be no regulatory distortions to the flow of product between buyers and sellers. Second, the market must be perfectly competitive, meaning that players can enter and leave at will, and no single player or group of players has any insight into future prices that allows them to set prices in a way that others cannot. Finally, the market must be information efficient; that is, all players must receive information at the same time, and it must cost them all nothing to get this information. Put this way, it becomes clear that few markets can meet these criteria or indeed come close to them. Therefore, within every market, players will be at different levels of understanding and readiness to deal with the risks; and hence, opportunities abound.

The fundamental inefficiency of most markets, and the opportunities for profit, are clear. Take, for example, the lending markets to mid-sized companies, the lifeblood of most banking markets around the world. To begin with, these are not frictionless markets. The cost of switching from one bank to another—that is, the cost of reeducating the loan officers about the particulars of one's situation and then paying all the up-front fees on a replacement loan—are high, so borrowers are not free to move from one bank to another. Friction also exists in switching between banks because the products are not all the same; the loans come with different terms and conditions, and with different levels of service. Even the quality of the loan officers varies. In addition, many markets have regulations that limit competition; for instance, the McFadden Act in the United States has limited the ability of banks to branch between states, putting out-of-state banks at a severe disadvantage in winning business from smaller companies that require branch services with their loans. Marginal competitors who somehow stay in the market are not able to influence prices the same way the dominant competitors do. Borrowers are not able to get multiple bids from many banks, since very few banks serve each market. Finally, such markets are certainly not information efficient. There is no high-quality, central clearing house for information about the credit risks of the borrowers. Each bank has to send out a field force to assess the condition of each present and potential borrower, and then guards its analysis jealously.

Combined, these factors mean that there is plenty of risk for the novice player in each market, and indeed, that success in one market may not lead to quick success in another, given the barriers to efficiency that have to be overcome by a new lender. The corollary is that for those who can surmount these barriers, great rewards can follow—as long as the fundamental competitive structure of the market is reasonable (for instance, as long as regulators do not continually subsidize uneconomic activity or recapitalize failed institutions).

Life insurance provides another example of an apparently competitive market that is far from efficient and, therefore, offers plenty of opportunity for those able to invest in understanding the risks. For a start, high transaction costs, in terms of commissions, repeat health checks, searches for different insurance companies, and the general bother of switching from one company to another, mean that buyers do not move swiftly from a poorly priced to a well-priced product. Then the products themselves are very complicated, with many twists and turns and exclusions in the small print that make it difficult for the customer to compare companies' policies. Finally, regulatory distortions are enormous, classifying types of coverage and setting bands of rates. There are limits on competition, since most countries, and many states in the United States, limit who is allowed to play in their life insurance markets. Finally, information does not flow evenly, simultaneously and at no cost to competitors. In fact, most competitors invest heavily to understand overall demographic and health trends better than other competitors so that they can have an advantage. They guard the results of health checks and other personal information, thereby disadvantaging any competitor trying to price away the business.

These two markets are clearly not efficient, and therefore offer opportunities both to exceed and to fall behind the average performance. Some would argue that this is only because they are not really markets in the sense that the efficient market theorists conceived. For these theorists, a market must trade securities or financial contracts (for instance, a foreign exchange contract). By excluding the financial markets of the day-to-day world of consumers and companies, the efficient market theorists give up a large part of the markets in which financial firms are interested. The problem is, efficient market theory does not seem to play out perfectly when applied to securities markets!

Take, for instance, the most liquid markets of all: the government securities markets. Surely here are markets where no one can win, where all available information is instantly reflected in market prices and nobody can expect to beat the averages. Certainly, the frictions in these markets are far less than those seen in the markets we have looked at so far. Transaction or switching costs are extremely low, and the product is quite homogeneous and divisible into bite-sized pieces for most of the major investors and traders. The primary dealer rules in the United States limit direct access to the Treasury auctions of new bonds to about 35 firms, make the trading less free than one would like, but compared to the other markets we have seen, there is little to worry about. But these markets do not have perfect competition; capital needs, technology costs, and the basic skills required to trade at all mean that not all can play in this market. Further, even the major government bond markets of the world are not information efficient. A key determinant of bond prices is the way in which central banks conduct monetary policies and thereby set interest rates. Not all competitors are as well positioned in every market to read the tea leaves of central bank activity. For instance, in London, the staffs of big banks and securities firms in the City that have regular access to the Bank of England, and may know many officials socially, are clearly in a better position to see which way the wind is blowing than the fund manager based in Manchester, Edinburgh, or even Geneva. Getting the news first and accurately is not free. It requires being at the right place at the right time and having enough staff members with the right contacts to cover all sources.

So, even the government bond markets are not perfectly efficient. Of course, this is not to deny that they have become murderously competitive for many, but only to say that the

opportunity does exist for some to take advantage of the ineffi-
ciencies. As a result, some major bond houses earn better
returns in these markets than do more peripheral investors and
unskilled banks and savings firms. Interestingly, many of the
most successful competitors have introduced *new* complexities
into the market, such as new derivative (for instance, futures,
options, and swaps) products. Although derivatives make trading easier, they can also reduce the homogeneity of the products, complicate information flows, and require new technology
few can afford. Introducing complexity, with its attendant risks,
is an intelligent move—if you can manage those risks better
than competitors.

Does all this mean that the efficient market theory is dead,
that we should now go out and try to beat the markets?
Absolutely not. Markets may not be efficient, but opportunities
exist only for some, not for all. First, in the stock market, most
individuals are probably on the wrong side of the information
barriers and transaction costs that can make those markets inefficient. Individuals do not have access to the best information
about companies as swiftly as do professional investors and
trading houses; on top of that, even when they do, they pay top
prices to trade stocks, so their incremental performance can easily be reduced by transaction costs. For most individuals, it
probably makes sense to invest in the stock market through
commingled funds such as mutual funds and investment trusts,
whose managers (hopefully) receive better information than
individuals do and can trade at lower cost. We should accept,
however, that even they are unlikely to beat the market consistently. Index funds may well be the best bet. Second, the best
markets today do reflect all available information very quickly
indeed. From a government policy standpoint, the securities
markets of the United States, for instance, are pretty efficient.
Regardless of these two caveats, however, it is still true that, to
date, no one has been able to build a *perfectly* efficient financial
market. In particular, most financial markets outside the cocoon
of the traded securities markets—the basic lending, deposit-
gathering, insurance, and payment markets that we all use—are

fundamentally inefficient. Risks, and thereby opportunities, abound.

The lack of efficiency in financial markets means that in every market, competitors' abilities to understand and price the risks vary widely. The reason for this turns out to be that competitors have very different perceptions of the risks in a market. Perhaps the easiest way to think about this is to divide risks into three categories: risks that are unknown and unmeasurable; risks that are known but still unmeasurable; and, finally, risks that are both known and measurable. In any given market, it soon becomes clear that different competitors have different perceptions of the same risks. The best players know all the risks in the business and can measure them very well; the weakest do not know all the risks, and even those they do know they cannot measure accurately. In the middle, most competitors may know the bulk of the risks but have difficulty measuring them accurately.

These three different states of risk can apply to all five types of risk: credit, market, operational, environmental, and behavioral. Starting with the potentially most dangerous risks, those that are both unknown to the competitor and unmeasurable, a wide variety of examples come to mind of situations where all competitors are blind to the risks for a time. These are risks that have not been identified to date because they have not manifested themselves or have not been perceived. An example of this is the pervasive effect of the increase in oil prices caused by the effective working of the OPEC cartel of oil-exporting countries. This was really an environmental risk, a risk in this case with a political foundation, that turned into major credit and market risks for financial competitors.

The 1970s oil shocks created a whole range of new risks, and thereby opportunities, in credit- and market risk-driven situations. Countries that had been large users of imported oil found that their balance of payments deteriorated very rapidly. The belief that "countries do not go bust" became a harsh joke for those renegotiating the debt of Latin American countries, many bowed down by the effects of the second oil price increase at the end of the 1970s. Companies that relied upon cheap energy to make their products suddenly found that their competitiveness was put under extreme pressure. The U.S. car manufacturers, which for years had provided a whole range of large, fuel-inefficient cars to the American public and had laughed at foreign competitors, were overwhelmed by the increase in customers' preferences for smaller, fuel-efficient Japanese cars. Airlines suddenly found that the cost of fuel, and the fuel efficiency of a fleet of planes, became the key determinants of life or death; a revolution in plane design ensued. Those that could not afford to replace their aging planes found they could not compete, and took their bankers with them.

New market risks emerged. Governments around the world grappled with the problem of responding to the oil price increases, and some were so concerned by the potential reductions in economic activity that they let their money supplies increase rapidly, setting in motion a period of high inflation rates in the major western economies that undermined bond and equity prices for prolonged periods in the 1970s. This inflation was reduced only in the early 1980s, when short-term interest rates were allowed to rise to nearly 20 percent in some major economies. Holders of bonds were in shock as their value crumpled.

So the boom in oil prices created a new series of credit and market risks that for most financial firms were initially both unknown and unmeasurable. The price increases caused severe tremors in major financial markets and within financial institutions. But they also created opportunities for those who could see through the fog and adjust accordingly. As financial firms modeled the results of different oil prices, those with the best insights found that the risks could be transformed from unknown and unmeasurable to known but very difficult to measure. Later, these firms were able to determine how different oil prices affected the risks about which they were most concerned. Those that made this transition most rapidly were the winners. They saw which companies would survive, and felt comfortable lending to them and avoiding others that they saw would not; or they had a clearer perception of how the combination of oil prices and tight monetary policies in the early 1980s would work out, foresaw the lower inflation that would follow, bought long bonds at depressed prices, and profited.

A smaller example of a risk that was at first unknown and unmeasurable is that of a new technology, the fax machine. Until the fax came along, text messages were sent via the telex, and in the United States this meant the dominance of one company, Western Union. This company, and later investors in the company, miscalculated how the fax would come to replace the telex in many situations and destroy the economics of the telex business and Western Union. At the beginning of the 1980s, the risk that the fax would have such an effect was both unknown and certainly unmeasurable. Western Union stuck to its core business, unaware that it was about to come under severe threat. By the mid-1980s, it was clear that some threat existed, but few could measure it accurately. By then, Western Union had invested heavily in capital equipment to diversify its communications offerings and had borrowed heavily to do so. Then on January 1, 1984, a new risk emerged: AT&T was broken up into the "Baby Bells" and a core long-distance telephone company (AT&T). Under Western Union's telex system, the final local link to the customer used the local telephone lines—and the new Baby Bells quickly boosted the access charges Western Union (and others) had to pay for these lines. Western Union passed on these costs by raising telex rates just as AT&T was lowering long-distance telephone rates. Telex traffic plunged, Western Union's cash flow dried up, and a long series of rescue plans came one upon the other.

The most dramatic of these plans was unveiled in December 1987, when Bennett S. LeBow took control of the company with a plan to increase the company's exposure to telex by merging its domestic telex activites with ITT Worldcom, the leader in international telex. LeBow hoped to extract enough cost savings from the combined businesses to make them profitable again, while repaying debt from general cost cutting and asset sales. While the proceeds from the cost reductions and asset sales proved to be disappointing, what really undid this plan was that whereas LeBow's team thought that telex volume was declining at some 10 percent a year, it was in fact declining at two to three times that rate as the fax became a common business tool. Soon the LeBow team was simply selling assets to survive quarter by quarter, with no confidence that at the end of the day they would come out ahead. They had known about the risk of telex traffic decline, but it was hard to measure. They took a risk—and in this case paid the price. In mid-1988 the coupon on Western Union's Senior Reset Notes was reset from a high 16 percent to an astronomical 19.25 percent. To repurchase the debt, the LeBow team had to hasten its disposal programs— eventually including selling, in 1990, the remnants of the dying telex business to, of all companies, AT&T.

For many firms, the October 1987 stock market break highlighted two new risks they had been unaware of and showed how dangerous these risks could be. Prior to the market break, a number of studies, some even sponsored by the U.S. Securities and Exchange Commission, had shown that such a collapse in prices was theoretically possible. But nobody had really thought through the operational and behavioral risks that would accompany this market risk to make it so much worse. As stock prices began to collapse in New York on Monday, October 19th, 1987, trading volumes increased to such enormous proportions that the market price monitoring systems and the ticker tape could not keep up with prices; a new operational risk had emerged. Investors suddenly did not know what the market prices were and which way they were trending. This produced an unforeseen behavioral risk: investor panic. Combined, the operational and behavioral risks led to further waves of panic selling removed from the immediate technical causes of the market declines on Monday morning. But the panic selling merely reignited the technical forces for price decline, and thereby created a reinforcing downward spiral of panic selling leading to technical selling leading to more panic. Nobody had been able to analyze all the complex interrelationships in the market to determine how everybody would perform, and as a result, fortunes were lost (or made), depending on whether one was long or short the market on Monday morning. Over time, as analysis of the October 1987 and October 1989 market breaks clarified what had happened, regulators and competitors became more skilled at dealing with the different risks they faced; they knew of them now and were able to measure them to some degree. The "circuit breakers" (or mandatory halts in trading when the market fell or rose a certain amount) introduced in 1988 were designed to give the panic a chance to disperse, while the immense computing and communications power added to the New York Stock Exchange was designed to make sure that the gap in market price information that had sown the panic in the first place did not recur.

So, risks that are unknown and unmeasurable can create havoc in financial markets, and those competitors who can move from this state of complete blindness most quickly will start to have some competitive advantage. At the next stage of awareness, risks can be identified but still not quantified. A good example of this is the risk of an earthquake and the way it affects the insurance and lending markets. It is well known that the West Coast of the United States is likely to have a major earthquake at some time, an earthquake that could do major damage to industrial, retail, and service industries in the region (a less well-known fact is that the area around St. Louis, Missouri, is just as vulnerable as California, lying on an equally great fault). The problem is, nobody can measure this risk very accurately; they are not sure of its timing and cannot predict its severity very well. For the financial firms providing loss control advice to companies in the area, or underwriting potential property damage, or lending to companies that are dependent on production in or sales to California, this uncertainty is a major problem. It illustrates how an environmental risk can become a credit risk for bankers and an underwriting risk for insurers. Interestingly, the best competitors are trying to convert this risk into one that is both known and measurable. They do this by developing close relationships with the academics creating the latest models of potential earthquake activity in the area, and combine the knowledge thus gained with detailed maps of every structure in a locality to see how they would fare under shocks of different strength. As a result, these insurers and loss control advisers are able to determine how a building they are planning to underwrite will fare under different conditions and what needs to be done (for instance, embedding heavy equipment in bedrock) to minimize losses from a major earthquake.

A very different kind of risk, one that was known but hard to measure accurately, was the risk in 1985 to 1989 of making loans to companies going through a leveraged buyout. The major risk was that during a recession, leveraged companies would experience such dramatic declines in cash flow that they would be unable to service their large debt loads. Even though this risk was known, measuring it was very difficult. Every transaction had presumably been structured by the bankers involved to work, and some "downside scenarios" had been analyzed to see if a deal would be able to survive a recession. Despite this work, logic indicated that increased debt would lead to larger defaults if a recession struck. Again, the best players tried to move beyond this stage of risk perception to risk measurement. They developed detailed computer models of leveraged companies based upon the most current information. Nevertheless, the opaque nature of the finances of many of these companies, and their unprecedented debt levels on going into a recession, meant that nobody was completely prepared for the losses that actually occurred in the early 1990s.

A similar situation applied to the real estate debacle at the end of the 1980s and the early 1990s, especially in the boom areas of the East and West coasts of the United States, London, and Tokyo. These areas had been the main beneficiaries of the financial market boom of the 1980s, and their real estate values, aided by some tax and regulatory encouragement for new development, had risen to unheard-of levels. Nearly all investors and developers in these markets knew that the rise in values could not continue unabated forever. There would be a break in the market, and in the process, some buildings would become uneconomic and some investments would be under water. But timing and measuring the size of this downturn was difficult. Throughout the 1980s, the markets kept rising, so holding back created a very large opportunity cost. The wisest investors and developers had been through this process many times before, most recently in the mid-1970s, and understood how to prepare. They liquidated their positions early, to be ready to come back into the market when it was about to revive. Others, who knew that there was a risk but could not tell when it would hit or measure its severity, suffered—from failed loans to developers and from investments that no longer paid any dividends.

Knowing that a risk exists, but not knowing when it will arise or how large it will be, is better than not knowing of the risk at all—but not much better. Luckily, in a number of financial markets, the state of knowledge has advanced enough that financial firms not only understand the risks but are also able to quantify them accurately. The prime example of this is the advances made in determining the life expectancy rates of a pool of individuals. The accuracy with which life insurers can predict losses on a pool of life insurance contracts is remarkable. Today, given basic medical and demographic information about a pool of insureds, a life insurer can predict expected losses precisely and translate this knowledge into better rates for each individual within the pool. An insurer without the latest understanding of demographic and medical trends—for instance, how a new experimental medical treatment might affect the life expectancy of today's 30-year-olds when they become senior citizens—will not measure the risk as finely and will be disadvantaged.

In situations such as life insurance, where there are many observations of losses, statistical analysis is used to predict future behavior. Credit card default rates by type of borrower can now be predicted quite accurately by credit card issuers because they possess a statistical base of experience from which to derive the likely course of future losses: they both know the risk and are able to measure it reasonably well. The same applies to automobile insurance. Because there are thousands of events to analyze, statistical techniques soon reveal patterns of experience—which cars in which locations are most likely to be broken into; which drivers, driving what make of car, are most likely to be involved in an accident; and so on. Insurers in these markets have moved beyond estimating the likely losses; they can predict them with reasonable accuracy. For them the risks are both known and measurable. In the securities markets, the same is true of some pricing relationships between stocks and their matching futures indices. Based on pricing experience and on mathematical formulas that underpin it, traders in these markets are able to see when an index and its underlying stocks move too far apart; they can then take advantage of this momentary disequilibrium to earn a profit before the two prices move back into a more rational relationship. This index futures arbitrage has earned a number of firms significant profits over the years, simply because they feel more certain about the risks they are taking than other firms.

Market perceptions of a risk evolve over time. What is at first unknown and unmeasurable for all then becomes known but still unmeasurable and then, after more experience and further research, becomes both known and measurable. For instance, after the spike in interest rates produced by the tight monetary policies of Federal Reserve Chairman Paul Volcker in the late 1970s and early 1980s, banks and their clients became very interested in controlling, or hedging, their exposure to interest rate volatility. It was around this time that the interest rate swap was developed, which among other uses provided a way for firms and banks with floating rate liabilities to swap them into fixed-rate borrowings. To service their customers, banks at the forefront of developing this product started to write large quantities of these contracts that were not recorded on the balance sheets of the banks. They were a future, hence off-balance-sheet, agreement to fill the gap in cash flows should the rates of the floating and fixed parties to the swap so diverge that one party had a problem meeting its obligation to the other. The bank stood in the middle, providing this credit guarantee.

When swaps contracts were first written around 1981 and 1982, little was known about the full nature of the risks, and certainly little was known about how to quantify them. Because they were written off-balance-sheet, at some banks central risk management personnel did not know or focus on the risk at all. The market was almost at the point of neither knowing the risk nor being able to quantify it. This situation soon changed. As the volume of swap contracts increased, the interest of senior management and the risk control functions increased, and soon everyone knew of the risk—but still found it difficult to quantify. During 1982 and 1983, all the major players in the market were in the middle of studies to quantify the risk. By the end of 1983, the best ones had the situation reasonably under control; they could both determine what types of risks they faced, and could measure them throughout the ups and downs of the interest rate cycle. So the market evolved, from an early, very vague perception of the risks to a much clearer quantification of them. This pattern of market perception and management of risks is repeated again and again in the banking, securities, and insurance markets.

It becomes reasonably clear in this context that the fundamental basis for competitive advantage in financial risk markets is to have a relatively better understanding and measurement of the risks in your chosen markets than do your competitors. In market after market, the winners are those who are one step ahead of the competition in being able to perceive and measure the risks. If the risks are unknown and unmeasurable for most, then the few who are at least aware of a new risk are at a clear advantage over the rest. If all are aware of a risk but only one or two can measure its intensity reasonably well, then again, the latter have a competitive advantage over the rest. Finally, if all can identify and measure the risk, then the few who can do so most accurately will price most finely, and at these low prices will know which loans, insurance opportunities, or securities offerings make sense—and which are to be avoided. As pressures increase in market after market, competitors often find themselves in this last stage, constantly honing their measurement of the risks so that they can provide the tightest pricing around the risk/reward line. New products, new markets, and environmental, technological, or regulatory changes, however, can introduce unforeseen risks that necessitate going through the evolution of risk perception from beginning to end until the risk can be measured accurately.

Financial firms face a whole series of uneven playing fields, where the winning players have built knowledge-based advantages around the risks in each market and earn excess returns through better pricing or lower losses. The goal is to have a better perception of the risks and rewards in each market (to know where the risk/reward line lies in each market) and be able to act upon this knowledge more rapidly and effectively than can competitors. This requires three core attributes or skills: valuation, flexibility, and resilience. These three risk/reward skills are the building blocks for creating strategies in financial markets. Each alone is of little value; it is only when they are used in combination that a competitor can create a viable strategy that can work in the market.

Valuation is the ability to identify, assess, and then structure risk opportunities in such a way as to earn attractive returns given the amount of risk involved in the event. Competitors in risk-based businesses are by definition faced with uncertainty, and need skills to manage and take advantage of that uncertainty. Valuation is the key skill that gives them the opportunity (but by itself not the certainty) to compete successfully in these markets. Specifically, valuation skills enable firms to identify possible future outcomes, assess their probabilities, and, finally, determine how to influence future events either by building in safeguards or by taking certain actions. Valuation tells a competitor whether to accept a specific opportunity, under what terms, and at what price. Valuation can be divided into three key components: gaining more information about risks; undertaking better evaluation of the information that is available; and, finally, using the evaluation of the information to create more options for action while the risk exists. Each of these three components builds on the others, although it is possible to build a valuation advantage by being particularly strong in any one of them.

Possessing information about a risk opportunity is obviously important. The information advantage comes in four ways. Winners can have a larger quantity of information than everybody else; the quality of their information can be superior; they can have finer or more detailed information than others; and, finally, they can have information that is available to them on a more timely basis than it is to competitors.

In the lending markets, if a firm knows more about an individual borrower, or more about that class of borrower, than others, it will probably be able to make better decisions than competitors. So, the established middle market lender in a community probably simply has more information about trends and conditions in the area than does the new entrant. Just having more information about the individuals who run the key businesses to which it might think of lending provides an enormous advantage for this established firm. Alternatively, a bank thinking of lending to cable television companies is likely to have a better sense of the key red flags if it has dealings with many such companies across the country, than if it is confined to lending to the few companies in its immediate locality. Similarly, in retail lending markets, the credit card company with a large pool of borrowers in many different segments is able to differentiate the sound borrowers from the unsound ones in each segment better than the smaller player with relatively few cardholders in fewer segments. In securities brokerage, the same rules apply: the best-informed brokerage firms are likely to give better advice than the less well informed, and thus will, over time, win clients away on the basis of a better track record. This is especially true in the more esoteric and less well researched areas like smaller capitalized stocks and overseas stocks. Here this information advantage can significantly increase the client's confidence in the broker. Again, in the world of insurance, more information can lead to an advantage. The company that specializes in insuring a particular type of boiler, wherever it exists, is likely to have so many more observations of the risks inherent in that type of boiler that it will have a risk selection and pricing advantage over the insurer that only bids on the boilers of that kind that exist in its particular geographic area of focus.

Possessing large quantities of data still leaves the competitor open to the "garbage in, garbage out" problem. Information has to be of good quality if it is to be of any use. Many a bank has suffered because, although it possessed large amounts of data about a potential customer, it was all irrelevant to the key issues. The infamous "desk lender," who conducts all credit research from a desk piled high with anonymous credit research and financial ratios about a target borrower, may possess large amounts of information but no quality information. The important facts may only be derived by visiting the management of the company in person, and taking a detailed tour of the plant to see if all their claims about efficiency and productivity seem to make sense given the actual state of the factory and the eagerness of the work force. The retail lender who simply relies on credit research by public credit bureaus may find himself at a severe disadvantage against the firm that uses data drawn from actual experiences of credit payments by borrowers of the type envisioned by the loan arrangement. The insurer who decides to insure a farm against the risk of fire destroying a new building will be at a disadvantage if he relies purely on the customer's description of the property and on a publicly filed building permit. Only by actually visiting the site and seeing firsthand that, for example, the new building is on the crest of a hill, so that getting fire engines to it in winter will be especially difficult, will the insurer realize that the risk of total property destruction from fire is larger than any public information suggests. So the quality as well as the quantity of information can provide important valuation advantages for competitors trying to choose the risk opportunities to pursue.

The next component of information content is the fineness or detail of the information. In the trading markets this is especially important, since often the difference between profit and loss in a large arbitrage trade can be determined by one or two hundredths of a percent (basis points) in the price of a security.

The trader needs to know the exact terms of the deal in order to capture that narrow opportunity. If the pricing information is not detailed enough, then the opportunity will be lost or the profits will become losses because the trade was done at the wrong price. Similarly, in the lending markets, a retail store thinking about extending credit to a shopper needs to know more than whether this borrower always repays loans. Whether the shopper pays them back on time is important as well. In insurance, a life insurer thinking about providing coverage to a 50-year-old man needs to know not only that the man has stopped an old habit of smoking, but also when he stopped, so that it can assess the extent to which his body has overcome the heart disease and lung cancer risks associated with smoking. With this greater detail, the life insurer will be able to classify the man more accurately in terms of life expectancy and provide the sharpest premium quotation. A merger and acquisition advisory firm helping a bidder value a potential target will be able to give a much better assessment of the potential cost savings from a merger if it understands in detail the types of computers and software the target company uses, and how easy it would be to convert all the key applications to the bidding company's systems, than if it only knows how much the target spends on computing.

The final element of an information advantage is that information is available more rapidly to one firm than it is to everyone else. Just as information fineness is crucial for the success of traders in tightly priced markets, information timeliness is often crucial to these firms as well. The trader who first notices that two securities that normally track each other closely have started to trade apart will be the first to have the opportunity to act on this aberration. The investor who hears first that a new wonder drug, on whose promise the manufacturer's stock price has advanced to new highs, is producing unforeseen side effects in clinical trials will be at an advantage over those who hear a few hours later. So today, we see that stock analysts at corporate briefings often carry cellular phones with which to call in the latest-breaking news to the firm's traders, rather than having them rely on the general news services.

In the corporate banking and advisory world, major firms such as Goldman Sachs and Chase Manhattan Bank have now developed systems to channel information about particular companies to the bankers covering these companies as rapidly as possible. The best of such systems alert the bankers to the latest news about a company and enable them to respond to a client's needs as rapidly as possible. At Chase, for instance, the Chase Information Exchange taps a wide variety of databases to bring information about companies to the bankers, but then adds to that the ability to develop models relevant to the particular situation at hand—be it a restructuring, merger or acquisition, or financing. At Goldman Sachs, the client database provides the bankers with rapid access to all external and internal information about the client or prospect. Therefore, a Goldman banker can not only call up external news information about the company but also review all Goldman correspondence with the company, as well as reports of visits and telephone contacts, in order to determine how to respond to a new opportunity.

In retail banking, rapid information about a customer seeking to extend his credit limit on a credit card can be crucial to making the right decision and retaining his business. When the customer calls, the bank obviously needs to know whether the borrower is a good credit risk to determine whether the credit line can be increased. The best credit card companies take up-to-date information about the cardholder's spending and payment patterns, which may give indications of his current financial stability, and then deliver it directly to the service agent taking the customer's call. Thus the service agent is provided with expert systems help to aid him in deciding whether or not to extend the credit line. Because this information is based upon the latest available facts about this borrower's use of the card, and because these facts are available to the service agent so quickly and backed by expert decision support systems, the best card companies are able to control mistakes in these situations and provide prompt service. This is a formula for success.

The same basic approach can be seen in the insurance industry, where the most advanced firms have introduced information delivery systems to support their claims agents in servicing customers. When a customer calls with a potential claim, the agent is able to provide rapid service, for instance by determining whether the claim seems to fit within the parameters of the particular insurance contract. The agent also assesses whether the claim is likely to require a claims adjuster to review it. Moving rapidly to involve the adjuster is crucial for holding down claims costs, particularly in situations that might at some point involve difficult legal wranglings about who is really to blame. The earlier the insurance company can get involved in the fact gathering that will determine the results of such arbitration, the more likely it is that the company's liability will be kept under control.

Information, in large quantities, of high quality, of sufficient fineness and available in a timely fashion, is a basis for making good valuation decisions. But it cannot guarantee them. Valuation is also dependent upon the evaluation of this information—weighing the risk/reward balance implied by the information. There are basically two types of evaluation. The first is based on tough analysis of large quantities of data, and has become more and more driven by computer-based analysis to discern patterns within the data; the second is based on "soft" judgment when the information available is still too opaque to allow the "hard," data-driven analytical approach. This distinction does not imply that the judgment-based evaluations are devoid of analysis, but merely that, in the end, some judgment has to force the final risk/reward choice because the information by itself does not lead to watertight conclusions. In reality, any risk/reward evaluation can be seen on a continuum. At one end is the hunch-based, "rolling the dice," gut-feel decision. At the other extreme is the decision that is completely automated, based on statistical analysis of past trends to determine how a firm should react in the present. Both approaches, however, essentially involve evaluation of information, and thus are essential to building a valuation approach in a market.

The analytical valuation approach is most often found when the data about a market is available in large quantities. The advantage is to be found in dissecting that data to discover patterns of behavior or outcomes that can drive decisions about the future. The life insurance industry, in its use of actuarial analysis, is basically applying the analytical approach to price life insurance for individuals and groups. The same can be said of the credit authorization process that banks, credit card companies, and stores use. They rely upon analyzing patterns of behavior and deciding which group or segment an individual falls into, and, as a result, whether or not he or she is to be trusted with a loan.

The judgment-based evaluation approach is used whenever the number of data points or observations do not support the statistical analysis found in the analytical approach. Essentially, what the judgment-based approaches try to do is to make up for this deficiency in the data by using expert judgments to re-create a statistically valid base. Judgment is meant to fill the holes where the data is lacking. Sometimes this works; sometimes it does not. Judgment-based approaches are found most often in situations such as lending to large corporations, where the risks of each situation are unique and the statistical experience to be called upon is weak. In such a case, a judgment has to be made about those unique facts to determine the nature of the risk/reward trade-off. In the related corporate advisory businesses, judgments based on fleeting and opaque facts constantly have to be made in a merger deal or in floating a public bond. The facts have to be analyzed, but by themselves they do not lead to obvious conclusions based on their patterns; additional judgment, probably based on intuition or experience, is required. Similarly, in the corporate insurance market, underwriters have to review each individual plant before providing coverage against damage or workers' injuries; they have to make unique judgments about the likelihood of tampering or other actions when providing products liability coverage for a particular food or drink product; and they have to review another financial firm's controls and processes before deciding what to charge for coverage against fraud. In the investment management business, fund managers are constantly making judgments about the future profitability of the companies they could invest in, knowing that the facts about the past do not provide certainty about the future. Thus they must make some interpretations and then decide which companies to invest in.

So valuation involves more than garnering the most or best information; it includes using that information to make evaluations of risk and reward opportunities, either through statistical analysis or through judgments. Yet, even then the process is not complete. Still open is the question of exactly how the firm will structure its involvement in the risk, and specifically, how it will bring into play options to escape or restructure its involvement in the risk as it unfolds. Building in action options when finally deciding to take advantage of a risk opportunity can be crucial for the eventual value of the transaction. There are two kinds of action options: those that can be put in place when the transaction is being arranged and those that can be applied while the risk is being incurred during the transaction.

Establishing action options while the transaction is being structured involves activities such as creating loan covenants to protect the lender should a risk start to trend in the wrong direction. In such covenants, the borrower is asked to abide by a certain set of financial and performance parameters; otherwise, the covenants give the bank the option of withdrawing the loan. In reality, of course, if the borrower has no way of repaying the loan, then the covenants are irrelevant. Therefore, covenants are most usefully thought of as early warning signals that may provide opportunities in some cases to exit, but actually they signal the need to intervene. This is, of course, not true in public bond offerings, where the ability of individual bondholders to intervene before the value of the bond is impaired by credit problems is very limited.

The weakness of public bondholders was dramatized during

the leveraged buyouts of the 1980s, when a large number of previously conservatively funded corporations took on large amounts of debt. As a result of this new debt, these companies' existing public bonds declined in value because the credit-paying capability of the companies was now under such strain. The markets trading these bonds quickly recognized the new facts, and started to trade the existing bonds as if they were junk. Because they had interest coupons of high-quality paper, the prices of the bonds soon declined to boost the yield up to junk levels.

The most well-publicized example of this problem occurred when RJR was taken private in 1988. On its balance sheet, RJR had a series of bonds, some with 30-year maturities. These bonds had no escape clause allowing for repayment should there be a change in corporate control or any other significant development; as a result, they declined dramatically in value just as the company's stock was soaring due to the takeover speculation and activity. Because the original bond-structuring team and the investors had no perception of this risk, they did not build into the bonds any action options to protect their value. Interestingly, such was the outcry of the investors, led by the Metropolitan Life Insurance Company based in New York, that in 1991 RJR came to an agreement with them that made them largely whole on the loss. RJR probably felt it had to do this if it was to retain access to the capital markets. Metropolitan Life, lacking adequate action options in the original bonds, moved to the second action option type—interacting with the risk as it occurred to try to turn it in its favor.

Interacting with the risk as it transpires occurs in all types of situations. In the corporate lending business, when a company breaks a loan covenant, the best competitors move quickly to work with the company's management to try to improve the company's finances. Cash flow usually becomes king, and the bank tries to convince the management to maximize cash flow and minimize discretionary expenses. In the leveraged buyout and venture capital businesses, the best firms work very hard to stay close to the companies in which they have invested to

ensure that the actions required to make the investment a success are taken, and that major risks are identified early and
managed. Of course, the venture capital firms also structure
their investments in tranches to match their confidence in the
fledgling technology or service they are funding. Nevertheless,
it is the continual interaction with the risks that enables them to
raise valuations. Finally, in the securities trading and investing
businesses, traders and investors are today interacting continuously with their risks through various hedges they apply.
Known usually as *dynamic hedging,* this involves not a static
hedge (for instance, simply taking out a put option to balance a
long position in a stock) but constant interaction with the risk as
your position fluctuates during the day. As relative and absolute prices change, you keep the overall net exposure the way
you want it to be. For example, a bond trading house might
find, perversely, that its inventory of bonds was rising as prices
fell because everybody in the market was a seller, and they were
one of the buyers of last resort. As this risk rose, the bond house
might intervene by increasing its short position in the bond
futures market. Again, having been unable to control its risk at
the beginning of the trading day, the firm has to turn to the second kind of action option, intervention, to manage the value of
the risk as it transpires.

Lack of action options can diminish or even destroy the value
of a risk opportunity. In 1988 the Chubb insurance company
entered into an agreement with Goodweather, an aptly named
insurance agency in the Midwest, to distribute drought insurance to farmers. Chubb actually authorized Goodweather to
issue $30 million of drought coverage. The coverage had a final
application date; if the insurance was not applied for before that
date, it was no longer available. What actually occurred was
that the spring of 1988 was very dry in the Midwest, and
Goodweather was inundated with 8800 applications for $350
million in coverage, more than 10 times Chubb's limit. Nearly
90 percent of these applications were received in the final few
days when coverage could be purchased, as the farmers waited
until the last moment to see what the weather forecast was like.

The farmers were led to believe by Goodweather that if they applied for the coverage by the deadline, they would be covered. That was not, of course, how Chubb had intended to structure the contracts. At this point, however, it was too late. The press had the story, and Chubb was faced with either paying for the claims that rolled in as the clouds did not, or trying to withdraw and facing, at best, a public relations disaster. In the end, Chubb settled with the farmers and sued Goodweather for overselling the policy. Clearly, Chubb had relied too much on Goodweather's internal controls, and it did not have in place the action options to escape its exposure should those controls be inadequate. Chubb had spotted what it believed to be a risk opportunity, but the valuation advantage (which for 1988 was illusory because the rain did not come) was undone by poor action options.

Action options are the least obvious ways in which financial firms can value a risk opportunity. They are, however, becoming increasingly important as financial firms develop ways to restructure and repackage risks into discrete pieces for hedging purposes. Without these action options, the valuation that a firm can attach to a risk opportunity must be much less than it would be with them, because it has no way of controlling or limiting the down side after the transaction is closed. Hence these two types of action options are crucial to the valuation skills that good competitors develop in their markets. With such action options, they are able to value a risk opportunity very differently than are competitors without them.

Valuation is a core skill for financial firms of all types—banks, securities and brokerage firms, and insurers. It is not, however, enough. Many firms can have the best valuation skills and still be unable to prevail. This is because there are two other core risk skills that are required in any mix that creates a strategy for a financial firm: flexibility and resilience.

Flexibility enables a firm to put its valuation skills into action. Valuation may enable a firm to recognize the value in a risk opportunity, but it is through flexibility that the firm is actually able to capture that value. Flexibility is the ability to bring to bear the resources required for success: assembling the people, technology, and financial capital required to capture an opportunity, and then being able to adjust as events unfold.

Flexibility is crucial in mergers or acquisitions of financial firms, where client or staff defections can sometimes take place quickly. A key to retaining the value perceived in the target bank, securities firm, or insurance company is to assure present clients, prospective clients, and staff that the new firm will serve their interests well. Otherwise, the bases of business and goodwill in the community that underpin the valuation of the target as an ongoing concern can quickly dissipate. In the 1980s in the United States, regional banking firms were given the opportunity to merge in a limited way across state lines; as a result, a number of major regional banking firms emerged. What distinguished many of the winners from the losers in this process was that they were able to move rapidly to retain the loyalty of the targets' clients and communities, while still capturing many of the cost advantages from rationalizing duplicate cost bases. They often did so by having the flexibility to flood their new partners with staff from the new parent firm within hours of the acquisition announcement, winning goodwill from clients and staff in the process. The key here was the ability to mobilize those resources very quickly. The laggards may have seen the valuation opportunity in the acquisition, but in moving too slowly, they frittered it away in lost clients and staff ill will.

The same flexibility requirement is at play in the insurance business. As insurance market prices fluctuate, opportunities appear that entice companies into selected markets because pricing is particularly attractive. The valuation skill tells them that there is an attractive risk opportunity. This is, however, a far cry from being able to take advantage of the opportunity. Unless they can apply the marketing and underwriting skills to this particular opportunity before others get to it and destroy the pricing, they will miss out on the benefits that their valuation skills identified. In fact, failure here does not just result in a lost opportunity. Even in stable markets, it is one thing to identify an opportunity and another to grasp it. An insurer may believe that insuring automobiles of a particular kind is an attractive opportunity from a valuation perspective, but getting the hundreds of agents and underwriters to move in unison to capture this opportunity across a large geographic area is a completely different skill. Too often, financial firms develop sophisticated valuation skills that they are unable to deliver to the market. They are too slow to bring the resources to bear, or the large number of people who have to be taught how to capture the opportunity, transaction by transaction, overwhelms their ability to transmit the valuation skill.

In the trading world, flexibility to capture the opportunity identified by valuation skills is often the difference between success and failure. Trading firms have internal controls to protect them from overexposure to particular risks, be they counterparty credit risks or market price movement risks. These are necessary controls, but at the same time, they must not overly limit the firm's ability to move when the valuation skills identify a real opportunity. If the traders are constantly waiting for authorization to trade, then the opportunity may well pass them by before they can act on it. An example of how flexibility can provide a competitive advantage in the trading world concerns a bank that was trading the Singapore dollar against the U.S. dollar. These two currencies are normally in a reasonably constant equilibrium, but this bank identified an opportunity to profit from a disequilibrium it saw coming. A major investor and trader asked this bank to deliver Singapore $500 million 2 weeks ahead, or forward. The bank agreed to do this but knew that a trade of that size would cause the 2-week forward rate to be depressed because of the size of the trade. So this bank hedged its overall position by going long the Singapore dollar in the spot market and in the 1-month forwards; at the same time, it went short the Singapore dollar in the crucial 2-week forward maturity. Then it took on the trade of the client, and once its positions were in place, it dumped the client's trade in the market. The 2-week forward price duly collapsed and the bank closed out its short positions, netting it $10 million in profit. The bank's valuation skills had correctly identified a risk opportunity.

What was remarkable about this performance was the way in which the bank applied its flexibility skills to capture the opportunity. The normal trading limit for the Singapore desk of this bank was about $200 million, so alone, it could not handle the trade. However, the traders called around and were able to get the trading desks in New York, London, and Tokyo to limit their activities for the period of this trade so that they could "borrow" their limits to make up the $500 million. Then the Singapore desk had to find counterparties with which it could do the offsetting forward trades. These trades, again, were large; for instance it needed about $100 million in the 1-month forward on the Singapore dollar. It found a bank that would provide such a large position, but again, this exceeded the counterparty limit with that bank that the Singapore desk had been given. More borrowing of limits from other locations, asking them to hold back trading with this client, was achieved and the trade went ahead. In retrospect this looks like a logical parceling out of risk limits to capture a valuation opportunity. But in the heat of the moment, few banks can do this, and so this bank achieved a clear advantage through its flexibility.

To capture risk opportunities identified by valuation skills, financial firms have to possess the flexibility to bring the resources to bear. But this is still not enough. The final core skill, resilience, is needed. Like it or not, in a business focused on absorbing, intermediating, and advising on risks, there will be losses and mistakes. Financial firms have to be able to survive these, and so they need resilience to garner attractive risk opportunities.

Resilience comes in two types. Obviously, financial resilience is a prerequisite in markets where large periodic losses can occur. For instance, in the property and casualty insurance market for large corporations, underwriters price the coverage on the assumption that the firm will make money over time. There will be losses, but over time, the premiums and investment income on those premiums will exceed the losses and operating expenses required to attract and service the business. However, given the laws of statistics, it is quite possible that the one-time big loss could occur in the first year of coverage, long before the premiums have been built up to make a profit. Only firms with large enough capital bases can absorb this type of loss and be able to move on to capture the full opportunity. In securities underwriting, there are times when markets do fall and the underwriters have to cover a large loss. Only those with the financial capital to survive this shock will be able to go on to reap the rewards of their valuation and flexibility skills. Banks must have the financial strength to survive major loan losses and move on to new risk opportunities. Interestingly, in developing new products, companies must often be prepared to experiment in order to see how the losses actually occur. Through this increased understanding of the risks, these companies are able to price and compete better than players that have not gone through the learning process. Only companies with the capital to survive such losses can benefit from the education. If they do indeed gain a valuation advantage as a result, they will be well rewarded for using their capital this way.

The other form of resilience is organizational resilience. Anyone who has been in a company that has suffered a major loss from a risk knows what this can mean: the whole company grinds to a halt, and all risk taking is practically forbidden. Financial firms need to be able to possess not only the financial resilience to absorb losses but also the ability to return to the fray afterward. They need to learn from and adapt to the loss. Otherwise, they soon cease to be real players in the market; they cease to fulfill the key role of financial institutions. This organizational resilience also involves the ability to establish the controls and procedures that forestall a panic, knee-jerk response in the first place. For instance, backup computer systems to replace those that go down because of a malfunction or power cutoff are institutionalized ways of building in organizational resilience to a crisis. There is a cost to this redundancy, but the companies that build or lease these extra systems believe it is money well spent to avoid a large crisis.

Valuation, flexibility, and resilience are the core building blocks that financial firms need as they enter the uneven playing fields that characterize most financial markets. Financial firms that focus their versions of these three skills on markets and risk opportunities where they have clear advantages can generate large profits; those that apply their skills in an unfocused way cannot expect to prosper, because they are unable to discern where the risk/reward line falls in their chosen markets.

In theory, of course, there are hundreds of ways to combine the many different types of these three core risk/reward skills in order to create a firm's unique strategy. Certainly, at first glance, financial firms seem to be pursuing all manner of strategies in the financial marketplace. In reality, however, the number of unique approaches is limited, and financial firms can combine these three skills in a few ways. Specifically, five core risk strategies seem to exist for financial firms; it is to those that we turn in the next chapters. If financial firms can master these five strategies, they will understand the key ways to position themselves in practically any financial market to earn profits from risks.

PROPOSITION II

FIVE RISK/REWARD STRATEGIES WILL UNDERPIN SUCCESS

4

Separating the Wheat from the Chaff: The Segmentation Strategy

When my wife and I were buying the house in which we live, like many home buyers we were complete neophytes on the subject of house insurance. Deciding it was best to get quotations from competing insurance companies, we found a couple of brokers and sought the best bids from the companies they accessed. For the same coverage from similarly strong, reputable companies, we were amazed at the range of premium quotations. Even more interesting was that the insurance company we had used to insure our previous house quoted a much lower premium for our new, similarly structured and sized house than it had for our old house, which was in a little town just 25 miles away. Planning to be loyal to this insurance company, we were nevertheless sufficiently intrigued to ask our broker why they were so much cheaper than everybody else and charged so much less than they had for our previous house.

The answer came back: "They know the segments in this market intimately." It turns out that the real risk from fire in wooden houses (the common breed in New England) is the speed with which the fire service can get to the house; this above all else will determine the extent of the damage. In this case, we had not only moved to the district of a full-time fire brigade, as opposed to the volunteer force in place just 25 miles away, but this insurance company had all the fire hydrants in the area plotted in its own proprietary database and knew that our new house was very close to a hydrant. Presumably, they were confident that in the event of a fire the firemen would arrive quickly, be able to access water swiftly, and thus be able to save the wooden structure from disaster. The other insurance companies were probably not able to divide the high-risk locations from the lower-risk ones as well as this company did, and so had to charge more average prices across the district. We chose the low bid.

Our insurance company, by dividing the high-risk houses from the lower-risk ones, was practicing the segmentation strategy, the first of the five core risk/reward strategies. Applicable in situations where there are perhaps thousands of individual risks to consider, this strategy is based on having superior knowledge of a particular market's segments of risk, and then avoiding or charging vast sums for the high-risk situations and pursuing the lower-risk or higher-profit situations aggressively. In particular, segmentation strategies rely upon analysis of thousands of pieces of "hard", numerical data. More and more often, these are computer-driven strategies. Only advanced computers with the latest statistical software can process the information finely enough to provide winning insights. It is no surprise, then, that the segmentation strategies are and will be most applicable to the mass retail markets—consumer banking, and insurance most notably—although, as we will see, they are also applicable to some wholesale markets as well.

An excellent example of the segmentation strategy in practice is provided by the credit and charge card industry. During the 1980s, the credit card became a key driver of earnings for many U.S. commercial banks. By the end of the decade, they had become such an important profit center that a number of significant nonbanks were entering the market, beginning with Sears Roebuck's Discover card, AT&T's Universal card introduced in 1990, and finally, cards from some of the regional telephone companies. Credit cards may appear to be a no-lose situation, but in fact, they are a complex business with many risks. But as in all financial markets, the risks were the attraction because those companies that could manage the risks would earn magnificent returns. In 1989, American Express, through its Travel Related Services group, earned $830 million, largely from its charge cards (Green, Gold, and Platinum) and its matching Optima credit cards; Citibank's Diners Club, Carte Blanche, Visa, and MasterCard earned about $600 million in the same year.

How did they do it? Credit and charge card economics are driven by a few key factors. First of all, there is the advertising cost to attract new card holders; the higher the hit rate of mailed solicitations, or applications left in stores, or cross-selling with other products, the better. Then there are credit losses—the lower the better. There are the costs of processing the charges flowing through stores, airlines, theaters, and other outlets, the costs of accounting for and tracking all these flows, and the cost of sending out statements to stores and retail customers. As these costs were largely fixed (with certain step function increases as a bank ran out of computing capacity), the more stores and card holders one could get, the better. (As long as it didn't cost a fortune to attract the new customers and they didn't turn out to be bad credit risks!) On the revenue side, a card company usually groups its customers into segments like "low user/pays off each month," "high user/keeps a regular balance outstanding," and "high user/pays off every month." Card companies are interested in high usage (they get fees from the stores for each charge) and in customers who do not pay off their balance all at once (they get very large interest spreads) but who pay some of the balance each month. They want to avoid the user who chews up processing capacity without keeping any balances, and they definitely want to minimize credit losses and defaults by those who borrow but do not repay.

While it is true that processing efficiency, low error rates, and low costs are important in the credit card world, segmentation is the key to this game. The winners are those who have been able to improve their marketing returns and lower their credit losses by using sophisticated segmentation techniques. These techniques have also been used to identify attractive customers within an existing card base to persuade them to upgrade to more profitable products (for instance, from American Express Green to Gold to Platinum cards) or to encourage increased charging on cards by increasing credit lines to customers believed to be good risks. The winners during the 1980s were the firms that invested in sophisticated segmentation technologies. In the mass retail credit market, such segmentation systems are based on *scoring technologies* in which each customer is scored according to a set of criteria that determine his or her creditworthiness; then the customers are segmented according to these scores. Two prime examples of users of such technologies in the United States are American Express and Citicorp/Citibank.

As we have all experienced, the usual way of segmenting the consumer market for credit cards during the 1960s and 1970s was to have the applicant fill out a basic form when he (or, increasingly, she) applied for the card, detailing items such as income, employment history, and number of years at the present residence; we have all filled out these forms. On the basis of this information, we were "scored"; that is, on the basis of the company's experience with people of similar backgrounds, we were assigned a risk score. That score determined whether or not we got a card and how large the spending limit was. The problem with this approach is that it is static, relying on data from one moment in time. In addition, it provides little protection against fraud by the applicant, does not protect against multiple simultaneous applications by overborrowing yuppies, and does not allow the bank or credit card company to update its files as customers' incomes and lifestyles change. American Express and Citibank were at the forefront in trying to correct these problems. By using advanced segmentation tools, they moved to a position where they were able to earn more attractive returns than the average credit card competitor. To do this, they invested in proprietary scoring systems. Most banks at the time relied on credit scoring services, such as those operated by TRW, that were available to all competitors. American Express and Citibank wanted to differentiate their risk/reward management skills so that they could outperform the competition, and they did so by developing *proprietary* databases. These firms were prepared to send out random mailings of credit card offerings to learn in-house about credit behavior. As you can imagine, they incurred significant costs as a result. One major player is reputed to have lost over $30 million in credit losses from such experiments. But the payoff was to be very big.

Proprietary credit files meant that these firms were able to segment the market in finer and different ways than the average credit card issuer. So, they had better knowledge of who to mail their fliers to, and what would entice each customer segment to apply. As a result, their marketing costs per new applicant went down, which, as noted earlier, is one of the key drivers of economics in this business. Once the applicant was in the door, they were able to assess his or her credit risk much more effectively than the average player. In practical terms, this meant they were able to assess who wouldn't pay and, on the other hand, who could support a large credit line. Their segmentation analysis showed that offering a large credit line on a card encouraged the use of that particular card over others the consumer might have in his wallet or her purse, so being able to differentiate the good risks from the bad ones was a crucial part of the competitive game. These firms simply had better information, and better ways of analyzing it, than the average credit card issuer. They still incurred losses, but they knew the reasons and were soon able to predict accurately what the losses would be from a new mailing of card solicitations, with certain credit limits, to a particular geographic or demographic segment. If a senior business manager demanded more cards and more loans to cardholders, the firm's analysts could segment the marketplace to determine where the highest hit rate for new solicitations would be and what level of credit losses to expect from such a mailing for any given achieved balance level.

By the end of the 1980s this approach, although still crucial for success, was starting to lose its effectiveness because there were signs that the market for new cards was becoming saturated. In fact, as AT&T showed, new (expensive) enhancements such as offering cards that had no annual charge and made available discounts on long-distance telephone calls would generate more applications, but the core market was not growing as rapidly as before. The next techniques to be added to the basic solicitation and credit-scoring approach were *dynamic* scoring approaches that would enable these firms to mine the customers they already had in greater depth. An example of this was the way these firms controlled losses from delinquent accounts.

The old way of dealing with delinquent accounts was straightforward and reasonably efficient. By careful monitoring of their consumer receivables, credit and charge card companies were able to spring quickly on those who were late in paying their bills or had exceeded their credit lines. A set series of actions ensued: a reminder letter was sent out, perhaps accompanied by a phone call to new customers; if that did not work, then more aggressive dunning letters, accompanied by blocking of further charges, followed. If there was still no payment, collection agencies were called in. In reality, these firms recovered only 25 cents on the dollar of delinquencies, and the typical new credit card portfolio was costing credit and charge card companies 4 percent of outstandings in losses each year. In fact, this level of losses was a deterrent to growth for many firms. In the mid-1980s, Bank of America (ironically, the founder of what became Visa) was so bowed down with credit losses in other components of the bank (farm loans and less-developed-country debt were the main problems) that it could not increase its attractive credit card portfolio as quickly as it would have liked for fear of raising its low credit loss history—even though this growth probably had attractive overall economics. Similarly, a smaller regional bank in the northeastern United States was hamstrung for fear of high credit losses based on the predictions of its antiquated credit-scoring systems. Although this firm believed that its credit card portfolio was growing too slowly given its market opportunity, and could see other firms increasing their card balances more rapidly, it was not convinced it could separate the strong credit risks from the weaker ones clearly enough to grow safely.

New segmentation techniques gave some firms the confidence to expand. Instead of the usual scoring approach described earlier, they constantly updated existing scores based on a cardholder's behavior and assigned *new* scores to each cardholder as time passed. These new numbers were based on the original demographic information received with the application but also on analysis of the customers' monthly charging history. This meant that these firms were able to differentiate among people who were late payers. Whereas traditional competitors had just one approach for every late payer, these firms were able to treat each payer differently. If the constantly updated behavior score suggested that you fitted the profile of borrowers at or near the limit of their financial capacity, then the card firm knew to act quickly if you didn't pay—the unpleasant letters went out fast, and every effort was made to recover the outstanding balance, even at the expense of your relationship with the bank. On the other hand, if the constantly updated behavior score put you in the category of a wealthy individual with little debt and easily able to pay your debts, then a late payment was treated with great care to ensure a potentially lucrative account was not given to the competition by too rapid and insensitive treatment. As all businesspeople know, one of the problems with constant travel today is that necessary chores at home, like paying bills, can go undone because you are simply away too often. Somehow the slim credit card bill is particularly likely to be overlooked. For the credit card companies without dynamic scoring techniques, which could alert them to differentiate the treatment of different types of late payers, this was a real problem. The company did not want to send the dogs to the home of a successful investment banker or movie producer who had happened to be traveling when the bill arrived.

Dynamic scoring techniques are applied not only to late payers but also every time a large charge is made. Once I had to make a trip to the Caribbean for a business meeting (hard to believe, I know, but in fact true—the whole day on the island was spent in a windowless conference room). As those who have taken trips there know, the airline schedules are not like those between New York and Chicago, Paris and London, or Tokyo and Hong Kong. If you miss the flight, you could be in for a very long wait. On this particular occasion, the business meeting was scheduled to start at 9 A.M. on the island, so my colleagues and I had decided to take the last flight out the night before and spend the night there, to give ourselves plenty of time in the morning to prepare for the meeting. This was in fact essential, as there were no flights early enough from New York to get to the island in time for the meeting. My colleagues made the flight with ease, but due to the delights of New York traffic, I missed it. Unfortunately, I had to be at the meeting; enter American Express. I needed to charter a plane to the island and charge it on my American Express card. Now, although I find the charge card useful, I am not in the habit of charging tens of thousands of dollars on it, so I waited with some trepidation for the response from American Express. As I expected, and probably as many of us have experienced at one time or another, the salesperson for the charter airline told me that "American Express wants to speak to you." The American Express representative asked me a few basic questions about the purpose of the charge and then authorized it. This amount was well in excess of my usual charge; how could the company expose itself to such risk? The answer was, of course, that they possessed sophisticated segmentation techniques.

Each American Express authorization agent has a detailed database (which is updated regularly) that can be accessed to determine the customer's credit record. Software supporting the authorization system determines where the person requesting extraordinary credit fits on the credit scoring system. That is what happened to me when I chartered the plane. (As an aside, even the best plans can fail. The plane duly turned up to take me to the meeting early the next morning, but then was delayed on the ground by a mechanical problem, so that I was late for the meeting anyway. Somebody had not segmented the good engines from the bad.)

The same approach is applied on a more regular basis for point-of-sale credit authorizations at shops and stores around the world. Whether it be American Express, Diners Club, Visa, MasterCard, or the Discover card, if you go to a shop today and purchase something with a card, it is very likely that your card will be put through a machine that reads the magnetic strip on the card and sends the information to a central database. This matches the request for credit not only against your limit on the card but also, in the more sophisticated scoring systems, against your past behavior to see if credit can be extended without any questions or whether some further inquiry makes sense. Every second, these companies put their balance sheets at risk through credit extension; multiple decisions per second around the world are required, and it is only through rigorous application of the segmentation strategy that this can be done.

Not only did this behavior scoring enable the winning companies to control losses, it was also the basis for future growth. Smaller banks found it harder and harder to increase their portfolios of credit card loans without incurring unattractive losses because the winners had segmented many of the attractive accounts out of the market. Small banks began to consider selling their account bases to the bigger players. With their advanced scoring technology, the winners were prepared to pay large premiums for these portfolios because they could take the mature account bases and safely increase them faster than the small bank could have done. As they developed experience with the newly acquired accounts, they learned who to advance more credit to and who to chase aggressively if they paid late. They made those accounts more active and more profitable. It was no surprise to see significant consolidation in the U.S.

credit card industry in the 1980s. This occurred because of the segmentation strategy.

The winners took their analytical capabilities one stage further. By the late 1980s, American Express was earning a significant share of its card-related profits from selling such goods as luggage, binoculars, books, and other products to card members through mail inserts provided with bills or from direct mailings. American Express realized that its true skill was in analysis and segmentation of data, and set out to apply that skill to a series of nonfinancial endeavors based on their card databases. Customers were inundated with mailings from American Express as the company used its behavior-based segmentation to decide who deserved an upgrade offer from the Green to the Gold card, who might like a subscription to a travel magazine (published by American Express), who needed and might actually buy (using their American Express card, of course) some new luggage.

The amazing example of the American Express segmentation strategy in practice was the introduction and success of the Platinum card. It is obviously a matter of personal taste, but this is really a silly card for all but a few. For an extraordinary $300 a year fee, the Platinum cardholder is offered some emergency travel services he or she is unlikely to use, with a "we'll do anything for you" attitude attached. In addition, the Platinum cardholder is able to signal to the world that he or she is special. The card has been an extraordinary success, building a base of high users who pay that high annual fee and do not come close to absorbing the level of extra servicing costs that outweigh the incremental fees. American Express was able to segment the market by understanding that people, or at least some types of people, would value the appeal of this card and were indifferent about the fee they had to pay. Some Platinum cardholders use the services extensively and are getting a good deal, but for the card to be an economic success, they have to be only a minority of those who bought the card. American Express took a risk by offering the open-ended service on the card, but they had enough test data to know that few would use it and many would pay an enormous premium for the snob appeal of the card.

American Express used their segmentation capabilities as a powerful competitive weapon when they moved directly from the charge card market into the credit card market. The traditional American Express cards were charge cards, requiring that the cardholder pay off the outstanding balance each month. Through its proprietary database on these cardholders' spending patterns, American Express decided to enter the credit card market, where cardholders are allowed to roll over their borrowings—at an interest cost. The problem for American Express was that this was already a mature market when they decided to enter. Their competitive advantage was segmentation. Based on their proprietary information on their existing cardholders, they offered the new Optima credit card *only* to existing cardholders, but at low fees and with a low interest rate. They reasoned that by controlling distribution this way, they would incur very low credit losses and, therefore, would be able to charge lower fees and interest. The card was a great marketing success and helped American Express win back some of the charge volume their cardholders were applying through their Visa, MasterCard, and Discover cards.

However, these databases are only as good as the data and the analytical software they use. In 1991, credit losses on the Optima Card resulted in a $155 million loss. There were signs of problems at the card's inception. When I applied for the Optima card, I was allocated a credit line of over $10,000—a result, I think, of the fact that I used my basic American Express card for my business travel expenses and was able to pay off very large bills as a result of travel in Asia through reimbursements. I was amused, therefore, when a senior partner of my firm started grumbling, soon after I was notified of this credit limit, that he had received a limit of only $1,500. He, however, was less amused that American Express thought I was a better credit risk than he was. The answer was obviously that he needed to do more international consulting.

A further use of segmentation strategy techniques in the credit card industry occurred when the airlines and the card industry joined forces. As a result of deregulation in the U.S. airline industry, the major airlines had invested heavily in data segmentation to work out exactly how to price each seat in order to get the maximum utilization and the best returns. Prices on routes changed continuously as the computer analysis suggested ways to earn the best return on each flight. This approach was supplemented by the "bonus miles" programs that attempted to woo frequent travelers to one airline over another, but ended up in many cases as simply a way of discounting. Some added attraction was needed to make fliers stick to one airline over another. Enter the credit card companies. By making each dollar charged on a card equal to one bonus mile on a particular program, both parties won. The airlines reinforced loyalty to one airline over another, while the credit card company found a loyal user who would use that card in preference to others because it came with a free vacation—as long as the user spent enough! But the card companies won something even better—a whole new group of affluent, high-usage customers to add to their existing card bases and to segment to their hearts' delight to gain more income. So, two masters in segmentation had come together to apply their technologies to each other's advantage. No wonder the smaller players felt squeezed out, and as a result many sold out.

Of course, this strategy of uniting two customer bases through an *affinity group card* did not always work. Football teams, charities, and others all tried to sell their unique customer bases to the card companies. These efforts were often expensive failures because the two parties had nothing to offer each other or their customers. There was a limit to the loyalty of a consumer to his baseball team, and if the affinity card offered nothing more than the team's logo on the front, and no nice benefits like frequent flier miles, then its attraction was limited.

Many such programs failed because they had not segmented the market in such a way as to offer anything special to the customer, and thus did not attract enough new cardholders or higher charges to justify the investment the card company had to make to get access to the customer base. The football clubs, charities, and others all required the card company to pay a fee and hand over a percentage of the income each year in return for access to the customer mailing list.

The credit and charge card industries in the United States are now sophisticated users of segmentation strategies. Cards are marketed to discrete segments of the market—for instance, travelers, and students—with corresponding features to attract these segments, ranging from low "teaser" interest rates for a certain period of time, to extended grace periods before interest is charged on borrowings, to a high-fee/low-rate card for the segment that likes to roll over the card borrowings. Other cards try to reward usage directly—most notably the Sears Discover card, with a rebate on charges of up to 1 percent, depending on the annual charge level. Segmentation will continue as competitors attempt to find opportunities in this increasingly saturated market.

The situation for these same businesses outside the United States can be very different. Most important, few markets have developed the U.S. consumer's insatiable taste for credit. At the same time, default rates in many countries are much lower. This does not necessarily give the companies much security, because the credit file information available to competitors in the United States is often not available elsewhere. For instance, due to lack of credit data, Citicorp is assuming that, in India, the relatively few people who have a telephone are probably better risks than those who do not, and in Indonesia they are using ownership of satellite dishes for television as the credit guide. As a result of these credit and economic pressures, many competitors decide to focus on the higher-income segments alone and try to develop a snob appeal for their cards. From this more wealthy base, they hope to attract high charge volume and borrowing, and to start building a proprietary database on their clients so that they can start offering higher limits to the more creditworthy customers and begin cross-selling other products on a targeted basis. This is the segmentation strategy applied to different circumstances.

If the credit and charge card industries were new or renewed devotees of data segmentation in the 1980s, they were behind an existing trend in both property and casualty and life insurance. When you step back from these industries as they affect the consumer world, it becomes clear that segmentation is the way to win. For life insurance, this is especially clear. The life insurance company gets a series of premiums that it can invest and reap the interest on—until the insured dies. At that point, the amount insured must be handed over to the named beneficiaries, be they the spouse, children, or some charity beloved of the deceased. The insurance company makes money as long as the insured lives long enough so that the annual premiums and interest, or other market returns accumulated over the years, exceed the amount paid out when that person dies. Forecasting life expectancies is therefore a key to success, especially in a competitive market. The firms that can identify the low-risk (e.g., target weight, nonsmoking women) groups and charge them less, and charge the higher-risk (e.g., overweight, smoking males) groups more, will do better than those that charge uniform rates across segments. They will win more of the attractive business and avoid undercharging the gourmands. To segment the market this way obviously requires access to past histories on life expectancies and a way to match applicants to this data. In a period of rapid advances in medical technology and with the emergence of new ailments and diseases, keeping up with life expectancies and adjusting life insurance rates is no easy task, especially when volatile investment markets make the calculations even more complex and risky. Life insurance is built upon the segmentation strategy, and application of that strategy becomes more complex every day.

If the life insurance industry is a net winner from advances in medical techniques and prevention practices, then the health insurance industry is a loser. Medical costs have grown at amazing rates around the world, especially in countries such as the United States, where the government does not set spending limits through some form of nationalized or socialized medicine. Heart bypass surgery, new treatments for cancer, new approaches for enhancing the life expectancies of the aged, new treatments for premature babies, and treatments for old diseases (Parkinson's disease) and new diseases (AIDS) have raised medical costs at a frightening rate. Under constant pressure from employers to control the rate of increase of medical insurance premiums or taxes, the insurers or governments that pick up the bills for hospital stays have to work out ways to control costs, or at least charge explicitly for the costs they do incur. The answer again is separation of the multiple risks—the segmentation strategy.

During the 1980s, the best health care insurers, and their cousins, the Health Maintenance Organizations (HMOs) which exist only in the U.S., invested heavily in segmenting two things: the likely medical costs from a population they plan to insure and the actual coverage provided. From these databases they learned important lessons. First, they could charge explicit premiums based on the medical risk of the population they agreed to insure. If an employer wanted to insure his staff but all persons were over 40 years old, then his premium would be much higher than if the staff included a large number of younger workers. If he wanted to provide full pregnancy and birth coverage, then the fewer women he employed the better. If the policy extended to family members of staff, then demographic groups with lower family sizes meant lower premiums. Second, the insurance companies began to monitor health services actually provided on a case-by-case basis. They also started to second-guess physicians to see if a patient really needed that extra day of recuperation in the hospital or if he could be sent home early. The insurer's database might show that an appendectomy should require only 2 days' hospitalization, so if the patient was in the hospital longer, the insurance company wanted to know why. Those insurers who could segment the market best could offer the best rates to the employers whose staff members were least likely to incur high medical bills. Those insurers that had the most effective monitoring of actual hospital charges against historic expectations would control their costs best, further enabling them to earn better returns and offer better rates. Given the extraordinary medical cost inflation of the 1980s, health insurance was a very risky business to underwrite, but the segmentation strategy offered the better insurers some hope of riding out the vicious cost and pricing cycles.

An example of this situation in action was (and is) the AIDS tragedy, especially as it played out for life insurers in the United States in the 1980s. Young, healthy, often prosperous males living primarily on the two coasts of the country were the first victims of the epidemic of this little-understood disease. They were also life insurers' prime market. They were young, so an insurer could expect high returns for a long period. They were often wealthy, so they wanted to buy more insurance than on average. Finally, they were good targets for cross-selling new products such as tax-deferred annuities and mutual funds that the companies wanted to build into major new businesses. Suddenly this scenario was going completely wrong—the target segment was becoming an enormous liability. During the early 1980s the data on this disease was so sketchy, and the projections of future life expectancies among this group were so varied and frightening, that many insurers decided effectively to withdraw from the market. Frightened by the hidden liabilities they believed existed in the insurance they had *already* written, these companies and their boards of directors were not about to place themselves further at risk.

But some stayed in the market, focusing considerable staff time and effort on building relationships with the medical community to understand the disease and its expected impact as best they could. As the research continued, a few facts became clear about high- and low-risk segments. Patterns of behavior, geography, and income grouping were among the key segmenting criteria. In the life insurance marketplace there were two components to a buyer's interest in buying one firm's term life insurance over another's: premium charges and whether a blood test was required. The insurance companies felt more reassured if they knew prior to granting life insurance that the buyer did not have AIDS at that time (although the blood test did not guarantee that they would not get it in the future, or that the infection had occurred too recently for the test to register the antibodies in the bloodstream). Customers, on the other hand, found the test an invasion of privacy or didn't want to go through all the bother just to buy life insurance. Therefore, the companies that could segment the market well enough *not* to require a blood test for certain groups, below a certain insurance dollar amount, would write more policies than those that did not understand the risks as well and required every applicant to have a blood test. This required constant updating of the insurance company's medical knowledge, applying that knowledge to the segment databases, and adjusting premiums and testing requirements segment by segment as far as regulators would allow.

Property and casualty insurers have been mentioned (as in the case of insuring our new house) as users of segmentation strategies. This industry finds the segmentation strategy useful because it too has to sift through large amounts of data to determine who are the good drivers, what are the risks of a house burning to the ground, and what theft and burglary rates are to be expected in each location. A fascinating example in the United States of this approach in action is that of the United Services Automobile Association (USAA), the insurance company serving military officers, former officers, and their families. It is the fifth largest automobile insurer, and the fifth largest provider of home insurance, in the country. USAA was able to produce below-average losses when insuring the automobiles and other property of the military and to charge below-average premium rates. How was this possible? Superior access to the customer was a big advantage; USAA enjoyed enviable loyalty from the military and a very high market share among them. But they knew how to use the data derived from this market share to their advantage. USAA used the data captured from their years of insuring the military to identify the good risks and to avoid the bad risks—or at least to get paid for taking those risks. So USAA could predict automobile risks based on factors such as the driver's rank, the location of his military base, and his tenure in the military. No other insurer had such a database. It could be developed only by actually insuring the customers, and USAA used its competitive advantage of having the data when others didn't to protect its data advantage; the company simply offered the best rates and kept the competition out! USAA also used its information advantage to cross-sell other products, starting with life insurance and moving on to mutual funds and credit cards. USAA Life Insurance Company relied upon direct marketing to USAA automobile and home insurance clients, and achieved an amazing 97 percent persistency rate (that is, only 3 percent of its policies lapsed each year). One MasterCard mailing produced a 52 percent response rate (most banks would be very happy with a response rate one-tenth of that!). This cross-selling success reflected the loyalty and trust USAA had built up from years of providing targeted service to its customers.

An equally dramatic example of successful segmentation is provided by the Progressive Insurance Company based in Beachwood, Ohio, which specialized in high-risk drivers and motorcyclists. Young men who wanted to drive souped-up Chevrolet Camaros or ride Harley-Davidsons found it very difficult to get insurance. However, their task was nothing compared to that of previously barred drivers, those with a record of multiple accidents or convicted drunk drivers. Given the appallingly low profitability of automobile insurance in the United States generally, mainline insurance companies had little interest in taking on these unfortunates unless forced to by a regulatory agency, as in some states. In places where that was not the case, enter Progressive. Again, the segmentation strategy approach is clear. Through years of study and experience, Progressive had developed its own proprietary database that enabled it to differentiate the merely very high risks from the truly suicidal ones, and to avoid the latter while providing (still expensive) coverage to the former. They knew obscure things about motorcyclists—for example, that men under 35 with a steady income who lived in certain zip codes were higher risks than those under 30 living in other zip codes. Because nobody else knew the histories of these groups of drivers and riders as well as Progressive, this company was often the only available choice and certainly the best-priced choice. They earned high returns not only because they knew what to charge the high-risk drivers, but also because they could recognize the lunatics and avoid them. The infamous state insurance pools that forced all companies to participate in providing coverage to the high risks *and* the lunatics produced enormous losses because they did no such segmentation.

To date, all the automobile insurance segmentation winners we have looked at have focused on which risks they will underwrite, at what price. The Travelers Insurance Company did this kind of segmentation, too, but also focused on the claims costs it incurred when one of its insured cars was in an accident. The typical way this works is as follows: When two cars are involved in an accident, they are towed away to the nearest garage and an estimate for repairs is prepared. Then the work is undertaken—beating out bashed-in wings, replacing twisted bumpers and fenders, replacing broken glass, even righting a twisted chassis. While medical and personal liability costs often can be the most traumatic costs of an accident, car repair costs run, on average, at 25 percent of an insurer's automobile claim costs. Travelers focused on these costs in great detail and found that it could apply the segmentation strategy to its advantage.

Having never worked in a car repair and body repair garage, I must admit that the practices of the industry are a bit of a mystery to me. So they are to most people, and that is the industry's secret weapon. It is a fragmented industry; no one national firm dominates any one national market. In addition, its customers are none too discriminating, having just suffered an unpleasant accident that has often left them in a state of shock. They are eager to get their cars repaired and unable to compare prices across markets because of the fragmentation of the industry. In addition, it is difficult to take a smashed-up car with broken front suspension on a grand tour from one garage to another to compare prices! Pricing in the market is, therefore, mysterious, and many consumers feel they are being taken advantage of and forced to pay exorbitant bills. The cynics among us might even say they are right.

Travelers tried to overcome this problem. In certain markets where it offered automobile insurance it had enough experience with accidents and subsequent repairs to be able to compare prices. What it found was very interesting. For some strange reason, some repair shops performed similar repairs for much higher prices than others. In addition, many used premium factory spare parts when generic spares would do just as well. It did not matter what brand of battery was used to replace the cracked original.

The research opened up a major segmentation opportunity. Travelers set up a system to intervene before repair work was done and either to have the damaged car taken to the nearest garage that was on their list of low-cost suppliers or to lower the original estimated repair bill. As a result of this research work, the resulting database of garages, and segmentation of the expensive from the less expensive, Travelers had an advantage, claiming to reduce repair bills by 11.5 percent because of its approach. Interestingly, it then began to sell this information to other insurers who would pay for it. Travelers hoped to get direct revenues from its segmentation skills. The service, called Systematic Auditing of Vehicle Estimates (SAVE), charged other insurers an average of $35 to review garages' repair estimates and give these insurers more facts with which to bargain. Travelers is no longer one of the only insurers with these segmentation skills; others have invested to control the risks of auto insurance.

When I first moved from London to New York, I was almost immediately the victim of the segmentation strategy—although a willing and satisfied victim. In London I had followed my parents when opening a bank account. Indeed, given my meager finances, first as a student and then as an overworked but underpaid new employee of a bank, my ability to control my spending and bring it anywhere near my income was limited, so this family connection was required to keep my account in good standing. When I moved to New York I had no such family reference to rely upon, so I used my own wits to determine where I should bank. My first approach was to walk outside both my apartment building on the Upper East Side and my new office in midtown. At both locations I noticed that there were Citibank branches and ATMs reasonably close by, so I went in and opened an account. I had been successfully segmented.

Market research survey after survey has confirmed that the average consumer desires one factor above all others when selecting a bank for basic transactions—that is, a checking or current account bank—and that factor is convenience. I had acted exactly in line with the surveys. The trick for the banks is to work out how to supply convenience at the lowest cost, because bank branches are very expensive to maintain. This requires the segmentation strategy—in particular, careful analysis of local demographics and of travel and commuting patterns to determine how to provide convenience to a neighborhood at reasonable cost. In my case, branches close to home and close to the office were required. As I explored Manhattan further, I also wanted them near shops, cinemas, theaters, and restaurants; Citibank generally obliged. They won my account and many more like it and generated extraordinary returns on their investment. Specifically, through careful analysis of local needs and careful placement of branches and ATMs (for instance, in the lobbies of new apartment buildings—guess where those tenants tended to bank), Citibank was able to build a market share of deposits that was much higher than its share of physical outlets. However, it had enough outlets, and they were so well placed, that for the average consumer there always seemed to be one nearby, and that was enough. From this disproportionate share of deposits per branch, Citibank not only earned great returns but also had the opportunity to cross-sell a wide range of other saving and lending products. Profits followed.

The principle Citibank was following was detailed segmentation of the demographics and travel patterns of the consumer. Branch positioning requires careful analysis of where the business is located during the course of a day and opening branches accordingly. Let's look at what I found when I moved to New York. I was interested in three main areas of town: the Upper East Side where I lived (and, in particular, the area near my apartment building), the one-block radius around the office building where my firm's offices are located, and downtown where I spent a good deal of time. In addition, I wanted to have a good number of branches around the city so that I could always find a branch if I needed it. From Citibank's perspective, I was an easy customer to satisfy inasmuch as my primary areas of travel and work were in relatively prosperous parts of town and were close to each other; it is tougher to locate branches when you have to cover a broader geographical area and locations of different economic strength. Here segmentation becomes crucial if a bank is to avoid ending up with too many branches in light of its income potential.

To most non-New Yorkers, New York means just Manhattan. In fact, of course, the city includes four other boroughs—the Bronx, Brooklyn, Queens, and Staten Island. Even within Manhattan, demographics and economics are very uneven, ranging from glitzy midtown to the struggling Harlems, the diverse upper West Side, and the East Village. Beyond the five boroughs, there then lie a series of unevenly prosperous suburbs and industrial areas. The challenge for the banks is to locate their branches across these districts to attract as much business as possible from consumers and small businesses without incurring exorbitant costs. Segmentation, if it is undertaken with great care, provides the answer.

New York banks analyze the basic demographics and banking statistics of an area: population totals, income levels, total bank deposits, and types of bank deposits. However, this information does not provide clear guidance for branch locations, so banks have to go a step further, just as American Express did in the credit card business. What the leading firms are able to do is to combine two key pieces of detailed data that the average competitor does not have or cannot afford to acquire. They are able to analyze the demographic data down to the zip code level, and then even more finely by using complex mapping software that models the likely capture of small business or consumer deposits and loans. Further, they incorporate commuting pattern data into their decision making to determine what the impact of daily flows of people across geographic areas will be on a branch's utility.

As applied to the New York region, this means that Citibank can determine what the likely catchment area for a branch will be on a static basis, and then factor in daily commuting patterns to determine which branches will be most productive overall. For Citibank this means deciding exactly where to place branches in the outer suburbs of New York, which may be very quiet during the day due to the commuters but crucial to winning their business when they are in the city. The surburban commuter from New Rochelle will choose his checking bank on the basis of convenience, which means convenience seven days a week. To win the profitable daytime flows, Citibank is prepared to establish branches and ATMs in residential surburban areas, where they are often used just to withdraw money.

This pattern is repeated in city after city in the United States. For instance, if you go to Detroit you find a few branches downtown and in the Renaissance Center, then a desert before the commuting suburbs begin. There are exceptions to this approach, of course—banks that have decided that their segment of the market is exactly the markets that others have left. One example is a savings bank in New York City that had a large branch in one of the toughest sections of town. The management of the bank always assumed that this branch, which was truly enormous in the style of the branches of old, was operating at a loss. In fact, further analysis showed it was the most profitable branch in the bank's network—primarily because it had no competition, and also because the local residents rewarded the bank with loyalty for staying in the area when others had moved out. This is a segmentation strategy, although one open to just a few.

But positioning branches where the wealthier segments of the population live and work is not the only application of the segmentation strategy to branch banking. It is also crucial for considering bank acquisitions. As banks in the United States, Europe, and Japan face reduced regulation concerning interstate or trans-Europe branching, many acquisition opportunities emerge and the segmentation strategy provides great opportunities. Perhaps one of the best examples of that situation in action was the acquisition of Crocker National Bank in California by Wells Fargo.

Crocker National was one of the top five branch banks in California in the 1970s and early 1980s, and was purchased in 1985 by Midland Bank of the United Kingdom as they tried a strategy of international diversification. This proved to be disastrous for Midland because they were unable to control Crocker's risk and reward judgments and the subsidiary incurred significant credit losses. At the same time, a talented retail banking team had taken hold at Wells Fargo and redirected its strategy toward the retail market, reducing its commitment to the wholesale market, including selling branches serving corporations outside the United States. As Midland considered its options for Crocker, the team at Wells Fargo determined that combining the branch networks of the two banks would produce a very attractive branch network for many consumers. The Wells team bid for and acquired Crocker for just over $1 billion, and at a stroke became one of the dominant retail banks in the largest state in the United States. This acquisition quickly paid for itself and established the Wells Fargo management team as a leader in the banking industry. They had succeeded by buying a particular bank whose branches meshed so well with their own that consumers found great convenience and moved accounts to the new Wells, which was also able to reduce duplicate costs very quickly. The same logic is behind the wave of 1991 U.S. banking mergers like

Chemical/Manufacturers Hanover, and NCNB/C&S/Sovan, and Bank of America/Security Pacific.

This is the whole point of the segmentation strategy applied to branch banking: Through careful analysis of consumers' overwhelming need for convenience, banks can win more customers per branch than less skilled competitors, and can do so *despite* the fact that the products offered through these branches are no cheaper than those offered by others—in fact, they are often more expensive. The banks that are good at segmenting the market often have only average products, for which they are able to charge premium rates because they have dealt with consumers' primary need. Relatively high spreads on loans and relatively high minimum balances on deposit accounts feed the profits of Citibank's retail branch system, but they are possible because of the superb branch network that keeps so many consumers loyal.

The value of segmentation does not apply to consumer markets alone. Many of the financing vehicles and infrastructure used to serve the consumer are also used in corporate markets. For instance, a large percentage of banking branch profitability is derived not from the consumer but from small businesses, and here again, careful segmentation is required. Not all tradesmen and small businesses are alike, and their different needs have to be understood and accommodated as far as possible. Unfortunately, some segments are more profitable than others, so banks are forced to try to discourage the unprofitable pieces of business and encourage the more profitable ones.

A number of services that local businesses value, such as availability of coins when needed and conversion of coins into notes and bills or into deposits, are very unprofitable for banks. Merchants, rather than small businesses, are the main segment demanding such services, and many banks now think of them as a distinct segment that must be treated separately—either discouraged through high pricing or encouraged and made profitable through careful pricing. The banks make their money from deposits and from lending, and they seek to serve the small businesses that will keep reasonable balances or borrow in sufficient quantities without defaulting. They accomplish this by the high pricing of these manual services to discourage use by all but the most profitable accounts, or at least to get the unprofitable ones to pay dearly for usage. So high minimums for free banking are set, and charges for service usage are levied against deposit balances to recover the costs of services used by the less profitable accounts. The latter are often the very small businesses, those with sales of less than $1 million a year, and careful segmentation of the credit and cost of service risks associated with this group often determines how services are priced and how much time bankers spend with each customer.

Segmentation strategies have been introduced to serve larger customers too. In the very-low-margin business of money transfer, the winning firms have continued to earn reasonable returns despite rapidly declining prices. They have succeeded because they have segmented the high-service users and now charge them explicit fees for the services. They have also identified the less price-sensitive customers and focus service on them to retain their float balances. In the past, when prices were higher, they did not worry about the large account that sent unclear instructions that required significant clerical intervention to clarify and execute. Now such offenders are explicitly charged for sending poor instructions. By careful segmentation of customers and services, low-cost, high-volume providers are still able to earn reasonable returns in this market.

Segmentation strategies have also entered the world of investment banking. Compared to retail financial firms, these institutions, particularly during the boom years of the 1980s, applied less focused management technique and discipline, although they could hardly be accused of being unprofitable. It was interesting to note, however, that, during the 1980s, the return on equity of most major U.S. investment banks declined despite the extraordinary opportunities they had. As the boom ended, they found that they had to find out precisely where they did and did not earn reasonable returns. In many of the trading businesses, this meant undertaking analysis of customer profitability and trading profitability that had never been done before, and then focusing salesmen and traders on the most profitable accounts and types of trades. Broadly, customers who submitted every trade to multiple bids were to be avoided, while those who were loyal to the bank and who could be cross-sold a large number of products were to be pursued.

In the mortgage-backed security market in the United States, the segmentation strategy was used earlier than in some other trading markets. During the 1980s, the provision of mortgages to the U.S. public went through extraordinary change. Up to then, savings and loan institutions had provided mortgages that they booked on their balance sheets. But the development of mortgage pass-through securities backed by federal agencies such as the Federal National Mortgage Association (Fannie Mae) and the Federal Home Loan Mortgage Corporation (Freddie Mac) meant that these mortgages could be packaged and turned into uniform, easily tradeable securities. The mortgage market tapped into the relative efficiency of the capital markets and thereby offered the promise of lower mortgage costs for borrowers. It also liquefied the balance sheets of the savings and loan firms at precisely the time when their liability interest rates had been deregulated. This protected them from interest rate mismatch that once came from funding long-term, fixed-rate mortgages with short-term deposits. Investors were also happy, as they were offered new fixed-rate instruments with near-Treasury credit quality but trading at higher yields than Treasuries.

Mortgage pass-throughs were, however, exactly what their name implied. Although Fannie Mae and Freddie Mac offered high credit quality on the instruments, they did not alter the uncertainty about when a particular tranche of mortgages would be repaid by the underlying borrowers. Thus investors found that they were receiving a higher yield for a good reason. They faced significant reinvestment risk, that is, the risk that the mortgages could be repaid, and thus their investment returned to them, earlier than they hoped. So a 4-year investment at 10 percent could easily become a 3-year investment, and equivalent 10 percent securities for the final year might not be available. For investors counting on an interest level for a predetermined period, this was a major problem. The collateral-ized mortgage obligation (CMO) was created to solve the prob-lem. The CMO took the mortgage pass-throughs and put the cash flows from a group of them into different tranches, with some components targeted at short-term investors, some at medium-term investors, and the final tranche at both longer-term investors and those prepared to take a higher yield, with the risk that their investment would be repaid earlier than they had hoped. By guaranteeing returns for each group and divid-ing the investment world this way, the CMO was able to attract new investors who until then had avoided the mortgage-backed security market. This invention was a major example of the seg-mentation strategy in practice in the wholesale markets, design-ing a new security to meet the different needs of different investors.

This segmentation approach became the theme of capital market innovations throughout the 1980s. Intermediary invest-ment banks developed detailed databases of their investor and issuer clients' needs and preferences, and then designed eso-teric instruments to match the two. Probably nowhere was this process of innovation more active than in the lightly regulated Euromarkets, where particular types of bonds, of particular cur-rencies, were issued in great waves as intermediaries discov-ered often short-lived pockets of investor interest and immediately scoured their issuer client base to find companies that wanted to tap the segment they had discovered.

This segmentation approach was taken one step further by Bear Stearns in the mortgage-backed security market, except that they applied it in the back office clearing function. As we saw earlier, CMOs are made up of groups of mortgage pass-through securities, each of which, in turn, is made up of hun-dreds of individual mortgages. The CMOs are in fact made up of pass-throughs of a particular *type*, not specific pass-throughs. When CMOs are traded, the trading firms have to give one another pass-throughs of a specified type, but not any specific pass-throughs. Although the individual pass-throughs issued at a time are very similar, they are not identical. In fact, these individual pass-throughs have slightly different prepayment expectations because they are backed by mortgages drawn from different locations, whose residents have different propensities to prepay their mortgages when interest rates fall. Those that prepay the least, and thus keep paying higher than market interest rates, back the more valuable pass-throughs within the generic type. Bear Stearns developed a proprietary database that stored this information and enabled them to identify which pass-throughs were most valuable. When they traded the pass-throughs, they traded the generic type—but their *back-office* staff in the clearing function knew to trade away the lower-value, more rapidly repaying pass-throughs and keep the higher-value pass-throughs for Bear Stearns. Thus, in a market with very tight trading spreads, Bear Stearns, through excellent segmentation of a very large amount of data, earned above-average returns for very little risk.

What does all this mean for the banks, insurance companies, securities firms, mutual fund companies, and other financial firms that want to earn adequate returns for the risks they take in markets where those risks are made up of thousands of individual decisions? In the consumer market, it means that many competitors have become very sophisticated, and that the unskilled ones will end up holding the unattractive risks or having to spend vast sums to attract customers because their marketing is too unfocused. More and more, the winning competitors know so much about the segments in the market that the new entrant or unskilled player must be prepared to incur major losses to break in. Technically, the segmenting winners have superb *valuation* skills, honed for data-intensive markets, and have the *flexibility* to take advantage of these skills. Finally, they have the *resilience* required to accept the losses needed to build their proprietary data-bases. In years to come, mass market financial services will rely more and more upon melding these risk and reward skills into segmentation strategies.

For wholesale firms, too, segmentation strategies will be important. The rapid process of new product introduction has slowed since the surge in the 1980s, and the long bull markets of that period and the growth in trading volumes that went with them have calmed down. Wholesale firms now have to search hard for profits. This means segmenting profitable customers from less profitable ones. This requires acquiring and analyzing data about corporate finance and trading businesses in very sophisticated ways. But those that have the data and the discipline to use it will be able to orient their expensive staffs and systems toward the best opportunities and to avoid the less attractive segments. In doing so, they will be using the segmentation strategy.

5

The Legal Inside Advantage:
The Insider Strategy

Throughout the history of investing, individuals and groups have been tempted to discover and use information that is not known to the wide circle of their fellow investors. Perhaps the most famous of these events was when Nathan Rothschild received early news of Napoleon's defeat by Wellington at Waterloo in 1815. Rothschild reputedly knew of the result some 40 hours before Wellington's official dispatches reached Downing Street. Prior to the news being known, the London markets were very fearful and prices were depressed. Rothschild took advantage of his special information to buy government bonds. When the news of Napoleon's defeat became widely known, the market rose dramatically. Rothschild profited greatly from using his advantaged information.

Since then, there have been numerous undetected cases of gains through insider trading and far fewer cases where the perpetrators have been discovered. In the more mature capital markets, especially those of the United States and Europe, insider trading involving corporate information (unlike Rothchild's timely use of general information) has become a criminal offense, and much regulatory time and expense is incurred in seeking out the insider traders who profit, for example, from advance knowledge of earnings news or a potential takeover. For instance, within the New York Stock Exchange organization, there is a specialist group that spends all of its time reviewing detailed records of trading activity to discern unusual trading around the time of news events and to then begin the process of pursuing those who may have profited at the expense of their fellow investors. These efforts are based on the belief that overall capital costs for industry and commerce will be reduced if investors can trade in the confidence that they are doing so on a level playing field.

In the 1980s, the surge in takeover activity and overall stock prices fueled an apparent increase in illegal insider trading (in fact, it may well be that investigation techniques improved so significantly that more insider traders were caught than before, rather than more actually existing). In the United States, a giant web of illicit trading activities was first unearthed with the arrest and subsequent conviction of Dennis Levine, who implicated arbitrageur Ivan Boesky. From there, a series of investigations eventually led to an enormous fine being levied against Drexel Burnham Lambert, the leading underwriter of junk bonds, a fine that was central to that firm's later demise. The head of Drexel's junk bond empire, Mike Milken, was also pursued and eventually accepted guilt for certain market manipulations.

In Europe, similar cases were unearthed. In London, the venerable merchant bank Morgan Grenfell was involved in an attempt to help Guinness take over Distillers, the leading Scotch whisky producer. Through a series of secret trades with guaranteed returns to the investors, Morgan Grenfell was able to hold up the share price of Guinness during the takeover period and make the bid, which included substantial amounts of Guinness stock in exchange for the Distillers stock, a success. In fact, the Guinness share price was artificially inflated, and Distillers shareholders who exchanged their stock for the Guinness offer were defrauded because they did not have this crucial inside information.

In Japan, the famous Recruit scandal illustrated how insider trading appeared to be widespread and completely accepted in that market, even among leaders of the government. These men were apparently happy to receive gifts of stock on an insider basis as recompense for the legislative and social support of a businessman. In the less mature and less regulated markets, of course, such insider activity is much more common, and markets move on waves of rumors about significant individuals and their business and investing activities. In all these cases, the investors are seeking an advantage over their peers; they are trying to change the risk/reward equation fundamentally in their favor by buying or selling stock at a price that reflects its value *prior* to the release of the news they possess as insiders. Immediately after that news release, the price will change to reflect the news—but they will have unfairly secured the profit from that price move.

These activities are widely frowned upon and in many countries are illegal. However, they are merely the extreme form of a core risk/reward strategy, the insider strategy. Insiders try to understand highly complex, uncertain risks by getting "inside" them through personal contacts, strong analytical skills, and an ability to build in up-front escape options should the risks go the wrong way. If the illegal insider takes this approach too far by applying it to the public, highly regulated securities markets, financial firms apply the perfectly legal approach in the field all the time as they try to assess individual risks that are not susceptible to segmentation into discrete groupings.

This is a fundamentally different approach from the segmentation strategy, where financial firms analyze hard data, often from a distance, in order to discern attractive risk/reward segments. Using the insider strategy, corporate lenders, property and casualty insurers, and leveraged buyout firms (to pick just three users of the insider strategy) all try to get inside the companies they are dealing with, by getting as close to the risk subject as possible, and are then prepared to rely upon soft judgments about it. For instance, the branch mortgage lender approving a very large mortgage on a house, of course, obtains valuations of the collateral value of the house but in fact relies primarily on a detailed history and a series of projections of the borrower's earnings, and a sense of his diligence and character derived from one-on-one meetings. Mortgage providers see turning to the collateral as a last resort. They really do not want to own houses, so the earnings of the borrower are the key determinant of whether a mortgage should be offered.

Some special insight is needed in all these cases where statistically valid segmentation will not work, and the financial firms that win often glean the insight from becoming privileged insiders. This approach is not illegal when applied outside the regulated markets that are designed to provide a level playing field for all investors; on the contrary, in the day-to-day world of financial risk absorption and intermediation, everybody recognizes that the playing field cannot be even, that the winning approach is to find the "unfair" advantage.

The leveraged buyout (LBO) trend of the 1980s was based on the insider strategy. An LBO takes a company that has a capital structure that is regarded as reasonably conservative in its use of debt, and then uses new debt to buy out the existing equity holders, replacing much of that equity with this new debt. The theory is that the company can survive this new debt load, either because its current performance will cover the debt payments or because the new debt will spur management to improve performance so much that all will end well. In the happy case, the debt providers receive significant fees and large spreads on the debt for absorbing the risks of this new leverage, and if the loan is indeed paid off, then they are well compensated. Their returns, however, pale against those of the new equity holders, who turn their position in a highly leveraged situation into a major holding in a more stable one. Truly spectacular returns can result.

The problem with this formula is that as more and more competitors seek to do an LBO, the price of the target company increases. Thus, the amount of debt the company will eventually have to cover also increases, and the margin for error declines to almost zero. To win in this business, an insider approach is clearly required if the bidding company seeking to sponsor the LBO is to be able to make the judgments required to justify its bid. Successful firms such as Kohlberg Kravis Roberts (KKR) in its mid-1980s heyday, Clayton & Dubilier, Forstmann, Little, and Gibbons Green van Amerongen (until its decline in the late 1980s) all followed a similar legal insider formula.

To make sense, LBOs have to be based on the insider strategy. The sponsor of an LBO is basically betting that it can beat the market, that it knows so much more than others about the potential of a company that it can pay a sizable premium over the market's valuation of the company and still earn attractive returns. LBOs fit perfectly into the insider strategy criteria: they involve a few crucial risk and reward decisions (rather than thousands a day, as in the segmentation strategy), and these few decisions must be based on incomplete information and soft judgments about people, as well as on hard facts.

To win in this field, the best LBO firms adopt very disciplined approaches from start to finish. First, they are careful in selecting the companies they will target. Often they limit their choices to those industries where they believe they have a deep working knowledge, and where therefore they believe they can assess the likelihood of success better than the average investor. In other words, they focus on areas where they believe they can develop an insider advantage. For a long time, Clayton & Dubilier told prospective investors in its LBO funds that it would not consider opportunities in apparel retailing, energy, or real estate—not because the firm believed these areas were inappropriate for LBOs, but rather because the principals of the firm had no special inside contacts in the areas and did not believe they could add any special legal inside insights to the transactions. Instead, Clayton & Dubilier emphasized its understanding of manufacturing, marketing, and distribution and said it sought opportunities to leverage those skills.

After selecting the broad field in which they will operate, the best firms then screen hundreds of opportunities a year against some core analytical and judgmental yardsticks they have in place to identify potential candidates. Essentially this is a segmentation strategy—but as we will see, it is just a small component of the effort. The best firms are very patient, resisting the temptation to alter their criteria just because prices are being bid to new highs by the availability of cheap and easy credit. The weaker firms, however, are less disciplined—and, as we will see, even the regular winners are sometimes tempted by the glamor of merely doing a deal. But most of the time, if no attractive opportunities are available, their money, and their investors' money, stays in the bank.

Eventually, however, an opportunity that fits both their hard analytical and soft judgment criteria emerges, and the firm moves to the next crucial stage—valuing the potential investment. It is here that the approach clearly parts company from the more traditional stock selection procedures, because the level of investigation of the investment is staggering. The LBO firm gets to know every detail of the operation: the age of the machinery, the character and viewpoints of key managers, the composition of discretionary expenditures, the loyalty of key customers, the age and skill base of the staff. All this data is used to develop a set of future cash flow projections, which are the core of any strategy to run the company with more debt than in the past. It is in this valuation stage that the investing company clearly tries to become an insider, for it will pay a price that vastly exceeds present market perceptions of the worth of the company. It can only do so if it is confident of something the market sees as much less certain. It is trying to build the confidence of an insider.

From this lengthy private investigation, the work soon moves into the public arena as new financing is put in place. It is here that the whole approach can run into difficulties if competing bids emerge and drive up the price of the company. Again, however, the insider approach can help in securing debt financing for the company's bid (through judicious arrangements with banks) and in convincing the lenders that only this bid, often supported by existing management, can deliver the revenue enhancements and cost reductions required to service the new debt. By being an insider with management, the bidder tries to frighten off outsiders.

Of course, the details of the financing are important to the success of the transaction (although, in fact, probably secondary to operating improvements, general market interest rates, and equity market trends). Replacing equity with debt immediately creates a new tax shield in many countries, raising after-tax cash flow. Beyond this step, the timing of cash repayments can be crucial to success. Limits on the rates of floating rate debt, and the use of zero coupon bonds and even exotica such as payment-in-kind bonds (where interest is in the form of more bonds), can help a company survive the early years of a large debt load. In a different vein, involving the operating managers in the equity portion of the financing can be crucial to their motivation for the long haul ahead.

A sense of the level of leverage in many of these transactions can be gleaned by looking at just two in the United States: Borg Warner, the automotive supplier, and Jim Walter, the house builder. Borg Warner had a total book value of just under $2 billion prior to the LBO; nearly 80 percent of its capitalization was provided by equity. After the transaction, the total book value of debt and equity had risen to nearly $4.8 billion, but only 4 *percent* of that was equity. The rest was senior debt, senior debentures, and a small amount of zero coupon bonds. The case of Jim Walter is just as startling. Prior to the LBO, the book value of its debt and equity was nearly $3 billion, of which just over 40 percent was in equity. After the LBO, total capitalization had risen to nearly $4 billion, of which, again, 4 percent was equity and the rest was an interesting cocktail of short-term debt, mortgage-backed securities, and subordinated payment-in-kind bonds and other debt. For the record, these transactions had very different outcomes. Borg Warner worked and earned the sponsors, a group led by Merrill Lynch, significant profits. The Jim Walter deal was one of KKR's least successful ventures, as asbestos liabilities mounted against the home builder and undermined its performance. With so little margin for failure, the company was forced to default on its debt.

In an LBO, winning the bid and structuring the transaction are probably only 20 percent of the challenge to wrest value from the company. Running the company and producing the operating improvements required to service the debt is the core of the effort (unless, as was the case in the mid-1980s, rising stock markets bail out equity investors in even marginal deals). In operating the company, the inside valuation is put to the test. Here is where LBO firms differ from traditional investors by taking a very active board role—for instance, moving quickly to replace managers who do not deliver the required improvements. Often these "improvements" include asset sales, cost reductions, repricing and marketing adjustments, and deferral of lower-priority investments and research, all designed to pay down debt or raise cash flow.

An example of this process in action is provided by the LBO of Safeway by KKR. In mid-May 1986, when it became clear that someone was accumulating stock in the supermarket chain, KKR contacted the CEO of Safeway, Peter Magowan, to suggest an LBO or management buyout (MBO). Magowan rejected the offer. That someone proved to be the Haft family, which owned a company called Dart. In July, Dart made an offer for Safeway at $58 a share, and quickly the board of Safeway reconsidered an LBO or recapitalization (i.e., simply buying back some stock with debt, avoiding some of the upheaval of a full-blown LBO). On July 21, Dart increased the pressure and raised its offer to $64 a share. It was at this point that KKR applied the insider strategy in earnest: it proposed to the board an offer made up of a cash offer for two-thirds of the Safeway shares at $69 a share, the other one-third to be exchanged for debentures valued at $64 per share. However, the offer was *dependent* upon the board's providing KKR with *sole access* to Safeway's internal management information and projections. This insider approach was given teeth by being subject to expiration within just 1 day of the offer! Given this alternative, and the ability to keep the present management involved with the company, the board agreed the next day; by the end of July, Dart had withdrawn from the situation, recognizing it did not have the insider advantage necessary to compete with KKR. The transaction turned into a major success for the new equity holders (although it involved significant layoffs, reductions in benefits and pay, and asset sales), as debt was swiftly repaid and the management was able to raise margins, improving internally derived cash flow. Interestingly, despite their legal access to inside information, the KKR team did not forecast Safeway's performance very accurately, but luckily they *underestimated* the operating improvements that actually resulted.

The final stage of an LBO is to exit the transaction by selling equity back to the market. If the transaction has been a success, the market will pay a large amount for the company, many times the original equity investment by the firm. The debt has been reduced and the cash flow stream preserved or raised, so the market values the equity at a significant premium to its value when the deal was first completed and the equity was swamped by the new debt.

The 1988 $1.8 billion LBO of Duracell, the battery manufacturer and marketing firm, by KKR illustrates many of the requirements for success in the business. At the time, Duracell was owned by Kraft Foods (itself soon to be purchased by Philip Morris, the tobacco company). Kraft saw the battery business as a commodity, cash-cow business and ran Duracell that way, starving it of investment. When Kraft and its advisers, Goldman Sachs, decided to sell Duracell, they valued the company at about $1 billion and invited bids. At the time, KKR knew little about the battery business, but from their experience with the earlier Beatrice Foods LBO, they had built up a series of contacts in the consumer products field and a sense that companies of this type could become successful LBO candidates.

KKR conducted a 4-month intense study of Duracell and believed it had found two ways to release value in the company so that it could support new levels of debt. The first approach was the obvious one of stripping away layers of management added to Duracell by the Kraft corporate management approach; the second was to devise a new sales approach to raise growth rates to over 10 percent a year. Combining these two performance improvements, and believing in their projections because of the insider status their work gave them, KKR bid $1.8 billion, well above the offers of competitors at the auction conducted by Goldman Sachs on behalf of Kraft. "Every company in America has projections that go straight up to the moon," said the KKR partner who valued the company, "Duracell was a rare company where those projections were accurate."

Why was KKR so confident about its projections, and why did it feel able to bid an amount that turned out to be so much higher than the bids of other firms? Basically because it was a legal insider and had developed an "unfair" advantage. KKR knew very well what had to be done and could be done to improve cash flow, and knew each manager well enough to judge whether he could deliver what had to be done to justify the price. Duracell CEO Robert Kidder and his team deserved the trust; Duracell met the aggressive projections, and when the market for junk bonds collapsed at the end of 1989 due to credit quality concerns, such was the market's confidence in Duracell's situation that the price of their bonds hardly declined at all. In May 1991 Duracell sold $450 million in new equity to the market, and it was soon trading at a price that valued KKR's original $350 million equity stake at about $1.4 billion. All the insider work had paid off.

LBOs received much criticism after the initial wave of activity during the 1980s, and it is certainly true, as we will see later, that there have been many expensive failures and that many of the "successful" deals of the 1980s were driven by falling interest rates and rising equity values. The performance of some LBO portfolios, against similarly leveraged passive equity portfolios over the same period, suggests that not all firms added value beyond that offered by the basic moves in capital markets during this time. Nevertheless, the successful transactions illustrate the effectiveness of using the legal inside advantage.

If LBO firms were the insiders of the 1980s, they were borrowing many of their disciplines from the venture capital firms of the 1970s. These firms also pursued an insider strategy, but perhaps with even more discipline and specialization than the LBO firms. Venture capitalists often lack the luxury of a long history of operating performance to analyze when they consider an investment in a start-up or fledgling company. Instead they have to rely upon their own judgment of the technology being brought forward, the business plan of the company, and the skill and experience of the principal managers in the venture. Given these complex and ill-defined risks, these are situations which absolutely require the insider strategy. The successful venture capital firms, therefore, are staffed with professionals who have multiple contacts in the academic and technical worlds in which they plan to specialize, and are able to draw upon their own experience and these contacts to help them evaluate the potential of each opportunity they see.

Again, like successful LBO firms, winning venture capitalists act with great patience in sifting through and seeking out opportunities. The best go out of their way to establish contacts with the scientists and engineers leading primary research work so that they can get a first, insider look at interesting new technologies that may warrant venture capital investment. Then, when they find a situation that seems to have some promise, they investigate it with enormous thoroughness to unearth every concern and contingency they can imagine. The problem at this stage is that potential outcomes are even more uncertain than in the LBO situations. The next step of the process after the initial financing, the actual management of the company, involves close involvement by the venture capital firm and a willingness to replace managers who do not seem to be able to deliver. By the very nature of these new businesses, an ability to be flexible is essential for success, so management has to be able to adjust its strategies and plans as technologies develop and as competitors try to usurp the market position of the new firm. The financing is structured to reflect the nature of the risk. It is provided in various tranches or stages that tie the level of investment to the maturity of the company. This is very unlike an LBO, where the investment is made in one large step, and then everybody hopes that the operating results will produce the required cash flow. In a venture deal, the insiders recognize the fragility of the projections and the technology, and structure their financial commitment to be in step with their confidence in the information on the technology and in the track record of the company and its managers.

The LBO, venture capital, and mergers and acquisition (M&A) fields all deal with complex and uncertain situations that require detailed insider knowledge if reasonable risk/reward judgments are to be made. So great is the uncertainty in many cases, and so important is the dependence on the character and integrity of individuals, that the financial firms involved in these activities have turned to private investigators to help them unearth the most detailed information available. In a way, they seek surrogate insiders.

In the summer of 1982, the then rapidly expanding Drexel Burnham Lambert underwrote some high-yield bonds for a charter airline named Flight Transportation. As the money was being raised, however, the airline's principals were arrested by the FBI. This was a very embarrassing incident for Drexel, as they were trying to establish the legitimacy of their high-yield clientele and the market for their bonds. So Drexel established a relationship with a firm called Kroll Associates, which specializes in investigatory work for financial and industrial companies. The firm is now staffed with former lawyers, security officers for major corporations, military intelligence officers, analysts, and investigative journalists. Working out of offices in New York, San Francisco, Los Angeles, London, Hong Kong, New Orleans, and Washington, D.C., the Kroll staffs help their clients get inside sensitive situations where the usual relationships and contacts will not suffice. Although the work can occasionally provide the plot of a good detective novel, in most cases it involves simply conducting the due diligence checks of character and business track records that the staffs of the financial firms do not have the skill or time to undertake themselves.

Kroll has developed significant databases of corporate information, but, if required, will supplement that with field work to unearth other inside information. In M&A work, especially hostile transactions, the details can become a little unpleasant, but in fact this work is not the bulk of Kroll's business. Most of the firm's work is in support of legal insider strategies—for example, for the bank about to make a loan to an overseas investor about whom they have only sketchy records. Kroll helps them understand the background of their potential customer, and does so at great speed. Competing against others, the bank that has used Kroll now has a better sense of the risks it is taking and can then judge the potential rewards in a clearer light. The insider strategy requires inside information.

Beyond information, however, the insider strategy also requires credibility. To have access to the flow of gossip and fast-breaking news in a local, national, or global market, a firm has to be seen by its peers as players. One of the problems of a new competitor in an insider market is that it cannot access information because it does not have the right contacts.

This problem is epitomized by the M&A world. For years these markets have been dominated by the same names, and if the top financial firms have changed, they often include the same individuals merely operating in different firms. The reason is that it is very difficult for new competitors to break in because these markets are built on credibility established by being one of the "movers and shakers." In the United States, the First Boston Corporation established a very strong position in the M&A market in the late 1970s and the 1980s on the basis of some strong, innovative work at the beginning of that period. Then, led by the joint heads of the M&A department, Joe Perella and Bruce Wasserstein, it developed a formidable array of contacts and a reputation as a firm to be aware of in any transaction. Yet, even after the split of Wasserstein and Perella from the firm (followed by the defection of many of the key staff), the First Boston M&A effort remained very successful because of the industry-by-industry credibility and contacts it had established. Against these insider relationships and market credibility, it is very difficult for new entrants to compete. An M&A transaction receives the attention of a company's CEO and may in fact be the career-breaking event for that individual. He or she is unlikely to chance that event on an untested firm. Hence the insider contacts and market reputation pay off as one insider refers clients to another. In Manhattan the restaurant "21" is well known as the frequent watering hole for this community. Eating there makes clear economic sense if you are to remain a visible member of the deal-making community to whom work should be referred. This is a real opportunity, inasmuch as in transactions with multiple groups, conflicts of interest can often mean that a large number of firms are involved in providing advice to one group or another. You get invited to these parties only if you are one of the "in" crowd.

In the United Kingdom this world operates even more intimately; the insider contacts often predate the days when the individuals became involved in finance at all. The leading example of corporate finance insider contacts is the stockbrokerage firm Cazenove. Unlike nearly all the other major firms, Cazenove resisted the temptation during Britain's Big Bang deregulation of its financial markets to link with a major merchant or commercial bank. Instead Cazenove has relied on its enviable corporate and institutional contacts. These contacts are known internally as *friends* rather than as clients, which is indicative of the way Cazenove sees the world. Cazenove has remained the leading corporate broker in the United Kingdom, being cited in 1989 by 242 companies as their corporate finance advisory broker; Rowe & Pitman, the second-placed firm, was cited by only 157 companies. Cazenove also possesses extraordinary influence over the investing institutions and is sometimes able to perform what appears to be the impossible. In 1984, the game manufacturer Waddingtons, which held the rights to, among other things, the game Monopoly, was fighting to reject a 500 pence per share bid from Robert Maxwell's BPCC group. Warburgs, a merchant bank, held a stake of 14.6 percent in the company, and Cazenove was able to place it with institutions at 508 pence, even though those institutions knew that

BPCC would withdraw their bid as a result and the price of Waddingtons stock would decline—which it did, to 445 pence within the week. These investors experience a 10 percent loss on their investment and yet have remained loyal to Cazenove.

The reason for this loyalty is that Cazenove follows the insider strategy par excellence; they know everybody in the financial community, and probably knew them well before they joined the City business community. Cazenove's partners are extremely well connected socially, and through a series of school, university, social, and family connections, they have a lock on the key decision makers in commerce, finance, and government. In a country where who you are is sometimes as important as what you know, this business approach is a basis for success. This is not to say that Cazenove's staff is not also very intelligent and skilled, but simply that the firm has an additional weapon in its arsenal. They are, in a very real sense, the inside themselves, and *others* gravitate to Cazenove.

The insider strategy is also crucial to the everyday lending done by banks around the world. Large corporations represent a relatively small (and, in many economies, a declining) share of lending activity. A very large share of activity is created by medium-sized and small businesses, a segment often referred to and targeted as the *middle market*. These companies have a very different relationship with their banks than do their large corporate counterparts. The very large companies, as long as they are reasonably healthy fiscally, have a wide variety of financing sources to choose from: domestic and international banks seeking the prestige of dealing with well-known corporate names, and securities firms that can offer them short-term financing (commercial paper), medium-term lending (medium-term notes and bonds), and long-term debt and equity funds. Offered such an assortment of funding options, these larger corporations feel relatively secure in playing one source off against another in order to derive the best terms and lowest rates. The middle-market company, however, has much less relative bargaining power, because often its financial well-being is less secure. Therefore, to see it through good times and bad, it is much more dependent on building a trust-based relationship with its one or two core banks. The middle-market company fears that if it is fickle with its banks in good times, it will be treated similarly by them when times get tough. Unlike the larger companies it has far fewer alternatives to turn to, so it cannot afford to cut off supplies of credit by constantly shopping just on the basis of price.

Just as the middle-market company has a difficult time controlling its banking relationships, the banks dealing with these companies have to adopt very different approaches than they use with larger companies. It all comes down to information. The large corporation is often publicly traded. It is researched in excruciating detail by many stock analysts, and its activities are well covered by the press and are often highly visible in the economy. In the late 1970s and early 1980s, for instance, it was obvious to everyone that certain major automobile manufacturers (Chrysler and American Motors in the United States, British Leyland and Talbot in Europe) were struggling; their cars were outmoded, and very few were to be seen on the road. For bankers, this level of research and visible public information provides a solid backdrop for their credit and investing decisions. It does not guarantee that they will always make the right decisions, and the high level of information leads to more competition and tighter pricing, but at least they have a reasonable basis for making their decisions. The middle-market company poses a very different challenge; it is rarely publicly traded, and even if it is, very few research analysts cover the company. Most often it is dependent on regional or specialized economic factors for its success, and may rely on the drive and experience of just one or two key managers for its organizational and even financial stability. The bankers faced with lending to or investing in such a company cannot rely on easily available information; to win, he or she must become an insider.

To be an insider of a middle-market company, of course, requires detailed analytical work, but also a willingness to learn about the personalities behind the numbers. A loan officer who is asked to advance a sum perhaps equal to the annual sales of a company must somehow be certain that this loan will be serviced and eventually repaid, or that the bank will have enough confidence about the company's future to extend a new loan when the original comes due. How does the loan officer become an insider? Very simply, by being inside the social and business community in which his or her clients operate. It is for this reason that middle-market lending has remained a geographically based business, often with regional competitors controlling local markets ahead of larger national banks. Local competitors have ties to the local communities, are members of the same social and sporting clubs, sit on the same local business and commerce boards, and even went to the same schools as their customers. National competitors may not have these local contacts and therefore have poorer information. By definition, they cannot compete in such a market, where they are outsiders and somebody else is an insider. The local players can make the crucial soft judgments much more successfully than the larger, more distant firms. In fact, the national competitors around the world that have succeeded in the middle market do so by essentially copying the local players. They build a network of local offices that try to attract local bankers and thereby develop the inside information, locality by locality.

Examples of this lending insider strategy can be found around the world. In New York City, the leading lenders to the garment manufacturers on Seventh Avenue survive in that volatile fashion-driven market by simply knowing who is hot and who is not, and lending and pricing accordingly. New entrants, with little knowledge of the personalities or the trends in that market, soon find either that they cannot make loans at what they believe are reasonable prices given their perception of the risks, or that they price too low because they do not understand the risks properly. Their peers in Scotland who lend to the smaller knitwear manufacturers have to be sensitive to the buying trends of larger firms like Dawson, as well as to the management discipline of each small firm. Again, a new entrant will find it very difficult to learn these facts and keep up-to-date with their evolution, and will therefore be at a disadvantage in pricing and weighing the risks. Further around the globe, the many textile manufacturers based in Hong Kong went through extraordinary transitions in the 1970s and 1980s. First, they rode the wave of exports to the West and then suffered hard times due to a combination of even lower-priced competition (some of it based on the Chinese mainland) and the effective protectionism provided to the Western manufacturers through the Multi-Fibre Arrangement. Again, the lenders to these firms have to be extremely diligent in learning about the management disciplines of each small firm in the face of these cycles of success and relative failure.

To put the insider strategy in context, imagine that the skilled bankers in these three textile markets were switched from one location to another: the Scottish bankers ended up in New York, the New Yorkers in Hong Kong, and the Hong Kong lenders in the highlands of Scotland. How well would they fare? Despite their knowledge of the industry, it is clear that they would not do very well. They simply would not possess the necessary inside information about each character and firm that brings the sterile financial numbers to life and gives them meaning. The New York garment man who always inflates his sales estimates—but who otherwise is a good risk once you understand this—would be an unknown to the newly arrived Scottish bankers. They would be unable to distinguish him from the more conservative manufacturers and would extend credit on the same basis, when in fact they should be scaling his projections down by 25 percent. At the same time, the Hong Kong lenders in Scotland would fare no better, since the tightly-woven relationships between businessman and banker would be closed to them. Denied access to this information, they would have to survive on public information and on the little they could observe while driving from one mill to the next—not a satisfactory insider strategy. But as if their plight was not bad enough, the poor New Yorker bankers in Hong Kong would have a miserable time, struggling in some cases even to find the site of the factory to which they are thinking of lending. In a market driven by relationships, contacts, and even favors, the naive new entrant, whatever his or her analytical skills, will simply not gather enough information to be able to compete.

New York provides a good example of how the insider strategy can be used to create a significant competitive advantage for a relatively small bank. In this particular case, the market was the commercial real estate market in the late 1980s and early 1990s. This market experienced a classic boom and bust cycle during this period, driven up by the expanding financial services and other services markets, which seemed to have an unending need for space as they hired staff to explore new markets and opportunities. Then came the October 19, 1987, stock market break, followed a couple of years later by the collapse of the junk bond market and a slowdown in the M&A business, the demise of firms like Drexel Burnham Lambert and Thomson McKinnon, and general cutbacks at the financial firms. The need for space dropped. This slowdown in demand for real estate was coupled with a tremendous increase in its supply, as usual lagging demand to some degree. Manhattan in particular during this period seemed to be one large construction site as glass tower after glass tower rose to accommodate the expected wave of new staffs. By the turn of the decade the problems were clear, with vacancy rates increasing and rental rates and purchase prices declining rapidly. Many significant lenders suffered badly from nonperforming construction loans backing buildings with few tenants or little hope of getting tenants. The boom that had produced attractive up-front fees and relatively large loan margins for bankers now produced loan write-offs, plunging bank earnings, and even dividend reductions by banks such as Manufacturers Hanover, Chase Manhattan, and Chemical. It was an all too familiar story, first seen in Texas and Oklahoma after the oil price declines of the mid-1980s and then in New England as that economy slowed.

Yet, in the middle of this upheaval, a small savings bank prospered in the New York real estate market—by using the insider strategy. This little bank religiously avoided all markets where it was either at an information disadvantage or where "feeding frenzies" led to a general deterioration of terms and declines in pricing as each competitor vied for the next piece of business. In other words, the bank avoided most of Manhattan and all construction lending. Instead, it focused on a market where it did have an information advantage—owners of second- or third-grade retail and residential buildings, to whom the bank could offer mortgages to free up their equity in these buildings. In addition, it made loans of no more than 3 years, so that its risks were limited to a time period it believed it could predict reasonably well. This bank won by establishing first-name relationships with these owners and understanding what they really required from their banker—a straight story about credit availability and the ability to lend quickly when the money was needed. Therefore this bank empowered its key lending officers with great authority; they were able to act with these landlords as if they had their own version of "My Word Is My Bond." At the same time, it made these officers operate within clear rules, for instance setting conservative loan-to-value guidelines that did not waver however swiftly prices were rising. To win, this bank relied upon close relationships, inside information about rental rates and future expansion plans, and quick service.

In the latter 1980s, growth of commercial real estate lending by this bank lagged well behind that of the leading commercial and savings banks in New York. These risk takers prospered from the major construction projects across the city, and were often happy even to fund speculative construction with no definite tenants, because real estate prices were rising rapidly and they were convinced that the buildings would be filled. The small savings bank was offered many opportunities to participate in these transactions, but turned them down at the clear expense of earnings in those years. Then came the market slowdown, and many firms were driven out of the market altogether as a result of their real estate problems. This savings bank reviewed its entire portfolio at the same time as major banks were announcing hundreds of millions of dollars of real estate write-offs in the region—and found that it had very few problem loans. At the same time, throughout this period, the bank was earning over 125 basis points after all costs on this business—a very attractive return. This performance was possible because the bankers in this institution had focused on a market where they could access legal insider information, and could constantly monitor the well-being of their portfolio in a way that a new entrant could not copy, simply because the relationships that provided the information would not be available to the newcomer.

A loser from this New York real estate experience was Chase Manhattan Bank. Yet Chase had repeatedly shown its knowledge of and comfort with the insider strategy in other lending markets. Although the basic insider approach is transferable from one judgment-based market to another, the actual contacts and sources of information have to be built with great care, market by market. Chase had great success in establishing those special information sources after the Second World War, when, like many other banks, it expanded into new foreign markets. One of its most fascinating efforts was in Indonesia.

Flying from the West, when you arrive in Jakarta, Indonesia, you know immediately that you have landed in a place where the rules are likely to be very different. The airport is new and impressive, but designed with an Indonesian flair that feels different from that of the steel and glass boxes to be seen worldwide. The ride from the airport to the center of Jakarta is likely to introduce you to small vans carrying 10 people or to motor scooters with 3 passengers, all driving or riding past the acreage still being tilled by ox-drawn machinery. A short rainstorm that sees the motorcyclists produce plastic bags to put over their heads and causes earthy runoff from the fields onto the road confirms the initial sense of difference.

Chase understood this market, no doubt through years of trial and error, and built a very successful and amazingly profitable strategy around becoming a true insider in the market. In this market, the key to successful corporate lending is often *who* you know as much as anything else, because who you know will lead to two results: first, who you know will give you access to some fairly reliable financial information, because often the publicly available information on companies is less than helpful; second, who you know will determine your ability in some cases to collect the loan principal at term, because collection will be much more likely if the borrower feels some sense of social responsibility and fears loss of face should he fail to repay. The only way a bank can succeed in this environment, therefore, is by following the insider strategy. Indeed, there is no other credible strategy in a market where even the facade of publicly available data of any quality often does not exist. Through careful and long-lived efforts to build exactly those types of relationships, Chase had developed a unique database of information about credit quality in the market, and at the same time was able to draw upon its friends to help collect in difficult situations. To an outsider the risks and rewards in this market were completely unclear, and the way in was equally mysterious. For Chase, an established insider, this information barrier provided a superb pricing umbrella that meant they were well rewarded for the effort they had made, and yet through their perfectly legal inside information, they felt they could control the risks.

The insider approach serves bankers well even after it has failed to protect them from more fundamental shifts in risks. During the 1970s, major commercial banks were the conduit for channeling dollars from the Middle East (as a result of the very large increases in oil prices) to the developing world, in particular Latin America. They were encouraged to do so by the various governmental and regulatory authorities. By the early 1980s, the force of economic events and the weight of this debt made many of these countries unable to service these loans; they either defaulted or imposed moratoriums on payments. This was an economic disaster for the banks, many of which faced enormous write-offs that threatened their very survival. Nevertheless, the relationships built up during this period of lending, rescheduling, and constant negotiations could also be turned into attractive profits. These banks were the ultimate insiders; in some sense, they had major equity interests in large parts of these economies. As a result of this position, they were able to build a dominant position in the restructuring work that flowed from the debt problems. So, it is no surprise to discover that firms like Citibank, Chase Manhattan, J. P. Morgan, and Manufacturers Hanover have built a series of highly profitable corporate finance and trading businesses around the Latin American markets.

The trading of Latin American debt, the very loans that these banks made and that have now gone sour, also uses the insider approach. The markets for this paper are very volatile because of rapid changes in sentiment and news about the creditworthiness of the underlying borrowers, and because ownership can at times be concentrated in just a few hands, suddenly expanding when new investors think they see an opportunity to buy at the bottom. This sort of market is a trader's delight, as it comes with wide bid/offer spreads and volatile trading prices. It requires, however, careful risk management to control positions and to find investors when markets go quiet. In addition, inasmuch as prices are not freely quoted on everyone's Quotron machine, excellent market intelligence about what was traded at what price is essential if the trading bank is, for instance, to value a portfolio that is for sale and bid for it in a manner that still leaves room for profit. It is an insider's market. To win, these banks have to know who is a seller and who is a buyer of what type of paper, and they get this information only by being close to the other banks that tend to be sellers, and to the few speculative investors and funds that might be net buyers. They have to build up close relationships with these players in the market, to know how they will react and how and when to offer them opportunities to trade their portfolios. At the same time, these traders have to rely on local contacts in the Latin American countries to keep them informed of developments that could alter the market sentiment toward one country or another. As one can imagine, given the paucity of information and the volatility of investor sentiment, this is a very risky market.

Insider strategies have also been successfully applied in the insurance world whenever large, discrete, and complex risk decisions are involved that require a high degree of judgment. Both property and casualty and life insurance offer many such risk/reward opportunities. In the large corporate market, property and casualty companies are offered opportunities to underwrite potentially enormous risks of chemical plants exploding, oil rigs bending under the seas, or a product being found to be harmful to the public. In life insurance, very large purchases are also made, like "key man" life insurance purchased by corporations to protect themselves from the loss of a key staff member, or large policies for the very wealthy or prominent.

Large corporate property and casualty insurance involves a multitude of complex, specialized risks, many of which are subject to global trends and shocks. Take the case of a typical chemical and pharmaceutical company with operations in Europe, Asia, and the United States. Such a company has a whole range of matters that need to be insured in some way. To begin with, it has property that must be covered against structural damage and collapse, flood, fire, and, if possible, earthquake. This includes coverage not only for the value of the plant, but also for the business interruption that ensues. A chemical company also has the liabilities it may incur from the sale or distribution of its products: drugs that are found to have unpleasant side effects or a company truck that runs into a school bus, causing carnage. Further, this company faces the possibility of fraud—either within the company or between its staff and that of another company. In a world where millions of dollars are regularly wired between companies and banks every day, the theoretical possibilities for fraud are significant. Companies also have to worry about their own workers and the costs resulting from injury to them during the production and distribution of the products.

If a chemical and pharmaceutical company has such risks, they are repeated many times, each in a specialized way, across large corporations around the world. Nuclear utilities have to find coverage for the value of their plants, as well as for compensation for victims of any plant leakage. Consumer products companies have to worry about production mistakes undermining the quality of products produced in vast quantities and distributed very rapidly; as Perrier found in 1990, bad publicity about a brand name can have economic consequences far beyond the immediate cost of the recall and destruction of the spoiled inventory. In addition, these companies face the risk of malevolent individuals deliberately tampering with their products, either during production or later on store shelves. Hotel and resort owners must worry about the liability cost of injuries over and above any property costs if one of their resorts is damaged. Companies that provide child-care services to working parents face enormous liability and damage claims should any of their facilities harbor staff who mistreat the children. Automobile manufacturers run the risk that one of their vehicles will turn out to have a defect that results in a series of accidents, producing a pyramid of claims from the injured and bereaved. On and on runs the list of specialized risks that are faced by each company and that must be resolved case by case.

The risks are real, but the factual basis for predicting losses in these areas is very weak. Unlike the case of insuring our house, discussed earlier, these risks are often not susceptible to statistical analysis of the type used in insurance segmentation strategies. Instead, the insurance companies that are called upon to consider and underwrite these risks must invest heavily in understanding the nature of each individual plant, distribution system, and packaging approach for a consumer product in the hope that this inside knowledge will enable them to earn more in premiums, and the interest on those premiums, than they pay out in claims. Their task is made all the more difficult by the fact that many of the risks they are underwriting have a *long tail;* that is, any losses or claims from the insured activity may not occur for some years after the activity is over. The asbestos problem is the most obvious example of a long-tail exposure. Asbestos manufacturers and the house builders who used the product were faced with claims for work they did perhaps 10 or 20 years before the asbestos problem was understood. They used the asbestos in the 1950s and 1960s, but the claims were made in the 1970s and 1980s.

In practice, the insurance companies have to adopt both an offensive and a defensive approach to being an insider in these complex situations. Offensively, they try to work with the companies they are insuring to reduce the risks they face. In the United States, the major underwriters of properties in the corporate world, the Factory Mutual companies like Allendale and Arkwright, are renowned for the loss-prevention advice they provide to manufacturers and processing plant owners to limit their risks of loss and worker injury. Everything from highly technical advice on processing flow risk control, to simple rules on keeping factory floors free from debris and oil to avoid falls, is provided and enforced to lower the risk, and thereby the companies' premiums. Defensively, the insurance companies work hard to understand the risks that remain. They cannot adopt a distant segmentation approach to the market, because the risks are unique and are constantly changing as plants expand and contract and as new products replace old ones. The best underwriters for these companies are industry experts with technical expertise, and the insurers rely upon their insider judgments of each situation to set the rates situation by situation.

In the mid-1980s, the property and casualty market in the United States went through a period of turmoil. Pricing in the market had always been cyclical, with premiums for the same risk rising and falling over a number of years on the basis of how much capacity, both from primary writers and from the reinsurance market, was available. Typically, a period of high losses would frighten away marginal capacity for a while and prices would harden, then these higher prices would encourage the marginal players to return, which would lower prices, until lower returns began the cycle all over again. In the mid-1980s, something more dramatic happened. A series of events combined to increase casualty and liability rates by extraordinarily high percentages year after year, and in some cases coverage was simply not available. One cause was the tendency of U.S. courts to award very large damages to the victims of product defects or individual professional error. This was compounded by the onset of some notable long-tail expenses (for instance, the costs of asbestos claims were becoming very clear to all) and some spectacular processing plant losses (most notably the Bhopal tragedy in India). Faced with this deteriorating underwriting environment, and declining interest rates that lowered the value of the premium income held in investment accounts before claims were paid, the insurance carriers raised their rates considerably or in some cases withdrew from markets. Such was the extent of the price increase that newspaper and magazines talked of the "insurance crisis" that would undermine American competitiveness.

As we have seen, the perception or even the existence of significant risks in a market often represents an opportunity for those who clearly understand the risks and can charge good prices for absorbing or intermediating them. As insurance rates increased, and for some chemical and product liability risks as coverage disappeared altogether, two very different financial institutions and a group of major corporations were teaming up to produce an entirely new answer. For many years, major corporations had recognized that they could save premium expenses by effectively insuring some predictable losses themselves, using what are called *captive* insurance companies, often located offshore to avoid onerous onshore insurance regulations and oversight. The captives were used to fund and administer payments on these predictable risks, and to avoid the costs of external carriers' bureaucracies and need to make a profit. For a time, they also provided some tax advantages. The less predictable risks, however, the large casualty and liability risks that were being priced in the mid-1980s at ever-rising rates, were not an area companies wanted to self-insure. The earnings impact of a large loss would be too much for a single company to accommodate, so the traditional insurance markets kept this business—until the mid-1980s. Then, as coverage disappeared or insurance rates rose to unheard-of heights, these major corporations began to see the self-insurance option in a new light. It was at this point that Marsh & McLennan, the world's largest insurance broker, and Morgan Guaranty, the prestigious corporate bank, teamed up to propose two *pooled* captive vehicles for major corporations to join.

One was called ACE, the other XL. ACE offered coverage of $100 million after the first $100 million of losses; XL's coverage went from $25 million up to the ACE attachment point of $100 million. They thus offered excess coverage above the regular working layers of repetitive losses from $0 to $25 million but did so on a self-insurance basis for those companies who wanted to join a pool of risks drawn from the great and the good of corporate America. To give the offer some sting, the major corporate members of the pool were asked to put up about $25 million to each vehicle to capitalize them—but they would then share in the profits if premiums exceeded paid claims. For these corporations, ACE and XL promised lower rates and also more stable coverage and pricing over time.

ACE and XL were possible because the highly skilled underwriters that Marsh & McLennan and Morgan Guaranty recruited for the venture understood that the market had overreacted to the events in the U.S. courts and to incidents like Bhopal, and that a policy could be written that would offer much of the coverage that leading corporations wanted without providing high-risk or long-tail coverage. Thus the policies did provide some pollution coverage, but only for sudden and accidental disasters that were discovered and reported rapidly. The much more insidious, and potentially more expensive, slow-seepage pollution or long-term pollution was explicitly excluded from the policies. Further, each member of the pool was individually assessed and underwritten by the companies, and was charged a premium according to this risk rating. Thus, ACE and XL adopted the insider strategy, weighing each risk with great care and understanding the intricacies of the various types of risk, so that the policy form limited the pool's exposure.

For Marsh & McLennan and Morgan Guaranty the ventures were also very lucrative. Directly, they led to large commissions for Marsh & McLennan as the broker received an override on all business placed with the companies, by any broker, for a number of years. For Morgan, all the investment funds, which soon totaled over $2 billion, were to be managed by the bank. Further, both companies had an equity stake in each venture that soon became very valuable. Indirectly, of course, the two financial companies had solved a major problem that was worrying the boards and CEOs of every major company in America. New or renewed connections emerged as a result, leading to further business opportunities.

The insider strategy can also be applied in the retail environment with great success. As we saw earlier, life insurance companies often have opportunities to underwrite large life insurance policies in the retail market. Although this is potentially very attractive business, it does pose some problems of medical and even mental risk. Obviously, if an individual increases the amount of coverage for himself or herself or for a relative, the company must be concerned either that they have just discovered some terminal medical news or that a murder or suicide plan is being laid. Again, however, the risks offer opportunities for the insurance companies that can remove these very large policies from their mass-market segmentation approaches and instead treat them as insider problems. In these cases, the insurance company must become familiar enough with the risk to understand the motivation for the insurance and the detailed health record of the insured. The winning players, then, are those prepared to invest in seeking significant amounts of medical information about the individual and to ask penetrating questions of the insured to ensure that the risks are fully understood. Only by building this insider case for each policy can a firm win in this large ticket, retail life insurance market.

In the retail banking environment, too, whole segments of the market must be covered with an insider strategy. As we saw earlier, middle-market corporate banking is built upon the insider approach, which differentiates it from the segmentation strategies that distinguish mass-market retail banking. Between these two markets, however, is the private banking market, where the very wealthy receive and seek financial services ranging from investment advice and custodial services, to personal loans, to advice and financing for their businesses. This market can become impenetrable to the competition if a bank is prepared to invest in it as if it were a corporate market and to build close relationships with the clients. This approach has been adopted, in different ways, in London, Zurich, and New York.

In London, banks such as Coutts and Company and Hoares serve the wealthier segments of the population. To win, they have adopted a relationship approach that they hope will justify the high fees and high minimum balance requirements they impose. At the top end of this market the bankers try to build insider, almost personal, relationships with their clients, at meetings regularly inquiring after the family's and children's progress, and applying a heavy dose of English genteel style to the process of taking deposits, managing assets, and making loans. At Coutts, all the front office staff still wear tailcoats, as if to communicate an old-fashioned style with time to spare. The approach is more than a facade, however; these bankers really do understand their clients much better than can the high street branch banker faced with hundreds of transactions an hour, and they are often called upon to use this detailed knowledge to make loans beyond the scope of routinized credit policies. Essentially these bankers are moving retail branch banking away from a segmentation strategy (even if it is overlaid by the *facade* of personalized service) to an insider approach, where discriminations are made on a case-by-case basis. To do this successfully requires knowledge of collateral, cash flow, or character, and these bankers are in the position to have that information.

In Zurich the approach is somewhat different, for the clientele is even wealthier and the transactions and style are even more private. Union Bank of Switzerland, Credit Suisse, Swiss Bancorporation, Bank Julius Baer, Bank Leu, and other domestic and overseas banks have built a reputation for quality service and privacy that has helped them garner large amounts of investment funds. Again, a private, insider relationship is developed with each client, and an investment approach and a code of conduct are created to suit every need. Often this includes efforts to disguise the true ownership of the assets, and it is certainly true that a fair amount of flight capital has turned up in Zurich—but this is because these bankers have adapted the insider strategy to the needs of their clientele.

These clients need, above all, confidential handling of their finances, and they tend to be very conservative in their investment preferences. Swiss private bankers cater to these needs. If you visit a major Swiss bank, there is very little evidence that it is a bank at all. You enter a discreet, elegant building in the heart of Zurich. Sitting in a pleasant waiting room, apart from some literature describing available services, you might almost be in a doctor's office. Then you are escorted upstairs to a private conference room, where your branch officer discusses your finances and options over coffee. After agreement, you depart. No queues, no noisy branch, no publicity. Of course, you pay for this service; the returns on your deposits are not quite as high as they could be elsewhere, the fees you pay are high, and there have even been suggestions that the corporate finance areas of Swiss banks have been able to place corporate debt they have originated at high prices with the private banking clients of the bank. Whether or not the private banking client is a "stuffee," one way or another he or she pays for the service provided—but that is the point. The Swiss banks work hard to understand the needs of each client, and are able to hold on to these clients as a result. They are taking the risk of all the costs associated with providing service at this level—but by being insiders to their clients, they earn very attractive returns on these significant investments.

In New York, private banking is again different, being as much a lending function as it is an investment advisory business. Again, however, J. P. Morgan, the Boston Company, U.S. Trust, Chase Manhattan, and others have adapted the insider approach to the needs of that market. At the center of their efforts, however, is the belief that in these more complex and esoteric situations, where the risks and rewards are relatively large, an insider strategy will lead to the best results. Therefore, these banks adopt a very different approach to banking than do the mass retail marketing forces, which rely on the segmentation approach. To begin with, they may be prepared to visit the client at his or her office or home, rather than requiring that all business be conducted at the bank. Then, as in London and Zurich, they will tailor the credit or investment package to the needs of the client as far as their understanding of the risks involved allows. The closer the insider relationship, the more likely they are to feel free to adapt policy on the basis of the insider information they have gleaned. If these relationships are truly strong, and the information allows the bank to extend credit in a way it would not normally do, then a long-time client, and a wonderful source of references, has been established.

In these three markets, and in private banking around the world, we also see other signs of the insider strategy in use. These bankers not only try to become insiders with their clients, they also become part of the professional network that can lead to further references. Just as the M&A movers and shakers regularly dine and meet together to reinforce their exclusivity and their source of mutual references, the private bankers deem it worthwhile to build a series of relationships with lawyers, accountants, and investment counselors so as to be able to refer their clients when required and to receive references in return. They are inside the private world of their clients at as many levels as possible.

The insider strategy, then, is based upon investing in understanding the complexities of discrete and potentially lucrative risks by becoming an insider, having access to information that is shared only with a few. On the basis of this legal inside information, the financial institution, be it a bank, securities firm, or insurance company, feels secure in assessing these complex risks and accepting or rejecting the terms as offered. Without this inside information in these private corporate and retail markets, a competitor is severely disadvantaged and is, in fact, effectively frozen out of the market.

Of course, the insider strategy does not always work, even when applied to situations that require the insider approach. This is usually because in a particular situation a financial firm did not actually receive advantaged information, or the information turned out to be erroneous, or the firm misinterpreted it, or the market was simply overwhelmed by exogenous events, and as a result the information lost its relevance. LBOs—transactions that are strongly dependent upon advantaged information—provide some good examples.

If you live in or around the New York area, Seaman's Furniture is well known to you through the aggressive advertising and promotions offered by this retailer of budget-priced furniture. The company had been driven to significant growth and profitability by its founder and chief executive, Morton Seaman, and in 1987 became the focus of a KKR-led LBO. At the time this appeared to be a perfectly reasonable deal, with KKR involving the Seaman family in the company's equity and in the ongoing management of the company, and with Seaman's possessing a firm hold on a section of the market and a well-established brand name.

In fact the deal turned into a disaster, with Seaman's missing its sales, profit, and cash flow projections to the point where, in 1989, KKR was forced to admit that the bondholders of new Seaman's paper would not get paid in full—the deal had failed. Why? One reason was that KKR had failed to tie in the Seaman family as well as they had thought. Morton Seaman, the founder and energy source of the firm, largely withdrew from a driving role once he received his payoff after the LBO. His brother Carl relinquished his responsibilities in 1989. From an earlier public offering of Seaman's, followed by the LBO, the Seaman's family netted about $225 million. They probably did not worry too much when the company started to struggle. KKR had overestimated their motivation when negotiating with them; their insider knowledge of the management capabilities of the firm proved to be erroneous. Then the projections put forward for the firm proved to be based on overoptimistic assumptions, and the firm simply could not grow itself out of the new $300 million debt load of the LBO. KKR presumed that they knew the company and its staff and management better than the average investor, and could therefore afford an insider bet. This proved to be untrue, and they suffered the consequences, as did the investors in the new Seaman's paper.

Home improvements figured in another LBO disaster, the deal led by the New York bank Bankers Trust to take Magnet, a British home improvement retailer, private through an LBO. In February 1989, Tom Duxbury, the chairman of Magnet, decided that the London stock market was overly nervous about his new high street retail focus for this building supplies/do-it-yourself store, and that a management buyout would allow his team to pursue its long-term strategy without the pressure to produce short-term results. Having seen profits rise from £26 million in the year to March 1986 to nearly £73 million in the year to March 1989, and possessing management's insider information on the outlook for the company, Duxbury and his team bid 330 pence a share for the company against a then market price of 180 pence. Interestingly, some shareholders vociferously fought the bid—arguing that management was trading on its inside information! Sun Alliance, a U.K. insurance company, argued that "by definition, if the company is good enough for management to want to take it over themselves, they must perceive that it's in their interests to do so. And if it's in their interest, it's against the interests of shareholders."

To win over holders of Magnet's different types of securities, the buyout had to be structured to provide a lot of cash up front. Yet even then, Bankers Trust found it difficult to syndicate the senior debt because there were signs that the retail furniture market was softening in the United Kingdom. At the time of the debt syndication, MFI, a U.K. furniture retailer, announced it would miss its sales forecasts. Bankers Trust ended up retaining over $100 million of Magnet debt, but hoped that Duxbury and his team knew what they were doing.

Unfortunately, Bankers Trust did not have the superior information they thought they had. They projected Magnet's performance and predicted that the company would produce enough cash flow to support the debt they had added through the LBO. These projections were based on an insider's perspective—but they were still wrong. In this case, management was overoptimistic about Magnet's ability to take market share while controlling its needs to finance inventory. This, combined with the

slowdown in English housing activity, created an impossible situation, and Bankers Trust was forced to admit that the deal had
soured. Within just six months of the closing, Magnet was
restructuring its debt and Bankers Trust, as a major holder, was
announcing that, as a result, its fourth-quarter 1989 earnings
would be reduced. Duxbury left Magnet. Bankers Trust's information had not been good enough.

Real estate woes were at the heart of perhaps the largest
failed insider strategy of the 1980s—the real estate lending
strategies pursued by many banks in the northeastern United
States. These strategies involved lending against construction
projects on the basis that the credit officers at the bank knew the
risks involved in each building so well that the banks could
safely extend the loans. Certainly, many of the best lenders in
this market (I am excluding from this example the frauds and
unprofessional work done by many thrifts and savings and
loans during the same period) had superb real estate departments that had worked very hard to become insiders in the
market. They understood the relative attractiveness of each site;
researched the retail and commercial business flows and how a
new, large building would affect these; and dug deeply into the
past, present, and potential creditworthiness of each major
developer. Nevertheless, they were being asked to finance projects that were essentially bets that real economic and job
growth would necessitate more use of office space, specifically
in the location and of the type they were financing. The biggest
question mark in these situations is often the macroeconomic
assumptions. This was exactly the issue in the northeastern
United States.

While the individual real estate banking teams were working
hard at being insiders in the individual situations they were
being asked to assess, broader variables were undermining
their market. Just as a spate of new office buildings became
available for leasing, the economy of the Northeast went into a
decline. First, the financial services industry was hurt by the
aftereffects of the 1987 market break and the decline in M&A
activity; then the cutbacks in defense expenditures slowed the

growth of the electronics and defense firms, many of them centered on Boston. Cutbacks in these two areas had knock-on effects in various services, and soon the new buildings had little hope of being filled. The bankers had undertaken detailed analysis of the opportunities for each building and understood the competitive dynamics of the market, but this insider analysis was overwhelmed by larger events. Soon developers such as John Portman and the Zeckendorfs in New York, and the Rich organization in Stamford, Connecticut, which had dominated the growth years, were having to pull back or even renegotiate their obligations. Many bankers' loans to real estate developers became nonperforming. Write-offs followed and bank dividends were cut. An insider strategy had been overwhelmed by larger events.

This problem was not confined to the northeastern U.S. real estate market. In Japan, real estate values had ascended at amazing rates because of a combination of a fundamental limit on supply (a result partly of antiquated regulations and unwillingness to pursue reclamation projects fully) and very low interest rates that produced high capitalizations of future leasing income streams. As real estate values increased during the 1980s, the whole market became somewhat self-reinforcing as investors and bankers depended upon each other and upon continued market value increases for their collateral and confidence. It was a situation that could not continue forever, especially in the most overheated market, central Tokyo. The trigger for the market decline was an increase in interest rates, brought about by increased inflation and money supply growth, which changed the capitalization rate on real estate. At the same time, the interest rate rise undermined the Japanese equity market, so that in early 1990 Japan saw both its real estate and its equity markets stall and then decline.

Although some significant investors were badly hurt by these twin declines, in a strange way it was once again the banks in Japan that suffered the most. During the late 1970s and throughout the 1980s, Japanese commercial banks had been able to expand their market share in core lending markets worldwide by expanding their balance sheets more than could the competition, often with lower margin assets. In wholesale market after wholesale market the major Japanese city banks were able to win market share during this period—first in the plain vanilla lending markets, and then, as they established more significant physical presences and experience in each market, in the more sophisticated credit markets such as credit enhancement of asset-backed securities and participation in LBOs. This whole approach was built upon the twin pillars of low required stock market returns on equity (underpinned by the low competing Japanese bond interest rates, which meant that equities were not expected to produce high returns by Western standards) and burgeoning capital bases. The capital growth came from two sources—retained profits and the growth in the investment portfolios of these banks, portfolios of equities and real estate. The decline in the real estate market and then in the equity market undermined this process, and the Japanese banks were required to withdraw from earlier growth strategies. Their capital squeeze was augmented by the 1987 global bank capital guidelines agreed to at the Bank for International Settlements (BIS), which stipulated minimum required bank capital levels. The Japanese city banks had relied upon their equity and real estate holdings to meet these guidelines, and now had to slow growth in loans because of the real estate and equity market declines. Again, the Japanese banks had excellent insider strategies in the local equity and real estate markets. Unfortunately, wider forces, especially the rise in Japanese inflation and the resulting increase in interest rates, undermined this detailed strategy. So we see how insiders can easily be overwhelmed by exogenous events.

The final cause of failure in insider strategies is simply that the whole basis for the insider approach was flawed. The perceived insider insights were irrelevant to the true situation of the risk/reward opportunity. Although it may seen extraordinary that such misdirection of effort can occur, in the frenzy of fast growth and intense competition for deals, this can happen.

An example illustrates the point. In the United Kingdom during the 1980s, British & Commonwealth was a fast-rising bank and information services firm that suddenly fell to earth, and then to bankruptcy, because of a completely misguided insider approach. British & Commonwealth had grown by knowing U.K. markets very well. Its chairman, John Gunn, had built up the money broker Exco during the early 1980s. In 1985 he joined British & Commonwealth and soon brought Exco into the fold. Then in 1988 British & Commonwealth decided to expand into a new business, and into the United States, by purchasing for £416 million a company called Atlantic Computers, one of the leaders in computer leasing—a very specialized market with which British & Commonwealth had only passing experience. Unfortunately, British & Commonwealth simply did not understand this complex market, especially the way Atlantic wrote its computer leases. They were called in many cases *Flexleases,* which effectively gave the lessee the opportunity to return the computer to Atlantic because of obsolescence or other reasons. This business, therefore, was completely driven by an estimate of the residual value of the computers over time and by an understanding of the likely evolution in computer technology. British & Commonwealth simply did not understand the insider risks they were assuming and saw Atlantic as just another, if somewhat specialized, financial firm. The reality was that they were buying into an extremely complex situation where knowledge of the computer industry was crucial.

Soon after the acquisition, it became clear that Atlantic was facing a mountain of returned computing equipment under its Flexlease scheme, and serious losses as a result. British & Commonwealth, burdened by over £1.3 billion of debt, tried to sell some of its profitable businesses to cover the emerging losses. In March 1990 it sold prestigious Gartmore Investment Management for £155 million. But soon thereafter, British & Commonwealth took a £550 million write-off for its investment in Atlantic. In early June, British & Commonwealth was turned over to outside administrators to be wound up. Its managers had not fully understood the market they were entering, and so had failed to evaluate Atlantic Computers as a proper insider;

their perceived insights were insufficient. They thought they were buying a winner; in fact, they bought themselves into bankruptcy.

Contrast the British & Commonwealth scramble to the care taken by a venture capitalist or an excellent property and casualty insurer, and we can see that under the cover of the insider approach, much nonsense is perpetrated. Luckily, events of this type simply make more obvious how the insider approach can, and does, work when it is applied properly. As we have seen, many facets of the banking, securities, and insurance worlds rely upon the legal insider approach. It is one of the core risk/reward strategies available to these firms, and if applied with care will continue to be so.

Financial markets that require detailed study of significant risks, the rewards of which can be very large, will move to the insider strategy. Regimented segmentation approaches will not work in these markets. The risks cannot be put into little boxes, and the customers require a more personalized approach if they are to choose one firm over another. The task facing the banks, insurance companies, and securities firms competing in such markets is to decide in which areas they can really be legal insiders—and then to put that detailed inside advantage in a wider context to make sure that broader events do not make it irrelevant. For those who can apply such discipline, the rewards have, and will be, very large.

6

Deriving the Future:
The Technical Strategy

A relatively new powerhouse in the world's capital markets is Chicago Research and Trading, or CRT. In 1977 the firm was founded with $200,000 of capital; by 1988 this had grown through retained profits to $225 million, and the firm employed over 600 staff members. How did the firm get there? By being traders par excellence of options and financial futures, often arbitraging them against the underlying or "cash" securities. Based in Chicago, the heart of the world's derivative markets, CRT became an enormous trading house, executing over 100,000 trades per day in the search for opportunities. To give some sense of perspective, a major Wall Street bond house like Salomon Brothers may execute only 10,000 trades on a busy day. At times CRT represented 30–40 percent of the volume on certain futures and options exchanges and over 5 percent of the volume of the Standard & Poors 500 stock index futures market. CRT was not looking for large wins on each trade, just enough to get by on—but with so many trades the firm did not need to win big on each one. Trading over $2.5 billion per day, the firm looked for momentary differences in options and futures prices against what a series of market formulas would suggest they should be. As one CRT trader said: "It's like picking up dimes in front of a bulldozer. You can make a lot of money, but you have to keep your eyes on the bulldozer."

CRT typifies what I call the *technical* strategy. The firm applies superb mathematical analysis and great organizational flexibility to the world's trading markets. CRT is headed by a charismatic leader, Joseph (Joe) Ritchie, who before founding CRT was a prison guard, a Chicago bus driver, and a deputy sheriff. More to the point, Ritchie is also a mathematical genius, able to carry out complex arbitrage calculations in his head and evaluate new opportunities with amazing speed. His real gift, however, may be that he was able to translate his personal capabilities into requirements to build an entire firm. For instance, Ritchie trusted in the power of the computer to copy his personal talent to identify opportunities and constantly monitor risks. He once said: "Equipment is vital in letting us know where our risks lie. There is simply no way we could do our kind of business without these machines."

In addition, Ritchie knew that to play the game the firm would have to be as nimble as he, as one individual, could be. So Ritchie, and the other three founders, Gary Ginter, Mark Ritchie, and Ron Bird, built a very close organization with a common sense of mission and little hierarchy. Some went so far as to say that the firm was based on hiring only born-again Christians like the four founders. This was probably unfair, but CRT did interview new recruits in great depth and put all new employees on 3 months' probation before retaining them. CRT put great faith in team play and did not build the typical trading firm's star system. The interview process was designed to discover whether an individual could retain his or her cool in a tough trading environment and remain a team player. As reported in Intermarket in February 1988, some questions that interviewees claimed they were asked in order to elicit their ability to stay cool under pressure included these:

"Have you ever taken narcotics or drugs?"

"Do you drink?" "Why do you drink?"

"Why do you wear pinstripes?"

"Have you ever stolen before?" "Why not?"

"Why did you leave your last job?"

Al Deibert, the bejeaned head of human resources at CRT, said that such interviews were designed to see if a new hire would fit into the CRT organization: "CRT employees enjoy responsibility. They view stress as adventure and hard work as satisfying. People at CRT basically experience work as fun."

Also noticeable in this firm is the absence of formality; no dress code exists, and everyone is on first-name terms. There is a country-style cafeteria where free breakfasts and lunches are served. The firm has as much of the aura of a university campus or camp as it does of a large financial firm—but that is just the point. Ritchie and his colleagues have built a very different firm that makes money in a manner that few other firms can sustain for as long.

At the heart of this effort lie a series of closely guarded mathematical formulas that CRT uses to determine the volatility of the options and futures it trades. One competitor said of these guides for traders:

> They are the most technically proficient traders I have ever seen. They guard those volatility tables as if it meant their life. You won't find one of those on the floor at the end of the trading day ever. My guess is that they evaluate each market on the basis of whether they expect their position to be disrupted, and have some sort of internal scoring system that evaluates each market.

Armed with these statistical insights, CRT then applies them with a vengeance. When the firm entered the Philadelphia foreign currency options trading market, it went from advising the exchange that it wanted to trade on a Wednesday to being one of the biggest traders on the exchange by that Friday! This kind of flexibility is possible only if you have superb analytical capabilities, constantly updated risk monitoring facilities, and great organizational flexibility. With these core skills, CRT moved from Chicago to trade its favorite exchange-traded instruments elsewhere (avoiding for a while the more judgmentally based, longer-term over-the-counter options). By 1988 CRT was trading at all three Chicago exchanges, as well as oil futures and options at the New York Mercantile Exchange, Institutional Index options at the American Stock Exchange as a specialist, and financial futures and options at the London International Financial Futures Exchange (LIFFE), the Singapore International Monetary Exchange (SIMEX), and the Pacific Stock Exchange. As a result, by then about one-third of its staff was working outside its home of Chicago, mostly in New York or London. To close out its development as a global firm, in 1990 CRT created a 50-50 joint venture with Mitsubishi Trust and Banking Corporation to trade options and futures for Japanese customers.

The technical strategy that CRT practices is one of two risk/reward strategies used in the worlds of trading and investing—the other being the inference strategy. Both of these strategies are practiced primarily in the trading rooms of the intermediaries and investors who populate the trading markets. The scene is basically the same in each city. The elevator doors open onto a huge floor lined with desks, where (often young) men and women stare at a bank of computer screens and occasionally yell at each other, or punch an incoming phone line to talk to other young men or women at other trading companies. In fact, such is the familiarity of the basic setup that the trading companies feel very comfortable sending their staffs from one location to another, believing that a good trader in one market will be a good trader in the next. The question is, what exactly are these people doing?

In many cases, they are making or losing their employers a lot of money! To outsiders, this is an impenetrable, magical world full of traders' jargon that is unintelligible to most. In fact, however, it is possible to discern patterns of activity that underpin reasonably consistent trading profits. Trading is not a black box.

Perhaps the best-known trading strategy is to act as an intermediary and take a spread or commission on the brokerage of stocks, bonds, currencies, and commodities between buyers and sellers. Whenever you or I buy stocks, we are well aware of brokers' commissions. Where such basic brokerage still exists, it becomes a segmentation game as competitors vie to discover the price-insensitive segments of the market and take advantage of them. However, in the past two decades, improvements in availability of information to investors and their concentration into very powerful institutions such as pension funds and mutual fund companies (instead of individual investors who are easily picked off) have made the basic bid/asked spread and commission game less and less attractive in market after market. Spreads or commissions have declined, and investors are demanding that brokers take more and more risk—for instance, by placing investors' sell positions on their own balance sheets prior to finding a buyer on the other side. To make reasonable profits, brokers have often found that the basic brokerage role has to be supplemented or even replaced by ways to make money through positioning for one's own account. The intermediary must become an investor too. The question is how to do this successfully, at reasonable risk. For the investors, this positioning is what they have been doing all along, but they too are now in search of ways to codify and improve their positioning strategies.

In this chapter and the next we will review how this can be done using the technical and inference strategies. Once again, we will find that it is adherence to the key principles of applying a firm's core risk/reward skills to the particular situation, and having a clear vision of exactly how these skills can be used to make money, that underpin success. Failures are characterized by a lack of clarity on how the firm had intended to make money in the particular market and why its skills were applicable to that situation.

The technical and inference strategies of the trading and investing worlds have an important link to the segmentation and insider strategies we have seen applied to the day-to-day affairs of banks, insurance companies, and corporate finance advisers. As we saw, the segmentation strategy is built on the detailed analysis of large quantities of hard data, creating segments that the company can approach differently and to which it can offer tailored products, thereby earning above-average returns. By contrast, the insider strategy depends upon judgments of individual situations that cannot be analyzed on a segment basis because each is large and unique. This split between one strategy that is analytically intensive and another that is judgment dependent is replicated in the worlds of trading and investing. We will, once again, start with the analytically intensive strategy, in this case the technical strategy, and then turn to the judgment-based inference strategy in the next chapter.

The technical strategy is often based upon timing investments in or out of a market or security better than the average competitor. If in all trading markets you are eventually trying to buy low and sell high, in using the technical strategy you are often prepared to act within very narrow windows of time—with some investments, lasting only a few minutes. However, what really characterizes technical strategies is a reliance on past or future calculated pricing movements to drive investment decisions. Such strategies are based on analysis of pricing relationships or mathematical formulas, not fundamental economic or corporate profitability trends. Therefore, these are not judgment-based approaches; instead, they rely upon the assimilation of large quantities of data, rapid statistically based analysis of that data, and often the ability to act quickly on the conclusions of that analysis to make an investment decision. Thus a technical strategy requires the core risk valuation skill to be applied with great attention to detail—since the positions being taken advantage of may be minute pricing discrepancies between two securities that will not last long—but also relies on the organization's flexibility, its ability to act upon this analysis before the opportunity is gone. This is not a strategy that works well in companies that have problems using information technology and assimilating it into the core of business decision making, nor is it a strategy for companies that have long-winded and multilayered decision-making approaches. Here managers must often be given the authority to make bets in short time periods; they cannot wait for headquarters to approve the transaction if it is to make money for the company. Headquarters has to be confident that the analysis is good and that the risk management approach will make the company win more often than it loses, and that when it does lose on an individual bet, the losses will be within an acceptable range.

Technical strategies have become much more important to financial companies in the last 20 years. This has happened because the trading markets have evolved to a stage where technical approaches are an important component of the way the markets work. There has been a broadening of both the availability of securities of all types and of the interest of investors in trading securities. This larger, more liquid environment is a technical trader's delight. It creates opportunities to compare pricing across markets, and within markets, with some certainty that if the trader sees an opportunity to buy a stock or bond that appears to be temporarily underpriced, there will later be a buyer when the trader wants to sell it. At its extreme, the increase in trading activity and liquidity in the last 20 years can be seen as the development of a global financial marketplace, including the creation of one single, unified market for some types of securities, and at least a much wider spread of interest in all types of securities, even if some markets are still priced locally. Broader interest in securities, and closer relationships between their pricing, create opportunities to arbitrage two markets or two securities with the knowledge that the price discrepancy the trader has noticed will also be noticed by this larger, often global network of other traders and investors. Therefore, at some point, the price discrepancy will be closed and the trader will make a profit for having noticed it first. A technical trader and investor would not succeed in an environment where trading is sporadic and where interrelationships between two markets or two securities are not constantly tested by the whirl of exchanges of stocks and bonds.

If increased comparisons between markets and the increase in trading volumes have underpinned the growth of the technical strategies, then the explosion in information technologies' capabilities and availability have been crucial to their actual implementation. A technical trader, huddled over trading screens, is dependent upon receiving price information at least as quickly as everybody else and then using computer analytics to look back over time and spot price relationships that appear out of line with particular parameters the trader, or the trader's research department, have decided are crucial. This discrepancy then has to be made visible to the trader, and he or she then has to be able to trade in the market very rapidly to take advantage of the opportunity. All this requires superb information technology—that is, the price feeds, the analytical software to identify anomalies in the pricing, and the communications capability to call a market maker and first take and then very quickly unwind a position. Until 10 or 15 years ago, this information technology was not available widely enough to make any one player comfortable that the anomalies he uncovered would eventually be corrected by someone else so that the trader could earn a profit. Now, of course, the problem is exactly the opposite: too many competitors possess these computer and communications capabilities, and the pricing anomalies are been corrected very quickly.

Not all securities offer the same technical opportunity. The key for a technical strategy is that through analysis it is possible to find discernible historic or mathematical relationships upon which to trade, and that tends to be easier when there are relatively few parameters or factors involved in the pricing of a security. If you think about the factors involved in security pricing, at the simplest level they are the risk of interest rate or currency movements—just plain market risk. Government bond prices, for instance, are driven by interest rate trends. As a product becomes more complex it starts to include other risks that affect its pricing—for instance, credit risk in the case of corporate bonds. The prices of these bonds are moved not only by general trends in interest rates, but also by the credit quality of the individual borrower, as investors in U.S. junk bonds are all too aware. Beyond corporate bonds are more complex bonds like asset-backed securities, mortgage-backed securities, and CMOs, which are influenced not only by general interest rate trends and the credit quality of the underlying borrowers (or their guarantors), but also by the likelihood that the underlying assets will be paid off more quickly than projected, thus denying the investors the projected yield for the full term. Finally, leaving aside esoteric derivatives like options on swaps, the most complex securities in terms of pricing are equities, which are affected by general interest rate levels, the credit quality of the company, and the level of profitability or performance of the company.

So, moving from the simplest short-term bond to the most complex equity, investors are faced with many new influences, or pricing parameters, to consider when deciding whether a security is cheap or expensive. In a similar fashion, technical strategists find it much easier to compare international short-term bond markets than to compare equities in different markets. In fact, in the simplest markets, technical strategies have become so popular that there are very few, profitable pricing anomalies to take advantage of left. Through a process called *covered interest arbitrage*, global foreign exchange and money market traders constantly squeeze out pricing anomalies, so that through the interest rate and foreign exchange forward markets it is possible to convert 3-month dollars into 3-month deutsche marks almost perfectly. Faced with this squeeze, the technical strategist has no profit to make, since there is no time or opportunity left to garner any pricing anomalies. The technical players have to move to markets where there are more risks to be considered when pricing an instrument, and therefore where the chance that there will be time to capture pricing anomalies between two similar securities in two different markets increases. Technical opportunities exist as long as, at some point, the pricing *will* converge. As they move to more complex securities, such as derivatives, the technical strategists also face more risks. As usual, therein lies the opportunity for those with the requisite skills.

Starting, for an example, in the longer-maturity government bond markets, technical strategists might compare long-term government bond yields across countries and try to find the bands within which these securities tend to trade against each other in order to buy when one country's bonds seem especially cheap and sell another country's that seem especially expensive. Technical players also test the relationship of different corporate bonds or different equities within a country. Most daringly, they look across countries in these markets in their quest for statistically or mathematically based pricing relationships that they can monitor and profit from through swift action. All the time, they are battling two pressures. The first is the steady march of techniques such as covered interest arbitrage that become so efficient that they squeeze out all profit; the other is the complexity and unreliability of some pricing relationships that make the technical process for more complex securities more of an art than a science. Between these pressures lie the technical profits.

The same basic patterns that technical traders and investors apply to the securities markets can also be applied to the commodities markets. Pricing linkages within a single commodity are reasonably secure, and the relationships between spot and future oil prices, for instance, can often be traded on with some scientific certainty. At the other extreme, pricing linkages between different commodities (for instance, oil and natural gas, wheat and barley, steers and pork bellies) reflect overall supply and demand balances but also discrete supply and demand issues. Timing the relationships between these commodities becomes much more difficult—and thereby rewarding for those who can do it. In the 1980s, a number of investment and commercial banks diversified into commodities trading on the basis that the technical approaches were analogous to the ones they were already adopting in their core securities and treasury trading businesses. Most obviously, Philipp Brothers and Salomon Brothers became linked, Goldman Sachs purchased J. Aron, and Chase Manhattan Bank and other major banks started to offer commodity swaps to producers and buyers of oil, copper, and other commodities as an extension of their interest rate and currency swap expertise.

The technical opportunity is to find pricing relationships between liquid instruments that can be quantified, to monitor them closely, and to act quickly when you (or your computer) determine that the prices have moved outside their historical or mathematical patterns. By buying or selling now, you will prosper when the normal pricing relationships are reestablished. Given the proliferation in securities and their derivative offshoots (futures, options, options on futures, swaps, options on swaps), the improved linking of information flows across countries, the increased interest in cross-border investing, and the improvements in the safety and quality of settlement and clearing procedures in many markets, the technical opportunity appears to be larger than ever. On the other hand, technical trading is its own worst enemy, because if a group of trading firms are too successful in linking a group of securities, other players will rush in to profit, and soon the markets will be forever linked. The pricing anomaly opportunities are squeezed out.

So if this is the opportunity, what are the requirements for success? To begin with, any technical strategy is dependent on the most superb analytical capabilities, which are, as we saw in the case of CRT, often dependent upon the best computer systems available. The technical trader has to be able to discern fleeting aberrations in market pricing and to decide when prices seem to be out of kilter. This analysis is often based upon detailed review of historical trends and analysis of mathematical relationships, so the ability to store accurate pricing histories, and to perform a wide variety of complex statistical analyses to determine the strength of potential pricing relationships is crucial. In an obvious analogy to segmentation strategy analyses, the best technical firms now apply dynamic updating to their historical analyses to determine how prices are linked. For example, if a firm has decided to study the price linkages between the equity securities of two chemical companies, it may conclude from historical analysis that they normally trade within a 25 percent range of each other. In addition, when one falls to a discount of more than 15 percent, then there is a greater than 60 percent chance that the price relationship will narrow in the next 3 weeks. This calls, under a basic technical strategy, for the trading firm to buy the discounted stock and sell short an offsetting position in the premium stock, thereby hedging out major market and chemical sector risks but locking in the spread differential between the pair of stocks. When the prices move back to their historical spread, the firm profits. A dynamic approach to this type of trading could take a number of forms, all designed to supplement this basic historically based analysis. The actual trading of the two stocks would be monitored, and if the price differentials continued to widen, the firm might first increase its positions. Then, if the spread between the two stocks continued to widen, the firm could conclude that new information about the relationships was emerging, and decide to liquidate because historical patterns were being broken and the statistical odds no longer applied. The trading firm might supplement its historical view of the world by analyzing the way in which options on these two stocks were priced, to see if they suggested that other investors were expecting any major changes in the way the stocks normally behaved. In all this work, fundamental economics or company performance do not play a role; in their purest forms, the technical approaches are based on rigorous statistical analysis of past price movements and mathematical formulas to predict future prices, rather than on softer judgments about future external events as guides to future securities prices.

Even if the analytics and the supporting information technology are in place, there is still no guarantee of success in implementing a technical approach. The individual organization may not be ready to invest on the basis of such a system. To succeed, a technical trading firm must have extremely short lines of communication and the ability to make rapid trading decisions.

A technical approach will be bogged down by overly bureaucratic decision-making. In situations where often thousands of trading decisions are made each day, a technical organization has to resort to much more programmed ways of devolving trading and investing authority, and must then be able to supplement these methods with a rapid exception system for the very large or higher-risk technical trades. Combined with this organizational flexibility must be a willingness to test new analytical approaches and to learn from initial losses. Just as in the segmentation strategies, the most valuable analytical databases are derived from proprietary analysis rather than generically available research. Some aspect of that proprietary analysis may involve pilot testing of the new ideas to iron out the problems and to see if all the risks in an approach have been foreseen by the theoretical analysis. Obviously, sometimes more work is needed. As a result, the winning technical firms are prepared to experiment, and incur some costs of experimentation, in order to build a unique set of tested insights into technical opportunities and determine how to take advantage of them with as little downside risk as possible.

If technical strategies have become more prevalent in the past 20 years as market and technological changes have allowed, they are hardly new. From the earliest period of stock market investing, the core discipline of fundamental stock analysis, the selection of stocks based upon their fundamental earnings potential or asset values, has been challenged by what is called *technical or chartist analysis.* This discipline has always rejected the judgments made by the fundamental school and instead had relied upon analysis of past stock market trends to decipher likely future movements. Although until the past 20 years or so they were not fully supported by sophisticated computer analysis of past pricing trends, the chartists have long practiced their craft.

Chartists try to discover figurative patterns in a market's historic price movements, and then to match present price trends against these historic "pictures" to predict future prices. A chartist's office will often be strewn with long line charts of past market price histories. From these charts will be derived shorter pictures of figures of behavior. There are many patterns that chartists focus on, ranging from momentum charts to the Japanese "candle." Perhaps the most famous of these is the *head and shoulders* pattern. This pattern of price movements has been observed in many markets and is often used by technical analysts when they are reviewing market movements and trying to predict the future. Figuratively, the head and shoulders pattern shows a period of gently rising market prices followed by a gentle decline back toward the level where the trend started (the left shoulder). This is then followed by a more dramatic uptilt in prices, which peak and decline again to their original level (the head). This more violent and dramatic price change is followed by gentle recovery and then decline (the right shoulder). This completes the head and shoulders price pattern. As you can imagine, this basic form provides significant potential for subbreeds of the species. Most important, the generic description does not specify the time frame for the pattern to be inscribed by the market, providing significant potential for interpretation. Is the head and shoulders to be created over a couple of weeks, a couple of months, or a couple of years? This basic quandary is at the base of the chartist's craft.

A good example can be seen in the advice a chartist might give to a succession of clients. Assuming that this analyst is an adherent of the head and shoulders pattern (among others), he or she is in a position to give a wide range of advice, depending upon the investment time frame of clients. If an investor has a long-term time frame, and is not seeking to churn the account but instead is prepared to accept some short-term losses if in the long term the portfolio mix is correctly balanced, then he can look at longer-term price movements of the major cash, bond, and stock markets of interest to the investor. Matching them to the chosen head and shoulders pattern, the chartist can provide projections for long-term trends and therefore give advice about the optimal portfolio mix for the investor. At the other end of the spectrum, he might have a client who is interested in catching short-term market trends. For this client he might look at a shorter, and therefore different, price history chart and give advice on shorter-term market movements—advice that might be the opposite of that given to the long-term investor. Finally, he might advise an investor with an interest in selecting individual stocks rather than trading between markets. Here again, the chartist can ply his or her trade over different time frames, and therefore with different recommendations for action.

The more you think about it, the more the technical possibilities are multiplied. We have focused on charting absolute price movements, the trends in the actual prices of a bond, a stock, a currency, or overall markets. The charting possibilities increase manyfold once chartists turn to the *relative* performance of markets or individual securities, and provide advice on the basis of patterns in these charts. At its most sophisticated, chartist approach can then combine the absolute charts with the relative charts, both over a wide range of time frames, to generate a multitude of potential outcomes for investors to consider.

For all its idiosyncrasies, chartist analysis must be hailed as the first widely used technical strategy. What is noticeable about this approach is that often the recommendations do not require rapid action to capture the opportunity; the head and shoulders patterns, for instance, can be played out over many months so that an investor does not have to move instantaneously to capture the opportunity. How, then, does this work qualify as the predecessor of today's rapid-fire technical approaches? Very simply, charting is a strategy based on comparing price histories using analysis of past trends, and then using this analysis, importantly devoid of any input about the fundamental economic or business conditions that might explain them, to drive behavior. The pace of today's very rapid technical strategies is a product of the quickness with which new arbitrage techniques close the windows of opportunity, but speed is not a necessary component of every technical strategy.

The most famous, and in some quarters infamous, technical strategy is the arbitrage that is done between the underlying securities in a market and the index future on that market—known as *index arbitrage*. This technique, often identified by the confusing label of "program trading"—which in fact covers a wide range of activities and therefore will not be used here—is very simple. It is at the heart of the way in which the futures markets are linked to the underlying cash markets on which the index future is written. When the Presidential Task Force on Market Mechanisms (the Brady Commission) was analyzing the October 1987 break in the U.S. stock market, a great deal of time was spent debating whether the cash and index future markets were one or two markets. At the heart of this question lay the problem the markets experienced on October 19 and 20. It was exactly when the two markets behaved as two markets, when their prices were not linked the way simple mathematics suggested, that investors panicked. The two markets are very much one market, and when they become delinked it is like an investor being given two prices on the same stock, both of which are declining. The immediate reaction is to assume that maybe neither price is right, and to panic and sell even more.

Index arbitrage is the technique by which cash and futures markets are linked and perform essentially as one. A futures contract on a security is a contract to buy that security at a given price at some date in the future. If you know the price of that security today, its past volatility, and what the interest carrying cost of the position would be for the time period between today and the exercise date on that contract, then it is easy to calculate at what price the futures contract must trade. Inasmuch as the same amount of stock today can be held with fewer investment dollars through an investment in a futures contract representing those stocks, the carrying cost on the future is much lower than on the stocks; for that reason, futures should naturally trade at a premium to the underlying stocks. The size of that premium can be mathematically derived with great precision. After accounting for different transaction costs, it is possible to equate the future's price with that of the securities it represents. Given this, many investors feel comfortable using the index futures market as a way to invest in, or hedge an underlying investment in, major securities markets. Most obviously, the bond and stock markets of the world have become linked to futures. As a result, two sets of investment activity, one directed at the real cash stocks and the other targeted at their derivative, the index future, are both influencing the price of the market. Index arbitrage unifies this pricing and creates a technical opportunity.

It works as follows. Let us suppose that a number of investors become nervous about the trend in the overall economy and interest rates and turn bearish on the stock market. Rather than selling individual stocks, they decide to reduce their exposure to the market by selling futures instead. This drives down the price of the index futures contracts to a level below that which applying the mathematical formula to the quoted prices of the stocks themselves would suggest. Technical traders react immediately and undertake index arbitrage. Seeing the price discrepancy, they simultaneously sell the underlying basket of stocks (in the case of the United States, a statistically reliable subset of the S&P 500 or 100) and buy the index futures. This action brings the two markets back into equilibrium and earns the technical investor a very small profit on either side of the hedged transaction. All the technical trader is doing is bringing into line what the futures sellers had wanted to align and restoring rational equilibrium to the markets. Of course, this effect can work in a variety of ways, creating many index arbitrage opportunities. Buyers of futures may open up the premium of the future and the cash stocks more than the formula would suggest. The index arbitrageurs buy the stocks and sell the equivalent amount of futures, and equilibrium is restored. Sellers of the underlying stocks may produce the same opening up of the differential, creating the same arbitrage opportunity.

Index arbitrage took off in the United States in the early 1980s, and the early players, the major U.S. investment banks, were able to derive attractive returns on the activity, as the futures premiums were often distorted, and there was enough spread, and enough time to capture it, to make basic arbitrage attractive. The risks existed, but the best players had the analytical tools to understand them and earn very attractive returns. This, of course, attracted more activity from second-tier investment banks and from investors who saw a way to put idle cash to use and earn a return on it that was higher than the return available from normal money-market deposits. In the United States, index arbitrage became a low-risk way to earn a premium return on cash. That was how good a job the multitude of index players did in controlling the risks.

Yet the game really did have some risks, and they were not always obvious. A major risk would seem to be that the analytical skills were not good enough and that the index arbitrage calculation would be incorrect. In fact, this was rarely the problem. Instead, simpler operational risks could create problems—for instance, failure to do the cash and futures trades fast enough to match each other and capture the opportunity. So the best players invested heavily in the information technology to deliver trade orders almost instantaneously after the analysis was done, and then developed with the New York Stock Exchange ways to deliver waves of trades in the underlying stocks to capture the arbitrage opportunity in time. The specialists on the floor of the Exchange who dealt in the individual stocks had to get used to these sudden surges in trades of whole baskets of stocks, trades driven by computer analysis of the spread between the prices of the futures and the underlying stocks. Index players who were slow in developing their operational approach found they were losers in this game; they did not have the key skills required to manage the risks.

As you would expect, index arbitrage was constantly refined. As more and more players entered the market, the price differentials were closed more and more quickly. The best players tried two responses to these competitive pressures. They tried to move even faster and do even more trades than the competitors to maximize the small spreads now available, or they tried to lower their costs so as to make the small spreads more attractive. They examined every aspect of the business and automated what was done by humans as far as was possible; at the same time, they tried to lower the fees they paid to outsiders for these transactions. For instance, some New York investment banks started to negotiate very low rates for these computer trades on the Exchange, and were prepared to look to regional exchanges other than the one in New York. These regional exchanges were often hungry for volume and were prepared to move quickly to capture some additional volume to bolster their market share—to the benefit of the most aggressive index arbitrageurs. This was a market where successful management of the risks demanded not only specialized analytical capabilities but also excellent operational and systems disciplines. Without these, the very small spreads available in the market would be eaten away in misjudged trades, operational failures, and costs. The best players focused on these requirements and eked out small profits on a multitude of trades.

The U.S. markets were among the first to develop these techniques in earnest, and it was no surprise, therefore, that it was the U.S. competitors who often profited when other markets developed sophisticated index futures markets. A good example of this occurred in Japan. By the end of the 1980s, the pressure to deregulate and modernize the Japanese financial markets had become impossible for the monetary and regulatory authorities in Japan to resist. A number of deregulatory moves were made during this period that in some respects mirrored the steps taken in the 1970s in the United States. For instance, the commissions brokers received on stock trades were not fully deregulated, but their price was reduced a number of times. Nevertheless, the major Japanese brokerage houses, led by the big four (Nomura, Daiwa, Nikko, and Yamaichi) were still very dependent upon commission income, derived both from individuals and from major investing institutions like the trust banks and life insurance companies. They had made only a minor transition to earning a living from risking their own capital in proprietary trades. They had no need to do so. The commission flow, especially during the boom times of the 1980s on the Tokyo Stock Exchange, was still enormous even after the cuts in commission rates. However, the markets were changing, and at the end of the decade, liquid stock index futures were introduced on both the Osaka and Tokyo exchanges. It was not the Japanese houses that led the way in profiting from the technical opportunity that index arbitrage offered in Japan. Rather, it was the *gaijin* or foreign houses, in particular U.S. firms such as Salomon Brothers and Morgan Stanley, that took the skills they had honed in the very competitive U.S. market and applied them to the less efficient Japanese arbitrage markets. At home, these U.S. houses had lost the large margins in customer commission trading by this time, and had been forced to develop the skills for trading for their own accounts. Basic index arbitrage was one of these skills, and the American houses earned large profits in the new Japanese market because they knew how to handle the analytical and operational risks and move fast enough to take advantage of the opportunities.

Index arbitrage was but one of the technical strategies developed during this period of dependence upon trading baskets of stocks. Another form of *program trading* (and thus the subject of much confusion) was the trading of baskets of stocks to reposition whole portfolios for a customer. The situation was as follows: an investor decided that he or she wanted to rebalance an equity portfolio by, for instance, selling all the consumer goods stocks and replacing them with a series of defense and industrial stocks. If the investor tried to do these trades one by one it would take far too long; further, the brokerage community would see what was coming and mark down the stocks to be sold before the trades were over, at a large loss to the investment house. To facilitate these trades, the basket trade was developed. Basically, the basket trade transferred much of the risk to the brokerage house.

Here's how it worked: the investment house would contact a number of brokers to announce, in secret, that it was going to sell a portfolio of stocks. It gave these brokerage houses just enough information to entice them, but not so much that they could depress prices before the trade. They might say that at the time the basket had a market value of, say, $100 million, was made up of 25 stocks, no position was larger than $8 million, no position was smaller than $1 million, and all the stocks were in the S&P 500. However, the selling firm would not tell the brokers exactly what stocks it wished to sell in order to preserve market secrecy and hold up the prices of the stocks. Instead, it would seek bids for the basket of stocks from the brokers, accepting that the vagueness of the description cost it something in the bids it would receive. The selling house wanted to rebalance its portfolio quickly, without the expense and market risk of slowly selling positions over perhaps a number of weeks, and found this somewhat disguised approach the best route to follow. The brokers bid for the roughly described portfolio, hoping that they could sell it at a reasonable enough price to make a profit. For them the transaction obviously involved large risks, but the gains in terms of commissions, potential positioning profits over and above the price they bid for the basket, and the goodwill generated with customers were what they were seeking.

To win in the basket trading business required the core skills we have already seen at the center of technical strategies. From the description of the basket to be sold, the brokers had to predict what the likely real value of the portfolio would be and how volatile it could be expected to be. In addition, they had to be wary of any individual positions that might be hard to trade. To develop this valuation of the portfolio, and thereby to create the basis for a bid on the stocks, the brokers had to have deep knowledge of the historic price volatilities of stocks and, in particular, of the industry sectors identified by the selling house as dominating the basket on offer. In addition, any proprietary insider information that the broker had gleaned about the selling institution might help them guess what was in the portfolio. This insider information would have been developed over the years by keeping track of what the investment house had bought and sold with the broker or had shown interest in; from this history, it might be possible to reconstruct good portions of what was in the basket. But this insider approach could not replace the core technical disciplines; the bidding brokers had to calculate what they thought the portfolio would be worth, how volatile it would be after they had purchased it, how much it would cost to hedge out major market volatility through a short sale of a matching value of futures or stock index options, how confident they were of being able to place the stock with other investors, how quickly they could do this, and what transaction costs they would incur in the process. Factoring all these elements into the equation, the brokers came up with their bids. As soon as the winner knew it had won, a team went into action to dissect the portfolio and decide how to unload it to the best advantage of the brokerage firm. The profitable winners in this game obviously had to have strong connections with other investors in order to place the stocks, but their core risk skill was the ability to analyze past pricing relationships with statistical rigor and then act rapidly to use this analysis to win the bid and then act in the market. The classic signs of a technical strategy in action: statistically rigorous analysis allied with organizational fleetness of foot.

Basket trading was hair-raising enough when practiced on the relatively liquid and efficient New York Stock Exchange. It was a completely different experience, however, when applied to many international equity markets at once. In many respects, however, basket trading of a global portfolio of stocks was even more popular among investors. During the 1970s, and especially during the 1980s, investment management houses around the world began to diversify their equity portfolios beyond their home markets. European investors had been the most aggressive at this, and were comfortable having 30 percent or more of their clients' money in markets outside the home market. Investors from the United States and Japan were slower to diversify their holdings, reflecting both their somewhat narrower perspectives on the world, the great size of their home equity markets, and, in the case of the Japanese and some public U.S. investors, regulatory or trustee restrictions on how much could be invested offshore. Nevertheless, by the mid-1980s, the volume of cross-border equity investing and trading had grown considerably, and so had the sophistication of the trading techniques available to the largest investors. Basket trading was one of the techniques on offer. This proved to be important, because market selection turned out to be the key driver of the returns achieved by a global equity portfolio. In nearly all cases, market selection was more important than which stocks were selected within each market, although the latter did have some effect on the returns achieved. Therefore, the best global managers were constantly assessing the relative attractiveness of each national market, and sought ways to rebalance their portfolios when they thought one market was likely to fall or rise relative to others. The short-term step they could take was to buy or sell futures on that market (if available; not all markets had developed stock index futures), but to lock in their new positions, and to avoid the cost of constantly having to roll over new futures positions, they needed to buy and sell baskets of the real, underlying cash stocks. As a result, the global basket trading market was developed.

As can be imagined, this market contained ferocious risks for the intermediaries undertaking the basket trades for their investor clients. In this case, the risks involved more than the complexities of undertaking large trades with baskets containing stocks from markets with very different volatilities; in addition, the intermediaries faced very different (and in some cases unreliable) clearing and settlement procedures market by market, as well as the expense of having in some cases to farm out the actual brokering of a stock to a local firm because they had no local capability. A successful global program trade, therefore, was made up of a multitude of little steps, each containing a measure of risk. First, the intermediary had to be comfortable with the prices of the stocks to be traded, not always a guaranteed event given the illiquidity of some markets. For instance, some markets had stocks that could not be owned by foreigners, severely reducing their liquidity. So the best players established local broker contacts (or their own local presences) to manage this initial pricing step. Then the intermediary had, as in the single-market basket trade, to calculate the likely volatility and holding period for the basket's components. This was a crucial and complicated task when dealing across multiple markets, and once again it relied upon the core technical strategy skill of superior analysis and understanding of pricing relationships. Once reasonably happy with these analyses on paper, the broker then had to turn to the real world, considering what it would cost to actually trade the stocks and how long it would take to clear and settle each national component. The longer it took to clear the stocks, the longer the broker had to wait for the money and the higher the financing cost of the transaction. Again, the best players worked hard, market by market, to establish their links with local players, or their own local trading and clearing capabilities, in order to lower their costs of trading.

These hurdles to success limited the competition to a few brokerage houses. Investors were simply not prepared to trust such trades to any broker, given the complexities and opportunities for major mistakes. At the end of the 1980s, the competition had settled down to a few houses, such as Goldman Sachs, Morgan Stanley, Salomon Brothers, and sometimes First Boston from the United States; James Capel and S. G. Warburg from the United Kingdom; and Union Bank of Switzerland through their owned British broker, Phillips & Drew. Advantage in these bids for basket trades went to the firms that could combine the analytics to determine potential risks and returns on a portfolio with the practical computer and operational skills to actually deliver the multiple trades at good prices and in good time—a classic mix for a technical strategy. Many of these trades, when they came, required the brokers to stay up all night to shepherd a trade as it went from market to market and to stay in close touch with their local contacts in each market. However, those brokers who constantly refined their analytics and their operations gained major competitive advantages, and being so far ahead on the learning curve created formidable barriers for new competitors. New players sought out traders from the winning firms so that they could short-circuit the development process. The best individuals moved among different brokerage houses very rapidly and at ever-increasing salaries.

Index arbitrage and basket trading are obviously technical strategies, combining statistical analysis with operational and organizational flexibility. Another trading activity, trading on the outcomes of potential takeovers, or risk arbitrage, may not seem to involve a technical strategy, but it does. This process is usually seen as an insider strategy; indeed, some risk arbitrageurs, such as Ivan Boesky, obviously saw it that way, stepped over the legal line on the insider approach, and used information in an illegal fashion. However, a significant aspect of risk arbitrage trading is not simple betting on the outcome of a deal but involves core technical strategies.

As the M&A and LBO markets became more sophisticated in the 1970s and 1980s, the role of specialist traders who spent their time trading on the likelihood of deals going through increased. These risk arbitrageurs ended up owning the swing shares in a transaction and were a crucial constituency for the key players in the M&A field to know and influence. At first, the key players could rely on rumors and manual reviews of trading activity to identify likely targets and take stakes in them. As the competition increased, however, these approaches were supplemented by more rigorous statistical analysis. Specifically, a number of competitors began to subscribe to services that analyzed share trading data and identified abnormal trading activity, either in price or in volume. It was once said that an arbitrageur should buy on the rumor and sell on the actual news of the deal being announced, thereby capturing the majority of the price increase. Such was the fervor of activity in the 1980s, however, that the best players tried to beat the rumors, indeed to get to the stage where they were *selling*, not buying, on the rumors, because by then most of the price appreciation had already occurred. To do this, they used some basic technical strategy disciplines.

Computer analysis can be undertaken for all parts of the risk arbitrage business. Most obviously, computers are employed to scan the equity and equity option markets to identify any unusual trading activity. Option markets can be particularly interesting, inasmuch as equity options are more sensitive and leveraged than the underlying stocks and are likely to reflect strange trading activity before the underlying stocks. So some firms subscribe to services that track the trading volume and premiums of thousands of equity options on the theory that if a transaction is in the offing, then one possible indication is that the premium on the option is overpriced relative to the theoretical level. Another early warning system consists of monitoring trading by insiders (the management of a company) in that company's stock to see if anything unusual is going on. Old-style arbitrage could not possibly cover thousands of situations this way *prior* to any rumor; it would be impossible to cover the market this way without extensive computer support.

Once a potential risk arbitrage situation is identified, further statistical analysis is required to determine if a potential deal is in the offing and at what price it could be done. This involves analyzing the shareholdings and financials of a company, as well as the financial strength of the suitor, to see at what price a deal could be financed. Given that the markets move very quickly when a deal becomes a public rumor, rapid integration of these various data feeds becomes the only way to set a possible strike price for the deal. On the basis of this rapid analysis, the best arbitrageurs are able to buy shares before the rest of the arbitrage community sees the same possibilities and bids up the price beyond the level established by the analysis.

Finally, once a merger deal is underway, a set of complex technical events are set in motion. The arbitrageur usually tries to take offsetting positions in the target and bidder, and computer programs are crucial in calculating and monitoring the spread on such positions and in identifying when a good time appears for selling out and taking a profit. They also aid in deciding the best means of participating in a takeover: is it through the underlying cash stocks, or do the options, or the convertible bonds, or even the preferred stock appear to be the best way to play? Computer analysis is required to factor in the volatilities of each instrument, the cost of carrying it, and the real-time prices to determine which is the best vehicle at each stage of the takeover.

Of course, part of the way an arbitrageur controls his or her exposure in such situations is to be involved in a number of transactions at once, and to build a probability tree on each to establish reasonably scientific risk and reward matrices for the overall portfolio. Continuous monitoring of prices, and of spreads between bids and achieved prices, is crucial if this portfolio approach is to allow for timely movements into and out of deals as they become more and less attractive. The key components of risk arbitrage—the analysis of thousands of situations against historical pricing to identify potential deals, the analysis of potential bid levels, the monitoring and risk weighting of a portfolio to maximize risk-adjusted returns—all exhibit the key components of a technical strategy: statistically driven decision making supported by an organization able to act quickly on the basis of that analysis. Now, as noted earlier, risk arbitrage also involves a good dose of judgment, and many players in the market eschew this computer driven approach. However, they are no longer the only players in the market; the technical strategists have their role.

The importance of a flexible organization in this field was underlined in February 1986 when Chemical Bank in New York stunned the investment world by hiring Timothy Tabor from Kidder Peabody to lead a new risk arbitrage effort at the bank. Risk arbitrage had traditionally been a domain dominated by investment banks. Commercial banks like Chemical had avoided the market because of potential conflicts of interest with their commercial loan customers and clients, and because they often did not have the organizational flexibility to put large amounts of capital at risk, at great speed, and focused on just a few transactions. Chemical's move in 1986 suggested that the bank had found a way to get around these problems. In retrospect, it seems clear that the bank may not really have thought through the implications of risk arbitrage in full before hiring Tabor.

Very soon after arriving at Chemical, Tabor and his team identified some transactions they wanted to invest in—but they discovered that Chemical had not yet put in place the basic capital and risk authorization procedures. Tabor was told to wait. This, however, was just the start, for soon members of the Chemical Bank board who disliked the arbitrage and corporate raider world applied pressure to the bank's management, and

Tabor was instructed to avoid all hostile transactions and to invest only in friendly deals. Given that most of the money in risk arbitrage was made in hostile transactions, this effectively put Tabor out of the market. He soon departed from Chemical, and the bank was left having made a public statement about its commitment to the investment banking world and being unable to follow through on it. Chemical failed in this venture because it lacked the organizational flexibility and dexterity to compete. Even if it could have applied the statistically analysis as well as any other competitor, the bank could not fulfill this other key requirement of a successful technical strategy.

If Chemical Bank on this occasion lacked the organizational flexibility to enter this technical market, its investment bank compatriots showed more agility. One of the most interesting examples of this in action is Morgan Stanley's use of an esoteric technical approach for the U.S. equity markets. In 1984 Morgan Stanley hired a rather unique gentleman named Nunzio Tartaglia. Tartaglia grew up in New York and put himself through Manhattan College by following in his father's footsteps as a laborer on construction crews. But Tartaglia's mind stretched beyond a construction site, and he went to Yale to earn a master's degree in physics. His reaction to the wave of social change that occurred during the late 1960s was not to go to Woodstock or the Isle of Wight, but instead to join the Jesuits. Five years later, not yet ordained and restless in the seminary, Tartaglia returned to the secular world and built on his physics degree, earning a Ph.D. in astrophysics from the University of Pittsburgh. He then spent 2 years at the prestigious Bell Laboratories before joining Merrill Lynch and beginning a frenetic career at one Wall Street firm after another, finally settling down in the world of quantitative analysis at Drexel Burnham Lambert at the end of the 1970s. Then the construction laborer, turned Jesuit, turned astrophysicist joined Morgan Stanley. His task: to build a high-technology, quantitative trading operation for Morgan Stanley's own account. Morgan planned to take these ecletic skills and use them for its own profitability directly, rather than selling the approach to clients.

A custom-tailored trading room, reputedly costing over $1 million, was built for Tartaglia's small team, which developed its own trading approach. Devoid of the usual ruckus of the trading floor, they ran the operation like a research and development department at a major pharmaceutical company. The ambience was quiet, and new ideas were discussed, researched, tested, and then introduced in full. At its height, the trading unit sent orders to trade over two million shares a day to the New York Stock Exchange, making it one of the most active investors in that market. All these trades were technical trades, based on analytics undertaken by a battery of computers at the team's disposal. These computers were used to discover new technical opportunities. Beginning with the basic equity pairs trading (for instance, trading the historic price spread between General Motors and Ford shares), the unit started to diversify and consider a wider set of interrelationships to be found in price series. The team looked at the interrelationships between certain equity prices and the prices of asset classes, such as the link between oil prices and groups of stocks, or the link between agricultural commodity prices and the prices of the major food manufacturers. Moving further afield, the team started to research whether there was a systematic way to profit from the market's reaction (or overreaction) to corporate earnings surprises.

Technical strategies, as we have seen, often involve taking many small bets to achieve a large return in the end. To make that approach work, however, one must keep the costs of each bet or trade to a minimum. Here again the Tartaglia team played the game fully, becoming the scourge of Wall Street by examining specialist commission rates and discounts to make sure they were getting the lowest possible execution costs on the New York Stock Exchange. Like other quantitative teams, the Morgan Stanley unit also used lower-cost alternatives when possible, like the Midwest Stock Exchange, which charged no floor brokerage commissions, and trading of U.S. shares in London.

For a period, the approach worked. The trades were relatively low risk, being hedged against each other and the market, and in the very volatile markets of the mid-1980s the unit ended up making large profits for the firm. But after the market break of October 1987, in the relatively calmer waters that followed, the unit was less successful and yet remained expensive to operate. At the same time, Tartaglia started to investigate futures trading strategies that would entail more capital risk for the firm. In 1989, as a result of lackluster returns and high costs (and probably reaping the wind of some rather rude comments about the cigar-and-suspender-type traders that dominated the more classical trading approach elsewhere at Morgan Stanley), Tartaglia left the firm. He had not given up, however, and reappeared in a very low-cost unit pursuing the same basic strategies on behalf of Japanese investors.

The Tartaglia experience at Morgan Stanley shows that a relatively large firm can be nimble enough to pursue advanced technical approaches, but that these have to be constantly watched to ensure that the conditions that allowed the approach to work still exist. In 1989 Morgan Stanley decided that Tartaglia's approach would no longer work. Tartaglia believed otherwise, concluding that technology had squeezed out all profits from the approach, at least all except enough to pay a small team and a few computing costs, not the infrastructure Morgan Stanley had underwritten. In that respect both were right, and both had reacted in their own ways to changing markets.

Morgan Stanley, of course, had the luxury of being able to drop the Tartaglia group because it had so many other strengths, many of them in its insider strategy-based investment banking group, that the profits of the unit could easily be done without once it lost its momentum. Not all firms that pursue a technical strategy have that luxury; if the strategy fails, the firm itself can fail.

Some technical strategies succeed for only brief periods before competitors began to whittle away the small arbitrage opportunities the technical strategists have discovered. But some fail because they have a fatal flaw. The most spectacular example of this problem was the concept called *portfolio insurance* that lay at the core of the October 1987 stock market break. Portfolio insurance was designed to protect, or insure, an equity portfolio's returns by dynamically hedging the fund's performance as the market moved. In a down or bear market, portfolio insurance was designed to protect existing returns by selling stock index futures as the market started to fall. Each portfolio insurance program had its own unique selling point, for instance triggering sales after the market fell 5 percent or more, that was designed to protect returns. As the market fell, the gains on the short positions in futures were designed to offset the losses on the long position in the underlying cash stocks and thereby protect returns.

Portfolio insurance depended on one key assumption: that, in a major crisis, the futures market would be liquid enough to absorb the waves of selling that would be unleashed. When just a few funds were using portfolio insurance, the technique could probably have worked, but by the middle of 1987 over $60 billion in U.S. equities were "protected" by portfolio insurance. During 1986 and 1987, the Securities and Exchange Commission reviewed periods of market volatility, and identified something they called the *cascade theory* as a potential cause of them and a potential future problem. This theory suggested that if a large number of portfolio insurers started to sell futures at once, the futures market would not be able to absorb the sales without marking futures prices down very rapidly. This dramatic decline in the indicated price of the stock index would produce major selling of cash stocks by the index arbitrageurs to try to bring the markets in line. This decline in the cash stocks would, of course, trigger further future sales by the portfolio insurers, bringing on a "cascade" of futures sales, stock sales, futures sales, on and on.

During October 1987, the U.S. stock market declined significantly; on Friday, October 16, it fell over 108 points, or 4.6 percent. Unknown to the general public, the major stockbrokers and the regulators worked over the following weekend because they were aware of some unsettling facts. First, despite the market's downward moves over the preceding weeks, the portfolio insurers had not been as active as expected. Some brokers had worked hard to try to discover or guess what the trigger points of the major portfolio insurers were. The analysts working over the weekend guessed that after the decline on October 16, the portfolio insurers would be forced to act on Monday, October 19. This analysis was reinforced by rumors that Fidelity, the large mutual fund company, was experiencing major telephone withdrawals from its equity funds that would force it also to sell equities in the market on Monday.

That Monday dawned early for the regulators and major brokers as they braced themselves for another bad day. They were not to be disappointed. At the heart of the problem was the failure of portfolio insurance to work safely for the entire market. As predicted by the cascade theory, the futures markets could not absorb the massive volumes of sell orders that were unleashed by the portfolio insurers. The futures and cash equity prices became disconnected, causing both failure to trade some stocks because of order imbalances and panic selling of some stocks. The decline in market prices, as expected, caused further portfolio insurance sales—the cascade theory in action. The portfolio insurers on balance did better than the average investor, but they did suffer major losses. The approach, based on computer-simulated dynamic hedging, could not work because in the real world over $60 billion in stocks could not be fully hedged. It may well be that the market was ready to decline on fundamentals by October 1987, and that the events of October 19 and 20 merely concentrated the decline into a couple of days. But for the portfolio insurers this was a disaster, producing a failure to insure funds on those days, as promised to their customers, and making the technique unacceptable to many and reducing its use dramatically.

Technical strategies play an important role in making the trading markets of the world act more effectively and efficiently. By finding and using ways to link market price movements, the technical strategists increase the ease and attractiveness of cross-market and cross-border investing, thereby allowing capital to flow more easily to places where it is needed. But as we have seen, these strategies are not just for the public good; they can produce fantastic profits or losses. But when a competitor has the ability to use hard analytical analysis of historic or mathematically predicted market prices, and has the organizational ability to move with great flexibility and speed to take advantage of this analysis, it can often make significant returns. For only a few, however, are these strategies the bulk of their activities. For most trading and investing firms, technical strategies are combined with strategies based on human analysis and judgment to produce overall returns. It is to these inference strategies that we turn in the next chapter.

7

Inferring the Future:
The Inference Strategy

At a race track, as the horses make the rounds of the paddock in front of the stewards and the local bettors, an eager bunch of people is to be seen examining every horse in great detail. As the favorite starts to act up, a frothy sweat rising next to the bridle and the saddle, a small murmur runs through this crowd. Some start looking to the second favorite. But he is looking subdued today; maybe that outsider with the glistening coat is the one to back. Final checks are made. The racing form is reviewed one last time—but the going is very soft today, so how relevant are all those times on good hard turf? The horses parade out onto the track and head for the starting stalls. One last look at them through binoculars—the favorite seems to have quieted down, so more money goes on him again. Then they are off. All these conjectures and analyses are put to the test.

Which bettors do best? They are making a series of judgments based on their experience, a little historical data, and as up-to-date information on the horses as they can derive. Inference-based trading and investing strategies are very sophisticated versions of the best horse betting—or at least, they are meant to be more sophisticated. Like the bettors at the track, the research analysts, investors, asset and liability managers, and traders who are peering into the markets are trying to make judgments about which assets will win over others. Will short-term interest rates stay high or will they fall, making long-term rates fall too? Will the domestic stock market outperform bonds? Which stocks in particular will do well? Energy stocks have been good recently, but have they now run their best race, and is it time to be looking at consumer goods stocks instead? Maybe the domestic market will outperform bonds, but will it rise as fast as overseas stocks, especially if the domestic currency declines in value as interest rates come down? Maybe the stocks and bonds of any country are no match for property. Is now the time to be going into a partnership to buy commercial property? But in which cities? On and on go the questions that the inference strategists have to ask. Unconvinced by the dry charts and statistics of the technical players, the inference investors and traders try to peer into the future based on their assessment of what everything going on around them in the real world and the financial economy means for the prices of financial assets.

The inference strategy is the twin of the insider strategy, just as the technical strategy is the twin of the segmentation strategy. Whereas the latter two are based on hard analytics of large quantities of data, the former two are based on judgments about often incomplete or uncertain information. The insider strategy is applied in the real economy in lending, venture capital, and large insurance underwriting. The inference strategy is applied in the worlds of investing and trading in markets. It involves inferring the future through analytical research, or, unfortunately, often from seat-of-the-pants analysis. It ultimately requires a good dose of judgment to lead to the final action. Whereas the technical strategy is driven by statistical analysis of the past to determine the future, the inference strategy is based on research of the past to infer the future. Some technical strategies feel clinical and "scientific"; the inference strategy, by contrast, always contains a good dose of art.

The inference strategy is what many financial firms execute in their investing and trading departments. When banks bet on interest rates on the basis of their economic forecasts they are applying the inference strategy. When investment managers judge that the stock market will go up, and therefore move their clients' money out of cash and into stocks, they are applying the inference strategy. When insurance companies decide to invest in bonds of a particular maturity because they expect interest rates for that maturity to decline, they are using the inference strategy. When stockbrokers advise their clients to buy one stock over another because their research department expects it to show strong profit growth, they are applying the inference strategy. In all these cases, firms may undertake extensive research of the past, but they are ultimately making judgments that depend upon their ability to see into the future. In contrast to the technical approach, the inference strategy relies upon analysis and judgments about *fundamentals* such as economic trends, companies' profitability, and interest rates.

This would all be well and good if everyone else was not trying to do the same things as you. The inference strategy is based upon the assumption that your inferences are better than those of others—which, therefore, assumes that you have some information, analysis, or experience advantage over others that will make such superior judgments possible. Unfortunately, it is often very difficult for outside investors in a financial company to tell whether it does or does not have an inference advantage. It is easy, however, as a manager of such a company to convince yourself that you do. For instance, portfolio managers can sound so wise; they have seen it all before and seem confident in what investment stance to take to bolster returns. Then the analysts supporting them are so knowledgeable about their industries, and seem to be on first-name terms with the senior management of the companies they are recommending. Finally, through your contacts covering the affairs of politicians and regulators, you are sure you have an edge on which way the policymakers will tilt the economy. With this team, how can you lose? Very easily.

In all too many cases, when a financial company analyzes its inference skills in more detail, it recognizes that it may not have any special advantage. Lackluster returns achieved over a long time, especially when the degree of risk taken is factored in, all too often show that the supposed advantage does not really exist. The key to pursuing an inference approach is to ask, using the most skeptical tone possible, what do we do, or have, that makes it possible for us consistently to make better judgments than the average player. How is it that when everybody else is still bearish about a market or a stock, we know that now is the time to move back into that market or buy that stock? When a new hot stock has been rising and rising, and many people believe it is time to take profits, how do we really know that it will go on rising, that its profit outlook is really so good? When our traders say they can earn us great returns if we would only give them permission to take larger positions, what do they believe will enable them to make superior bets? Do they have better information about the fundamentals underpinning the securities, or do they have special insights about where the smart money is heading?

The key here is not that any of these investors or traders has a single formula for success; there is not just one inference approach that will work. Rather, they must be able to articulate clearly, and support with convincing evidence, what it is that will enable them to make better judgments than others and act on them in good time. Once this basis for success is articulated and understood, then it is possible to monitor whether the conditions required for success exist and continue to exist. Without a proper articulation of the inference approach, the whole scene becomes a pointless set of claims and counterclaims about the "skills" of the analysts, portfolio managers, and traders. Meanwhile, the firm keeps investing and trading without any real sense of why and how it can be a winner.

Inference strategies focus on the contacts and valuation judgments made by people. For that reason, they are the hardest to analyze. The data on the skills and track records of the key players, and on whether the information sources are really superior, is thin and full of conjecture. But the managements of all types of major financial institutions constantly rely on the inference approach—for instance, when they make interest rate bets or select particular stocks for a portfolio. What evidence is there that this strategy works? Frankly, the evidence is spotty, and this is because in only a few cases is it possible to see that an investor or trader really has the information, analysis, or judgment advantage to underpin a consistently successful inference approach.

In the last chapter we looked at the precursor of modern technical strategies, the chartist approach to investing. The counterpart to the approach is fundamental analysis, the inference strategy applied to the investment management world. Ever since an organized, professional investment management system was devised and applied, the fundamental research, inference approach has been the core discipline used.

Fundamental investors act as their name suggests: they invest and trade on the basis of fundamentals. By this is meant the fundamental economic, political, and corporate activities that make up the investment world. The fundamental investor tries to stay ahead of everyone else on developments in these areas, analyzes their trends, projects those trends into the future—and then makes a trade or investment that will make money if the judgment about the future is correct. To do this, the fundamental investor uses a number of techniques.

Fundamental stock investing is based on recognizing stocks that are cheap or expensive on the basis of what the fundamental investor or trader believes the future holds for the company. The classical approach used to make this determination is to analyze the future earnings potential of the company and then divide an earnings per share number into today's share price to develop a *price-earnings ratio (PE)* based on both present and future projected earnings. Comparing these PEs to those of other companies, the fundamental investor decides which stock is cheap and which is expensive—and invests or trades accordingly. The problem with this approach is that it is very difficult to be sure of these projections; hence, a good dose of judgment is required about what will affect future earnings.

During my time at a merchant bank in England, I was a fundamental research analyst for the portfolio managers in the bank's investment department. This department managed the accounts of major pension funds, and my job was to cover a number of industry sectors of the British economy, advise the portfolio managers on the earnings outlook for those industries, and then, within each industry, identify which companies looked like better investments than others, given their relative future PEs. One of the industry sectors I covered was the brewing industry in Britain, and my experiences illustrate the limitations and problems of the inference approach.

The portfolio managers were looking to me for an overall assessment of how attractive the brewing industry appeared to be at any moment in time. Then they wanted me to advise them, for instance, on whether Bass or Whitbread looked like a better investment, whether Guiness would continue to grow, and how long regional brewers like Greene King in East Anglia could continue to take share from the nationals. Finally, they wanted me to tell them which stocks to buy and sell, and to monitor these recommendations constantly as prices moved from day to day. To produce this advice, I had a number of resources to rely upon. First, as a buy-side analyst, I could call upon all the brewing industry analysts at the sell-side stockbrokerage firms, ask their opinions, and read their research reports on the brewing industry and the major brewing companies. I had our own files on these companies and the opinions of other analysts or portfolio managers who had held my position in prior years. In addition, I scanned the newspapers and brewing industry trade journals to try to stay ahead of everyone else on the latest technologies, labor relations, and sales news that might affect one of the companies. Finally, there were company visits when a group of analysts were invited to take a tour of a company's facilities and ask questions of the top managers to help us understand the company better than we could from the numbers and few pictures in the annual report.

As you can imagine, brewing company visits were particularly interesting. I remember one occasion when a group of us were bused out of London to the facilities of one of the fastest-growing regional brewing firms that was about to make a foray into the London market. Investors were very unsure what this meant. Would the company incur enormous new distribution costs, come face to face with national competitors' cutthroat pricing, and suffer serious losses? Or would the London pub dweller leap at the regional brew, find its Old World taste superior, and create a surge in sales? The visit was part of a concerted attempt by this brewer to convince the investment community of the latter, but we hard-bitten analysts were not going to be taken in. We boarded our bus with every intention of asking tough questions of the management. As we passed out of the suburbs of London and headed through hedge-bounded roads for the brewery, each of us studied the annual report one more time, looked at our earnings projections and our key assumptions that lay behind them, and prepared the questions that we hoped would help us discern the future more clearly. Then we arrived at the brewery, and our best-laid plans withered away.

We were ushered into a large refectory, wood-paneled and hung with portraits of (noticeably red-nosed) former patriarchs of the firm. At one end of the table at which we sat stood the ominous truth—three large jugs of the local brew and 12 beer mugs. We were certainly here to understand the company better! The problem was, it was still only 10 in the morning. In strode the chairman of the company, and immediately he filled the beer mugs and passed them around. There was no escaping the ritual—indeed, the peer pressure to consume was enormous. The chairman's ability to fix those who only sipped with a look of disgust was remarkable. So was the speed with which he refilled half-empty mugs. So the meeting moved on, but somehow in that refectory, with the lukewarm beer settling uneasily on the eggs, or cereal, or toast consumed not too long before, the questioning was a little less acerbic than had been planned on the bus.

An hour later, we stumbled from the refectory and started a tour of the brewery, focusing too much on the details of the process with which we were unfamiliar than on the economic implications of it all. Finally, after a few more questions, we returned to the refectory for an excellent lunch accompanied by an extra special (and extra potent) batch of the brew. Duly affected, we returned to the bus and London. Now we faced the hard task—determining what did all this mean for the stock of the brewer.

The problem with fundamental analysis and fundamental investment approaches is that, to be legal, they cannot be based on clearly advantaged sources of information. If they are, and if this information is not freely available to all investors, then in most markets they fall foul of the insider trading laws and regulations. Inference strategies cannot be illegal insider strategies. Therefore, from a mosaic of incomplete information, the inference investor tries to develop the wisdom of an insider, but by definition is unlikely to do so on a consistent basis. As a stock analyst for the merchant bank in London, I sometimes made very successful investment recommendations, and the stocks I recommended were bought by the portfolio managers and improved the returns of the investment funds. At other times, however, my recommendations were less successful. How could I really be expected to fare better than average? I had no better information than anyone else, and our economic research was not consistently better than that of other firms. I certainly did not have years of wisdom in the markets. It was hard for the management of the bank to tell whether I was just on a lucky streak when I did well, or whether I had found some new source of special advantage.

This problem has not stopped the fundamental investment community around the world from inventing a barrage of inference techniques. In the 1970s, the major Western economies suffered a severe burst of inflation as the aftermath of the Vietnam War deficits in the United States mixed with sharp oil price increases and lax monetary policies worldwide. As inflation rose to double-digit levels around the world, stock research analysts started to tinker with the way they viewed earnings. These analysts started to adjust the earnings accounted for on the basis of historical costs to reflect the current costs of replacing equipment and inventory. So depreciation charges and the cost of goods sold were both adjusted upward. On the basis of these revised (usually depressed) earnings, analysts drew an entirely new view of the corporate world. Particularly in high-inflation environments like that of the United Kingdom, this was a world where manufacturing firms with rapidly aging plants suddenly looked very unattractive, and where companies with less need to replace fixed assets, and those with appreciating assets like property and natural resources, looked very attractive. Current cost earnings analysis became the rage, and investment portfolios started to be repositioned to emphasize companies that performed well under this analysis.

No sooner had current cost earnings become the new orthodoxy than Volcker and Howe on either side of the Atlantic burst the inflation bubble. Suddenly, current cost earnings analysis was pushed aside as analysts focused on companies that would benefit in a less inflationary environment. The new focus was on cash flow. Real cash generated by the business was seen as the true driver of value. So if cash was king, the researchers went out seeking him. They built complex models to project cash flows of companies, full of assumptions and informed guesses, and on the basis of these models advised the portfolio managers who made the investing or trading decisions. As each new analytical technique was introduced, first a few, then all the stock market analysts adopted it. The whole quality of the research effort improved, but the long-term advantage gained by one firm over another was minimal.

A similar trend was to be found in Japan. Throughout the 1980s, the Japanese stock market perplexed all the Western researchers who tried to equate its valuations to those found in Europe and the United States. The problem was very simple. Western stock markets tended to value companies at between 8 and 20 times earnings; the Japanese market valued them at closer to 60. Even allowing for different accounting procedures, the Japanese valuations seemed to be at least twice those in the United States. As cross-border investing increased during this decade, more and more investors and traders from the West were exposed to the Japanese market and came to believe that it must collapse. How could it survive at such outrageous levels? Surely it would slip back closer to *our* valuations. So at several times during the 1980s, Western investors were major sellers on the Japanese exchanges—and saw the market simply keep rising. What was going on? The Japanese market worked somewhat differently than the Western markets, and was propped up by very large investment flows because investors in Japan had few alternatives. At the time, the different approach was based partly upon the real asset values that were hidden in the balance sheets of companies. For instance, as Japanese real estate values increased, so did the value of hidden assets on the balance sheets of these companies, and so then did their stock prices.

So the inference approach in Japan was based upon different analytics than the one used in the West. But the two were joined when, in the 1980s, *the weight of money* analysis was adopted by researchers in the West who were trying to predict overall market trends. Instead of analyzing individual stocks, or even industry sectors, these analysts focused on overall flows of funds in the economy and on how much was likely to end up in the equity markets. From there they predicted the direction of the overall market. Of course, the flow of funds was always at the margin, and therefore could cause violent price effects because a change in cash flows to or from the market could represent a large percentage of the stocks actually traded in a week or a month. So these analysts tried to predict cash flows into pension funds, insurance company stock funds, mutual funds, or investment trusts and, finally, individual investors' behavior, to assess the overall demand for stocks. They balanced this against the withdrawals from the market (for instance, to pay pensions or to fund insurance claims) and the expected new supply of stock from rights issues and initial public offerings. Finally, they factored in how much stock would be withdrawn from the market through corporate buybacks, LBOs, and mergers or acquisitions. Balancing these estimates of supply and demand, the analysts predicted the price of the market the same way supply and demand analysis would be used in predicting the trend of oil prices or the price of consumer electronics.

Where did these various inference approaches lead? Unfortunately, not very far. As we saw earlier when discussing perfect and efficient markets, it has been shown that few inference investors can consistently outperform the market when information is reasonably equally available to all participants. In any particular period, after factoring in all their costs, the average mutual fund company and investment counselor in fact slightly underperforms the market averages. Even more disconcerting for the inference advocates is that winners in any one year are unlikely to remain winners for long. The winning formula cannot be sustained or is in fact a mirage.

So overwhelming has been the strength of this research that it has spawned an entirely new approach to investing—index investing, where the investor consciously does not try to beat the market but merely hopes to mimic it. This is done by holding a basket of stocks—for instance, the *Financial Times* 100 stocks on the London stock market or the S & P 500 in New York. Indexing basically assumes that the inference strategy, when applied to open and relatively efficient stock markets, will not produce superior returns—so why incur all the costs of the analysts and portfolio managers? Of course, indexing has within it the seeds of its own destruction. It assumes that a highly competitive set of inference strategies is taking place and that, as a result, the real economic information is rapidly translated into stock prices that reflect a synthesis of investors' expectations about the future. Because all these inference strategies are in place, and because very few of them can outperform the others consistently, lower-cost indexing makes sense. But should the inference strategists wither away because of their lack of success, should more and more money be applied to indexing approaches, then some real inference opportunities might open up due to lack of diligent research. Too much indexing at the expense of fundamental research makes the latter very attractive again.

Inferring the future, as we have seen, lies at the heart of what stock market investors do every day. Many market traders have followed a similar route. Many brokers and traders have turned to supplementing their declining brokerage income with positioning profits. In effect, they have become investors as well as brokers. In the previous chapter, we saw how some try to earn positioning profits by applying technical strategies of one form or another. Many other brokers, and in some cases the same brokers pursuing two positioning approaches at once, have opted for the inference approach to positioning.

The theory for traders is that they *really* will have an information advantage over and above that possessed by the average investor. The supposed information advantage for traders is that they see a very high percentage of trades going across their desks or offered to them by their customers. This flow of trading orders is seen by many as an opportunity to detect which way the market is going, and which sectors and stocks are hot, before the average player. On the basis of this advantaged information, the trader is then able to take a series of bets that, on average, will work out well for the firm. But as with so many inference strategies, when we examine these so-called information advantages in detail, they turn out to be illusory for all but a very few brokers in each market.

The work of Lynn Feldman and Jack Stephenson on positioning profitability in the U.S. government securities market* illustrated how fragile the positioning advantage of traders can be. For the U.S. Treasuries markets, they showed that very few trading firms have such a large share of total trades that they

---

*"STAY SMALL or GET HUGE—Lessons from Securities Trading,"
Lynn Feldman and Jack Stephenson, *Harvard Business Review*, May–June 1988.

have advantaged insights into the overall trading trends in the market. These few leading firms, most obviously Salomon Brothers in New York, probably can say that they have a tangible and sustainable information advantage over the average investor. They can expect to make above-average returns by pursuing an inference approach to trading Treasuries, although even Salomon is turning to technical strategies in this market. At the other end of the spectrum are market makers with minute shares of the total trades. To the Salomon Brothers of the world, these theoretically competing firms are practically customers, and are treated very much like any other investor customer. They get all the information that Salomon traders feel comfortable giving to their investor customers, secure in the knowledge that these small market makers cannot use the information against them. These very minor market makers have only an average chance of earning attractive inference returns.

In the middle are the "pariahs," the trading firms that are clearly far from the first tier, but aspire to it and may have the financial wherewithal to get to the top if they are determined. At one time or another, the major New York money center banks have threatened to become such a presence in the U.S. Treasuries markets. To these pariahs, the first-tier type of competitor will give as little information as possible. As a result, with too little information from their own relatively meager customer trading, these players in the middle are at a severe disadvantage in the inference positioning game. In fact, they may have the least information about trading trends of all the market participants, given that the leading market makers try to close down all sources of information to them.

Unfortunately, it is often these middle-tier competitors that embark upon inference approaches. As new competitors with aggressive ambitions (and some pride), these players often build up significant costs in the research, sales, and trading of the securities they have chosen. Often they pay well above market rates to attract some of the best sales and trading professionals to their new enterprise or pay multiples of book value for an existing firm. Probably they then invest in the latest technological support for these salespeople and traders. London, Tokyo, and New York all have examples of firms that have entered a trading market this way. Around the time of Big Bang, London was littered with many such expensive expansions by competitors with little direct experience in any of the markets they were entering.

Then the trouble starts. On the relatively low levels of customer trading volume that the new enterprise can garner, such expansion is simply not economically viable. Armed, however, with a mandate to build market share in order to become a power in the market, the new team sets to work. At first, they will probably try to win share through finer and finer bid/asked spreads and by offering to take more and more risk to win customers' orders. This will still not lead to acceptable profits. So, the inference approach is called upon. Accompanied by claims that all the leading players make their big profits through positioning, not brokering, the new team will initiate a proprietary trading strategy. Confused, perhaps, by their individual success when they were part of a firm with much greater access to trading flows, the new team probably believes that the proprietary returns achieved by the leading players in a market are available to them as well. All too often they are sadly wrong, and the new trading effort suffers more dramatic losses than in the past. Then perhaps even the proudest parent firm will start to question the wisdom of proceeding.

At the root of these middle-tier sales and trading firms' inference failures is the fact that they really do *not* have an information or evaluation advantage. They do not see a large enough share of the trading volume to be able to detect overall price trends earlier than the average investor, nor do they have a fundamental research advantage that allows them to make better investment judgments than others. Driven, however, by the costs of sustaining a credible presence in the market, they find that effectively "rolling the dice" is the only route they can follow. Of course, the managers of these trading efforts do not see the situation that way. They sincerely believe they can take positions which place the firm effectively and profitably at reasonable levels of risk. The reality is that in market after market, very few trading firms have the necessary valuation advantage required for such a strategy.

What is interesting about the inference trading winners is that they are rarely the same firms across different markets. Information gleaned in one area is unlikely to lead to an advantage in others. Competitors cannot make blanket statements about their "trading strength"; it has to be earned market by market. Examples of leaders abound, however, if one looks at individual markets.

Probably the best-known recent example was Drexel Burnham Lambert in the junk bond market in the United States. In many respects, Drexel was the inventor of junk bonds, and certainly the first firm to popularize the instruments. Drexel's returns from this market (that is, their legal returns, leaving aside the dealings that led to their severe fine and final demise) were obviously made partly from the large initial underwriting fees they received. But in addition, they earned very attractive returns by trading these bonds after they were issued. In some years, Drexel possessed more than 60 percent share of the junk bond underwriting market. Examining overall trends in the junk bond market, and understanding the financial condition and investment appetite of the key investors, Drexel was able to predict likely overall market movements reasonably well, although this did not protect the firm from holding significant inventories of junk bonds prior to the market's collapse in the autumn of 1989. But the firm's real inference advantage was that it had the best information on trading and investing in individual junk bonds. For each issue for which it had been the lead underwriter, Drexel knew who had been the major initial purchasers. In addition, as the dominant firm making a market in that particular security, Drexel was able constantly to update this database with the latest trading information. No other firm could match Drexel's knowledge of the market in an individual junk bond; hence, Drexel was able to garner all the trading information that existed and position itself effectively. Spectacular trading profits followed.

Inference advantages accrued to leading players in other trading markets as well. For instance, after Big Bang, the U.K. equity market moved to a market-making system. Initially, a large number of new competitors entered the market, seeking to become major players. But this over capacity produced very low market-making spreads. At the same time, the extreme fragmentation of the market meant that very few competitors had enough information from trading the stocks to gain a real inference advantage. However, S. G. Warburg and Smith New Court emerged as examples of exceptions to this rule. These two market makers had developed significant market shares in key stocks, and thereby had a large flow of trades from which to determine the mood of the market, in effect an instantaneous update on the weight of money. Whereas the new or weaker market makers were often unaware of the real trends in the stocks in which they made markets, these two stronger players emerged with a much clearer view of trends. As the remorseless vise of excess capacity and declining overall trading volumes after the October 1987 market break crushed the profitability of many market makers, some significant firms were forced to withdraw. Chase Manhattan Bank, Citibank, Hill Samuel, Lloyds Bank, Midland Bank, and Morgan Grenfell all either withdrew from or radically curtailed their market-making activities in London. Meanwhile, Warburgs and Smith New Court gained market share at their expense, and thus reinvigorated their inference strategies.

A third London broker that attempted to use an inference approach in the U.K. stock market after Big Bang was James Capel, a subsidiary of Hong Kong and Shanghai Bank. Capel was different from the first two, however. From the outset of the new trading world post Big Bang, its management had decided to avoid being a market maker. Building on its leading position in researching British companies, Capel planned to continue to act as an agent, trading stocks in return for commissions. The firm proclaimed that it would be able to retain a large share of trading through the quality of its research and because investors would know that it was not a market maker trying to trade at their expense. The approach was at first very successful, and the firm was able to garner an increasingly large share of London's market activity without incurring the costs and risks of the market makers. In early 1986, Capel held 6.3 percent of equity trading; by the middle of 1987, its share was over 8.5 percent. Over time, however, this position came under pressure as investors became more comfortable with the market-making approach. Capel had to respond by effectively becoming a market maker without registering as such. Market rumors were rife that Capel's "agency, risk-free trades" were increasingly involving taking positions for customers in order to facilitate their trades. In effect, Capel had become an "upstairs" market maker. Obviously, for this additional risk to make sense, the firm must have expected an additional reward. The combination of existing agency trading volume and positioning for key customers gave Capel a firm base for its own proprietary inference-based trades. Although Capel's earnings, like those of nearly all participants in the U.K. equity market at this time, were weak, and although by 1989 the firm was forced to slim down to improve profits, it retained a strong market presence, a significant share of trades, and the basis for an inference strategy.

This basic trading approach has long been at work in the U.S. over-the-counter (OTC) stock market run by NASDAQ. In the OTC market, a few market makers dominate the trading in individual stocks. Investors know who understands the market in these often illiquid securities best, and hence tend to concentrate their trading with those few firms, further reinforcing their advantage. New entrants wishing to trade a particular OTC stock find that they simply cannot make adequate returns given the volatility and risks of the stock, as well as the risk that they will be left with inventory of declining value that they cannot sell. But the few dominant players earn enough, both on the pure bid/asked spreads on the large volumes they see and on the positioning profits they are able to make as the trading day unfolds. Here, however, the rule that each market must be viewed independently is taken a stage further. Here each stock is a market unto itself, and leadership in one stock is not necessarily the basis for leadership in another.

So far, we have focused our analysis of the inference strategists on the competitors in the world's stock markets, but in fact, the inference approach is just as active in the bond, foreign exchange, and money markets of the world. Sitting at the center of these activities are the commercial banks, savings banks, and building societies that daily have to match their assets (loans) and liabilities (deposits) and decide which way they think interest rates will go. This process is often surrounded by magic at these firms, but the basic positioning decision is really a judgment, based on the best information and evaluation available, on the direction of interest rates. There have been great successes and failures.

One of the most dramatic successes was the decision by J. P. Morgan, at the height of Volcker's tight monetary policy period at the beginning of the 1980s, to buy a large portfolio of long-dated municipal bonds in the United States. This turned out to be a brilliant move that served them well over a number of years. As the Federal Reserve started to loosen monetary policy and interest rates declined, Morgan had locked in years of high spreads on its interest income account; the bank had guessed right. At the other extreme, prior to the lending debacle of the late 1980s, the savings and loans in the United States participated in some very unwise asset and liability management, often locking in mortgages at low interest rates and then funding them with floating-rate deposits that were repriced upward and created a severe squeeze on the interest margin account. They had guessed wrong.

Of course, not all players in the interest rate markets are equal. A bank like J. P. Morgan is as close to the Federal Reserve policymakers as any private institution can be. In addition, it has sophisticated operations in the other major money centers of the world and is able to add perspectives on overseas monetary policies. Finally, Morgan can attract and retain some of the best economists and traders to worry about the trends in the economy. Combining this supply of quality information with the quality of its people means that Morgan is in as good a position as any bank to predict trends in the economy and thereby in those all-important interest rates. Given the risks, Morgan has many of the attributes required to play the inference game in this market.

Now look at the local savings bank. Made up very often of 10 or 20 branches in the suburbs of a growing new town, with a headquarters building set off in a new office park, this bank is about as far away from the Federal Reserve as any banking institution can be. It is completely reliant upon the information received from the news wires and what is passed down by the local Federal Reserve officials. Its staff may be good local lenders with excellent local contacts—in other words, it may have the necessary raw material for the insider strategy in its local lending markets—but it cannot claim to have special economic insights or a special line to the key policymakers in Washington. But this bank too, under pressure from declining loan spreads and perhaps from losses on its portfolio of loans, may someday feel driven to try the inference strategy on its assets and liabilities. Its managers will "sense" that rates are coming down, and the bank will decide to lock in present loan rates by issuing long-term mortgages and issue short-term deposits to take advantage of the expected decline in rates. All too often, this disadvantaged inference approach comes undone.

Many were inference losers just because they could not see that success in one period was as much luck as anything else. First Bank System, based in Minneapolis, Minnesota, showed how difficult it is for banks to profit from the inference strategy over an extended period. In the mid-1980s, many U.S. regional commercial banks like First Bank System were suffering losses from loans as a result of the national recession at the beginning of the decade, as well as from the ongoing Midwestern problems in manufacturing and agriculture that continued on into the middle of the decade. To control these problems, the chief operating officer at First Bank System, Dennis Evans, pursued a strategy of investing in bonds instead of loans. To make sufficient profits on these bonds, however, Evans had to replace interest rate spreads earned for taking credit risk on loans with the spreads earned between long-term and short-term interest rates. He took interest rate risk. Specifically, from 1984 to 1987, First Bank System's bond portfolio increased from just under $3 billion to nearly $8 billion. Most of these extra bonds were of long maturities and were funded by short-term deposits. So Evans was betting on a decline in interest rates, which would both increase the spread between the bonds and the deposits and make the bonds more valuable.

Between 1984 and 1986, Evans was a hero. He correctly forecast that interest rates would decline, and the bank earned large profits on the positions he had taken. At the end of 1986, the bank was able to take a capital gain of $417 million by selling $3.5 billion of bonds. Much of this gain was used to clean up the bank's loan portfolio. Evans had gained the best of both worlds as far as many could see; he had lowered risk in the loan portfolio while raising overall profitability. In fact, he had taken significant risks but been lucky. Could he repeat the feat? Unfortunately, he tried to do so.

In early 1987 he refunded the bond portfolio, again on the basis that interest rates would decline. He believed that the United States was about to enter a recession and that the monetary authorities would lower interest rates as a result. He was wrong. Interest rates moved much higher during the second and third quarters of 1987, and First Bank System's bonds quickly became worth $600 million less than the amount Evans had paid for them. At this point, the bank decided to hedge its position, only to see exactly the decline in interest rates it had hoped for (brought about by the stock market break in October 1987 and the worldwide efforts of central banks to avert panic); due to the newly purchased hedges, the bank did not profit from the interest rate decline. It had guessed wrong twice.

The bank soldiered on through the rest of 1987 and most of 1988 hoping for some respite, but on December 19, 1988, faced up to a $500 million loss. As reported in the *New York Times*, the chief financial officer, Gerald B. Fischer said: "The likelihood of lower interest rates had declined over the past few months." The chairman, De Walt H. Ankeny, Jr., admitted that to take advantage of any lower rates that might come about, the hedging positions on the portfolio would have to be removed: "As soon as those hedges were eliminated, there would be tremendous risk to the organization if we were wrong and rates were to rise instead of fall."

This, of course, was exactly the risk that Evans had exposed the bank to in the 1984–1986 period. During that period he had been a winner; hence, the risks seemed manageable and Evans appeared to be a great seer. In 1988 it became clear that neither the bank nor Evans had any special inference advantage in predicting the trend of global or even U.S. interest rates. Why should they have? But the bank had acted as if it had, and paid the price. A month after the announcement of the sale of the portfolio, Evans resigned. First Bank System's experience illustrates how hard it is for top management to abandon a "successful" inference strategy even if they believe it is built on quicksand. In bull markets, most inference players make money, and it is hard to argue at this time that the profits are a mirage, that on a risk-adjusted basis they are unattractive. Unfortunately, this difficult task is exactly the responsibility of managers overseeing an inference-based strategy. They constantly have to check that the information or evaluation advantages that are presumed to underpin the strategy still exist. Otherwise, the whole effort could unravel, and yesterday's bull market profits (much of which will have disappeared in compensation to the traders) will be overwhelmed by today's losses.

The inference advantages some possess in the interest rate and money markets are mirrored in the foreign exchange markets, and the results have been truly spectacular. Throughout the 1980s, a group of major money center banks achieved superb records of profitability in this market, profits that in fact covered many sins in their businesses elsewhere. These banks, the well-known ones in New York, London, Frankfurt, and

Tokyo, were able to achieve these returns largely because they used the inference approach with great success. As in so many trading markets, the large players derive their returns from numerous sources. Certainly for the major foreign exchange dealers, customer business is very important. Building profits from customer business involves the segmentation strategy, as competitors strive to find the segments of customers that are less price sensitive, or are price sensitive but provide very large volumes. For many of the significant foreign exchange dealers, this customer flow brokering gives them a steady source of income, and they encourage their sales forces to discover corporations, investors, and even wealthy individuals who will give them significant volumes at attractive spreads. They find that they can take this approach further by adding the complexity of different cross-currencies and foreign exchange products (spot, forwards, options, swaps) to their segmentation analyses to find the cells of the product/customer market where they can make the most money. For instance, a French bank may find that local French corporations hunt around for the best spot dollar/ French franc quotes but are far less price sensitive when it comes to their occasional dollar/French franc forward hedges. Hence this bank might compete aggressively on the spot foreign exchange business to win the lucrative forward hedging business. However, these customer segmentation returns are very often supplemented by positioning profits. Here again, no single approach is followed; some players may use a technical approach, researching and charting past price relationships to discover statistically attractive bets that prices will move in a particular direction given past trends. Many others, however, employ an inference approach with great success.

The foreign exchange markets have, in fact, presented wonderful inference opportunities for the money center banks. The reasons are that the basic components for a winning inference strategy—advantaged information, many disadvantaged players to take advantage of, highly talented staffs to evaluate the information, and the ability of the organization to act upon the information—are available in abundance to the leading players.

Their sources of advantaged information are two. First, they see a very large percentage of the volume in their currencies of focus, either directly or through their contacts in the market. They can clearly discern the trends in order flow, whereas smaller banks and corporate customers are locked out of this world. Second, they have the best contacts with one group of key players in the market, the central banks. The trading banks know that the central bank is not playing on the same field as they are. It has a policy mission to fulfill, and once the trading bank can work out what this mission is, it can take advantage of the forced position of the central bank.

During the 1980s, the major foreign exchange rates (dollar, deutsche mark, yen) moved in great waves as the combination of monetary policies, central bank interventions, and the following trades of the trading banks sent the rates from historic highs to historic lows in the space of just a few years. The volumes of the trading banks overwhelmed those of the central banks or the foreign exchange activity required to clear real trade in physical goods and services between countries. At the center of all this activity, the major money center banks were able to discern which way the central banks were leading and to follow very quickly. Then the second-tier banks saw the trend and followed suit, putting into action the famous trader phrase "The trend is your friend." The large money center banks were able to monitor this activity too, and bet on it keeping the trend going even if it overshot the original target of the central banks. Then they saw the turn in central bank policy or market sentiment earlier than the average player and took advantage of that too. Given their position at the center of the foreign exchange whirlwind, these money center banks were clearly advantaged and used their position to earn attractive, inference-driven returns.

This approach was taken one step further by the New York money center bank Bankers Trust. During 1986 and 1987, Bankers Trust recorded very strong profits in foreign exchange trading. The results in 1987 were amazing; the bank recorded nearly $600 million in profit before operating expenses simply from trading foreign exchange, $338 million of which came in the fourth quarter of the year. Then, in July 1988, embarassingly an internal investigation resulted in Bankers Trust reducing these earnings by $80 million—to a mere $513 million for the year! Truly extraordinary performance, and to a large extent the result of the inference strategy in practice. Bankers Trust earned these superior returns by taking risks, but knowing how to manage them through a very advanced version of the inference approach.

A large part of Bankers Trust's returns were earned in a then esoteric part of the foreign exchange market, the long-dated OTC options market. In this market, a bank offers its customers options on foreign exchange rates perhaps 5 years into the future. The bank might offer to sell a call option on the pound sterling against the dollar. The buyer of this option has the right to buy pounds at, for instance, the rate of $1.50 to the pound 5 years from today. The buyer would find this option very valuable if the dollar weakened to a rate higher than $1.50; the option would expire worthless if the dollar strengthened to a rate of $1.49 or less required to buy a pound. Writing these long-dated options was not a simple matter; there was no high volume exchange to which Bankers Trust could hope to sell its exposures. The trick was to have enough such deals that the risks were counterbalanced and to hedge the exposure by taking offsetting positions as far as possible in other instruments. Finally, the whole operation was made worthwhile by the large prices that the bank was able to charge for these options. Assuming that the bank knew the history of the trading relationship between the two currencies well enough and could predict the likely volatility of the option, it could expect to make very attractive returns. So the basic approach required a good dose of the technical approach (to take historical price relationships and mathematical formulas and turn them into attractively priced options). It also used segmentation skills to identify the currencies the bank could excel in and the customers who would pay the most for this service.

Bankers Trust, however, took use of the options market into

the inference world. Or rather, Andy Krieger did. Krieger was a particularly expert foreign exchange options trader at Bankers Trust who came to the firm in 1986 from Salomon Brothers and became a power in his own right. Krieger's adult life had begun very differently. He entered the University of Pennsylvania in 1974 and stayed there for 10 years, studying Indian philosophy and Sanskrit at the Ph.D. level. In 1982 he entered the university's business school, Wharton, and graduated in 1984, joining Salomon Brothers to trade currency options. A long-time vegetarian, Krieger now returned to eating meat, reportedly explaining that trading was so aggressive that worrying about hurting animals seemed silly. His trading certainly was aggressive. The typical trading or position limit for a foreign exchange trader at Bankers Trust was $50 million, set against the bank's capital base of just under $3 billion at the time Krieger was active. By limiting the positions any one trader could take, Bankers Trust, like most other trading firms, tried to limit its exposure to individual error or malfeasance. These limits, however, also reduce the profits that a very successful trader can generate. Krieger was so successful that Bankers Trust allowed him a limit of $700 million, or nearly one quarter of the capital of the firm. Krieger engaged in some of the most esoteric trades imaginable. After he had left the firm and there was time to unravel his trades, Bankers Trust came to realize that sometimes he had about $2 billion at risk (although his positions were hedged and more liquid than $2 billion of loans). In a way, Bankers Trust's whole future was riding on the judgment and trades of one 32-year-old banker! Even though the bank hired a full-time assistant to keep track of Krieger's dizzying trades, as one Bankers Trust executive told the *Wall Street Journal* in 1988, "Nobody understood what Andy was doing."

What exactly was he doing? We saw earlier that the OTC foreign exchange options market is basically a technical and segmentation market. Krieger used options for the inference strategy, sometimes by inferring how the market would react to his own actions. Krieger focused on short-term rather than long-term options, and earned his returns more from judging which way a market would move than from mathematically calculated spreads. He focused on using options for leveraged investments on trends in the market. He often chose to write options in the less liquid, lower-trading-volume currencies—for instance, the New Zealand dollar against a more significant currency. What Krieger realized was that if he took enormous positions through options in these currencies, he alone could create a market distortion that he could reasonably well predict and therefore profit from. So Krieger took positions of up to $1 billion in these esoteric options and stood ready to profit from the expected reaction in the market as word of what he was doing got around. He built a pyramid of offsetting trades through the spot, forward, and options markets, and then profited as these various contracts repriced in response to his major position. Such was his market power that the New Zealand central bank is said to have complained to the Federal Reserve that Bankers Trust, specifically Andy Krieger, was affecting the New Zealand dollar exchange rates!

Krieger was not using just a technical strategy. It was certainly true that to succeed he had to be an expert in the complicated mathematical formulas that bound all these complex contracts together, and that past pricing volatility guided the offsetting and hedging positions he took to control risk as market conditions changed. But Krieger was operating outside the lessons of history. At the center of his approach, and the core risk in what he was doing, was his reliance upon his judgment that markets would react in a particular way. Krieger inferred a strategy from the way he saw markets reacting to his new form of options writing. Through large trades in relatively illiquid markets, Krieger realized very large profits for Bankers Trust; about half of the $513 million in foreign exchange profits they made in 1987 was attributed to Krieger alone.

For Bankers Trust this was a bittersweet experience; the profits were very attractive, but the wrath of major central banks was not. The deficiencies exposed in their risk control systems, on which they prided themselves, were both embarrassing and worrying. In early 1988, Krieger was awarded a $3 million bonus for his efforts in 1987—just 1 percent of the profits he had made for the bank. He resigned from Bankers Trust, but it may well have been a mutual parting of the ways. Krieger would no doubt have come under much closer scrutiny, and probably would not have enjoyed the close attention. On the other hand, Bankers Trust was probably happy to be free of the risk he represented, especially as to date they had not been too badly hurt. They probably decided to get out of the Krieger approach while they were ahead.

As Bankers Trust realized in the Krieger case, compensating traders for inference profits before all the results of the investments or trades are fully recognized is a serious problem. In most firms, traders and corporate finance officers are paid a salary and a bonus largely dependent upon their effectiveness in that year—but the risks of their actions for their employers may lie many years in the future. In the late 1980s, this discrepancy became nearly fatal for one major firm.

During the 1980s, the First Boston Corporation grew to be one of the major competitors on Wall Street. It was one of the five "bulge bracket" firms that dominated the underwriting markets. It became one of the leading M&A houses and a major force in the debt and equity trading markets, particularly dominating asset-backed securities. As all these markets boomed during the 1980s, First Boston produced enormous wealth— much of which, however, was paid out in bonuses to employees. As a rising tide lifts all ships, all First Boston employees enjoyed rapidly rising and in some cases lavish compensation; at the same time, the firm more than doubled its staff from 1980 to 1987. The great driver of this cash flow became the M&A effort led by Bruce Wasserstein and Joe Perella. They led a department of well over 100 professionals that consistently was at the heart of the major mergers of the go-go years in M&A. They produced fabulous wealth for the key officers of the firm and for the firm as a whole.

First Boston was, however, very dependent on the inference strategy, and by the end of 1987 was starting to pay the price for investing where it had few real advantages. Its major trading activities, which balanced the income earned by the M&A team, started to run into problems when the U.S. bond markets turned down in early 1987 after the prolonged bull market of the previous years. First Boston's traders were beginning to come under pressure from the M&A team because they required so much expenditure on systems and used so much capital compared with the M&A team. The downturn in the market reduced their profitability and increased the M&A team's frustration. In reaction, the traders did what so many inference investors and traders do under pressure—they took more risk. The results were disastrous. Trading in complex, highly volatile Treasury bond options with which the traders were not fully familiar produced a loss of over $100 million in early 1987. The traders had hoped to earn attractive returns by taking an interest rate bet in these new instruments, but ended up getting both the bet wrong and misunderstanding how the new instruments would trade and the risks to which they were exposing the firm. For the individual traders, of course, the loss was limited to their compensation that year or perhaps to their jobs; for First Boston, it was the beginning of a long descent toward financial hardship.

During 1987 and 1988, the relative proportion of total profitability provided by the M&A team continued to rise, and the fragility of the trading profits became clearer and clearer. The inference strategy on the trading floors was not working. Exactly at this point, the M&A team exposed the firm to a new inference risk, but under the guise of an insider strategy.

During the 1980s, the M&A markets in the United States had matured to the point where major firms like First Boston had built up large departments and enviable track records. But these large teams had a ferocious appetite for money. The major contributors were used to earning over $1 million a year, and many professionals with less than 10 years of experience were earning at least $500,000. To feed these hungry mouths, the departments needed an endless supply of transactions. At first the M&A market, supported by junk bond financing for a large number of transactions, obliged. But as the market matured and the hungry mouths became more numerous and demanding, the leading players decided that they needed to kick-start the process. They indulged in something that was called *merchant banking* in the United States, but in fact is not to be confused with the British term for an investment bank. This involved the M&A teams of the major investment banks no longer just acting as advisers and agents in deals, but actually investing in and initiating them. The M&A teams argued that this was a more attractive use of the investment bank's capital than the "risky" trading markets. Anyway, it was argued, the approach did not require much capital, as the investment by the firm could be highly leveraged.

At first this was a bonanza, because they could become the investment bank of choice to the firm in which they had invested, and thereby chalk up a string of advisory fees from the company. After the initial transaction that would lead to this investment, there would often follow a wave of further recapitalizations, spinoffs of divisions, and new security offerings that would be led by the "captive" investment bank and for which that bank would be paid large fees. But apparently this was still not enough for the M&A teams. At First Boston, Wasserstein and Perella pioneered an extension of the merchant banking concept.

In addition to the equity investment made in the deals, they introduced the concept of *bridge loans*. These were supposedly short-term extensions of credit by the investment bank to a company in the middle of a merger or recapitalization prior to the issuance of permanent financing. With large spreads, these loans were also attractive to the investment bank in that they effectively further locked the company into using it for all new securities transactions and corporate finance advice until the bridge loans were unwound. The M&A teams now had the ability to prime the pump. They could invest in and provide credit for deals on which they were paid large fees, and these transactions turned into large bonuses. The temptations and risks were obvious. The M&A teams were using their employers' balance sheets to begin transactions for which they were paid large bonuses mostly *in the year the deal closed*—but the bank could be exposed to the risks for a much longer period.

What exactly were the risks in the deals? The M&A teams described them as basically the risks of an insider strategy. Could the teams get close enough to the target companies to size up the management? Could they get inside information on the companies' prospects and thereby be able to make wiser investments than the average investor? Of course, this was part of the risk involved. But in fact, the M&A teams were taking much larger market risks than specific company risks.

By making loans to very indebted companies, they were relying on two factors to work in their favor. First, they were hoping that the long U.S. economic expansion would continue and that interest rates would stay reasonably low. Second, they were expecting the public junk bond market to continue to thrive, allowing them to unwind the exposure to the bridge loans by issuing public junk bonds. First in 1986 and then again at the beginning of 1988, Wasserstein and Perella, while still at First Boston, put these theories to the test by involving First Boston in bridge loans to the Campeau Corporation as it went on its wild acquisition spree in the retailing arena. The two professionals closed transactions and collected the initial fees. However, continuing friction with the rest of First Boston, particularly their reported perception that they were subsidizing the trading operations, caused Wasserstein and Perella to exit in February 1988 to set up their own firm—leaving First Boston with the bridge loan habit and some significant exposures.

By the end of 1989, the two key assumptions upon which the bridge loans were made were no longer valid. At the end of 1989, the junk bond market fell apart as credit concerns and the demise of Drexel Burnham Lambert produced nearly panic price declines on some days and a collapse of liquidity. Soon thereafter, the reasons for the credit concerns became clear. The United States was heading into a recession, and highly leveraged companies would have major problems servicing their debt obligations. Defaults in the junk bond market were expected to rise significantly.

This left the investment banks holding bridge loans for years that they had originally expected to hold for only a few months. The value of these loans plummeted as the companies to which they were made began to suffer from serious economic problems. For First Boston, the situation became acute in the middle of 1990 as all their major businesses suffered from the downturn in the securities and advisory businesses. Poor earnings and bridge loans of dubious value threatened the core of the company. In the autumn, the company was effectively taken over by its longtime Swiss bank ally, Credit Suisse. The poor earnings and losses on the bridge loans filtered through to the Swiss holding company CS Holdings, which in 1991 cut its dividend by a third and announced plans to sell 20 percent of Credit Suisse to the public. As reported in the *Wall Street Journal* when expressing confidence in the new management team in place in 1991, a CS Holdings executive board member said of the 1990 losses: "These guys were not instrumental in these losses. These losses arose because of silly decisions one, two, three years ago. All the people really responsible have left First Boston."

But for poignancy, no failed inference strategy can match those pursued in the U.S. equity market over the weekend before the stock market break in October 1987. The Friday before the major decline on the following Monday saw a decline of over 100 points on the Dow Jones Index, and as a result, the newspapers over the weekend were filled with speculation about what might follow. Given that the market was about to decline nearly 23 percent on Monday, in retrospect some amazing predictions were produced:

"With about four minutes to go [on Friday], we're buying. And we'll continue to do it on Monday. There is absolutely no reason for this. It's gone down tremendously," said a trader at one firm.

"Historically, you get that type of activity prior to a turning point in the market," said an investor at another firm.

These investors were all professional, well-intentioned peo-

ple. Unfortunately, they were pursuing an approach, the inference approach, that is prone to error and is successful only for
those who really have an information or evaluation advantage.
They did not have such an advantage on this occasion, and they
and their clients paid the price.

Across trading and investing markets, the inference approach
based on judgments about the future will always be a core strategy used by banks, securities firms, and insurance companies.
This approach lies at the heart of many asset and liability, trading, and investing activities of these firms. It also underlies the
strategies of many investment funds. Yet this popular approach
is in many ways the most difficult one to apply with consistent
results. It is also the hardest for top management to dissect to
see whether it is based on real information and evaluation
advantages or on quicksand. This constant checking of inference approaches is crucial. Those who truly possess such
advantages in particular markets will prosper and grow, while
those who apply the inference approach without any advantages may well face serious problems or even bankruptcy.

8

Prize Size: The Scale Strategy

Sheer scale. Some competitors are so large or strong that they possess an advantage even if they are no more skilled than everyone else in the market. This is the basis of the *scale strategy*, the fifth core strategy used by financial institutions. Nomura Securities in Eurobonds, Goldman Sachs in commercial paper, CIGNA in corporate insurance, and State Street in mutual fund processing all use or have used the scale strategy. Obviously, if the competitor is large but fundamentally unskilled, it will fritter away its strength; to prosper, it must have the ability to take advantage of the staying power that size allows. But if such a competitor can combine great strength with an ability to learn new skills, then the scale strategy is a formidable approach.

The scale strategy involves leveraging a company's scope of activities, breadth of business, and capital base to enter a market or to grow and sustain share in a market where the firm is already a player. Initially, the scale strategy can lead to depressed returns until the firm's competitors are forced to exit or at least confine their efforts to a narrow section of the target market. Scale strategies can be used in retail and wholesale markets, in banking, securities, and insurance markets. Indeed, the scale strategy has its natural home in the universal, multiline financial institutions like Deutsche Bank in Germany that developed in Europe after World War II and may be seen in the United States in the 1990s and beyond. These firms fit the scale strategy definition to perfection. They combine different lines of business under one roof, hoping to achieve efficiency in areas such as staff overhead and centralized technology support. At the same time, they have large enough earnings to make long-term investments and stable enough earnings because of their product diversification to weather storms in one market or another. These universal firms, supported by very large capital bases, believe they can defeat most competitors and come to dominate market after market.

The scale strategies, then, are based fundamentally on the third risk/reward skill, resilience, which is applied as a key competitive weapon. Obviously, this strength can be undermined. It can be wasted on unwinnable wars against other scale players in similar markets. Or it can be squandered through lax use—for instance, from poor underwriting in markets where the firm has no valuation or flexibility advantages. Successful scale strategies imply some skills in chosen markets that can be *augmented* by the addition of scale to the point where the competitor is unstoppable.

Discipline is probably the watchword when considering the scale approach. When reviewing strategies being proposed or pursued by financial firms, it always seems sensible to lay aside all arguments about scale advantages until the end of the review. Scale is such an easy excuse for weak or misguided business ventures that it should be seen as the icing on the cake rather than the cake itself. If a bank, securities firm, or insurance company cannot explain why it can at least expect to compete at parity with many of the leading firms in a chosen market without resorting to arguments about scale advantages, then the proposed strategy should be viewed with some skepticism. Long-term profitability will always be underpinned by the ability to select attractive risk/reward opportunities, and in particular to reject, or richly price, the higher-risk situations. The firm should be able to describe how it will make these superior risk/reward selections through the use of core valuation, flexibility, and resilience skills combined into a segmentation, insider, technical, or inference approach. Only when this articulation is clear and accepted should the issue of scale enter the argument as the final reason to justify the strategy. Discipline in pursuing this logic identifies those who successfully execute the scale approach. Wishful thinking, often combined with grand schemes for corporate growth, are the telltale signs of misguided scale arguments.

With this important proviso, the core requirements of the scale approach can be examined in more detail. At the center of the approach is an ability to use financial or physical scale to do what cannot be done by smaller players. The strategy essentially comes in three forms: scale within a market, scale across markets, and financial scale. Thus successful scale competitors *within* a market have significant market share or outlets to support intense activity. As a result, they have such high levels of service and customer contact that smaller firms with less market presence have, at best, to retreat to a niche approach. Alternatively, the scale competitor may not have scale in a particular market but may in total be a larger firm than others in the market. In this case, the scale approach is to use the earnings from other businesses or to leverage the centralized costs associated with the other businesses to *cross-subsidize* the new business until inherent scale and skills in that market become self-supporting. Finally, scale strategies can simply involve being more *financially resilient* than the competition in order to live to fight another day if a market experiences periodic or cyclical losses and several firms are driven out. The financially strong players will be left to pick up the market share of the losing firms and prosper as a result thereafter.

The three forms of the scale approach can be used in interesting combinations to produce a self-supporting cycle of improvement and growth. From a secure capital base, a strong player in one market can use the earnings and shared cost base in that market to *subsidize* entry and initial growth in another market. Then, however, as performance in the new market improves and significant share is achieved, a *within-market* scale approach can be applied to squeeze out some weaker competitors and improve the business's cash flow. The firm now has two pillars of strength. While continuing to defend them and upgrade performance in the two markets, it can seek to apply the scale cross-subsidy approach to a third market. All this time, the financial strength of the firm positions it to take advantage of periodic or cyclical losses in one of its chosen markets and to further consolidate its operating performance. One scale advantage, therefore, can be used to lead to another, so that competitors of less stature are never safe.

This logic, as argued earlier, is very dangerous for most firms. Putting such an approach into practice requires enormous discipline and an ability to manage many different situations simultaneously. Few firms can succeed at this task, and mediocre returns have resulted for many who have tried it. Broad mediocrity, undifferentiated competitive positions in market after market, and slipshod application of risk/reward management skills all too often characterize scale players trying to compete in multiple markets. This perception of larger firms deprives them of the best talent in each market, which further reinforces the downward spiral to mediocrity. Finally, the financial markets become both depressed by the lackluster earnings of the firm and confused by the real risks this multidimensional firm is exposed to, so its access to capital becomes either constrained or expensive. So, one by one, the supposed scale advantages—within markets, across markets, and financially—slip away from the "scale" competitors. This tendency to mediocrity and decreasing performance is the antithesis of all the theoretical scale advantages enjoyed by large firms. To be successful, scale players require the discipline to apply the scale argument only where they already have a reason to be competitive without it, and then to check constantly to ensure that scale is not being abused to achieve growth at enormous cost.

The scale strategy requires a firm to be able to survive periodic or cyclical losses in order to sustain or build market share and profitability. Probably no financial industry puts that concept to the test more fully than the property and casualty insurance market. In that market, giant insurers like CIGNA, Aetna, Tokio Marine and Fire, Allianz, and the Lloyds underwriters agree to underwrite a property or casualty loss on the basis that, over time, the premiums and investment income on those premiums will outweigh claims that have to be paid. Some parts of this insurance market, like small individual and corporate claims, involve some of the core strategies we have already reviewed, most notably the segmentation strategy. But the high end of the market is different. Insuring oil rigs in the North Sea, protecting companies from lawsuits resulting from defective products, or writing earthquake insurance is an insider market. The underwriter must make individual judgments about each case.

But the firm also must be large enough to play. In this market, there is a true transfer of risk. This year's premiums in no way cover possible losses during the year. An insurance company can choose to underwrite property on the South Carolina coast on the basis that it is well protected against fire, is well constructed, and is well protected against burglary or other man-made risks. It can accept a premium just 1 percent of the value of rebuilding the property should some disaster occur. Then, as in 1989, a major hurricane can hit and wipe out that premium 100 times over.

In such a market, those without sufficient financial scale will be forced to exit, either forcibly through excess losses or because they fear the consequences of staying in the market. Those that have the necessary financial strength will win out over time. In the insurance market, however, that strength is not derived only from the resources of the insurance companies dealing with the claim. These companies try to mitigate their exposure to such events as major hurricanes in two ways. First, they seek to reduce risk through diversification, and work hard at modeling their exposure to natural events to try to make sure that trouble in one location, or from one type of pollution, or in one kind of company, will not cause too severe a problem. (As an aside, it is interesting to note that this natural limiting of exposures both constrains and increases competition. No one company tries to dominate a single market for fear of overextending its exposure to that type of risk, but this very restraint encourages others to enter a market and compete in the hope of earning attractive returns from the business the leading players cannot accept.) Second, looking beyond their own strength, the insurers then turn to the reinsurance markets of the world as a means of increasing their capacity to compete for business without incurring unacceptable risks. Reinsurance basically involves the transfer of business, or certain types of risk across a book of business, in return for ceding to the reinsurance company a percentage of the premium on the business. Through the process of swapping and reinsuring their exposures, the primary carriers, and the reinsurers themselves, are able to increase their capacity to weather periodic or cyclical losses and retain a competitive position. Weakly capitalized firms, or firms that regularly accept business that no reinsurer will accept, are at a severe competitive disadvantage in these markets. Yet no matter how good their underwriting skills, however well they think they know the weather patterns off the South Carolina coast, insurers face the risk that a once-in-a-century event could occur at the very beginning of the underwriting period, before they have earned much premium or interest on those monies. Without a sufficient capital base to cushion the shock, they are unable to compete. Scale is one important differentiating factor in this particular market.

This insurance situation is particularly bad in the U.S. property and casualty markets. Reinsurance capacity flows into and out of the market so easily that very cyclical boom/bust pricing has emerged as the norm. In such a market, financial scale relative to the risks being taken is a prerequisite for success, since exposure to rapidly deteriorating risk/reward conditions is a natural part of the market's structure. Unless insurers in this market can be sure their underwriters will always catch the turn in the market, and will be able to withdraw as prices collapse without alienating clients, they have to accept boom and bust returns. A few notable exceptions, such as the American International Group, may escape the cycle to some degree, but even their returns are cyclical, merely with fewer severe down-turns than those experienced by their competitors. In the United States, then, insurers in the corporate property and casualty markets have to have financial scale to play at all.

Scale is an obvious necessity in a business subject to severe periodic and cyclical losses, like corporate property and casu-alty insurance. It can also become a necessity in otherwise stable markets in which competitive quirks have produced murder-ously low returns for most players. The major capital markets of the world produce some superb examples of this problem and the scale strategy in inexorable action.

In capital market after capital market, returns available to many competitors have shrunk to the point where the question is not whether they will lose money, but only how much they will lose. Be it Gilt trading in London, Treasury trading in New York, or government bond trading in Tokyo, most competitors are losing money or earning unattractive returns on capital. Equity trading in London and New York is unattractive for most players, especially in London after the effects of Big Bang. Municipal bond trading in New York became so unattractive that even Salomon Brothers decided it was not worthwhile to compete as a wholesale house. Commercial paper and Euro-commercial paper trading have produced unattractive returns for most firms for years. As we saw in reviewing the technical and inference strategies, a number of firms have found ways to leverage particular information, evaluation, and flexibility advantages to wring some money out of even the most mature markets, but in total, these markets are becoming less, not more, attractive for the combatants. Yet still they soldier on.

Around the world great firms, to name but the most obvious, such as Credit Suisse, Swiss Bank Corporation and Union Bank of Switzerland (UBS) from Switzerland; Deutsche Bank, Commerzbank, and Dresdner Bank from Germany; Barclays, National Westminster, and Warburgs from the United Kingdom; Credit Lyonnais, Paribas, and Indosuez from France; Hong Kong and Shanghai Bank from Hong Kong; Nomura, Daiwa, Nikko, Yamaichi, Sumitomo Bank, and others from Japan; and

Goldman Sachs, Merrill Lynch, Salomon Brothers, Morgan Stanley, Lehman Brothers, J. P. Morgan, Bankers Trust, and Citibank from the United States crash against each other to produce unattractive returns in many of these markets. In some cases these firms may compete indirectly, as does UBS through Phillips and Drew, Hong Kong and Shanghai through James Capel and Wardleys, and Credit Suisse through First Boston and Credit Suisse First Boston. Most have a vision of being one of the five or ten global wholesale trading firms in the world. They believe they can win in this war of attrition and emerge holding enough market share in enough markets to see trading spreads widen and their sources of information for proprietary inference or technical strategies improve. They commit extraordinary resources to this quest. Millions upon millions of dollars of capital are made available, and a good deal of it has been lost. New information systems are created to support the expensive traders and salesmen as they ply their often unprofitable trade.

How can these markets continue to function this way? What is in fact in motion is a grotesque but logical functioning of the cross-market scale strategy repeated over and over again. Each of these major firms is relying on dominant positions in other markets to cross-subsidize its losses in the global trading markets. As long as they are secure in the highly profitable markets that provide the cross-subsidy, and as long as they retain their long-term global ambitions, they can be expected to continue to compete and invest in the global capital markets. If one steps inside a major financial institution and examines its performance in more detail than is possible for the outside observer or investor to do, it often becomes clear that the fantastic profits advertised to the world are earned from a few core franchises and customer relationships. A good deal of the firm's activity is marginally profitable at best. The core, often old and well-established franchises subsidize new ventures and failed efforts. Such is the strength of these old franchises, however, that these major firms can afford to keep the less attractive efforts going as long as they feel fit.

This is exactly what is happening in the global capital markets. Most of the major players are able to cross-subsidize their efforts from elsewhere, and so, despite amazing losses, capacity retreats from these markets very slowly. The Swiss banks are able to call upon cartelized profits in their home banking market and their worldwide private banking franchise as a source of strength. The Germans can also look to a relatively protected home market, combined with their relative dominance of it, as a source of strength. The British divide the retail banking market among just five major players, and have established enviable local market density from which to reap attractive returns if costs are controlled. The French banks have a similar lock on their domestic retail market, and have been able to parlay the loyalty earned from consumers into successful forays into selling mutual funds and life insurance. Hong Kong and Shanghai Bank controls much of the retail market on the island and lives in a world where retail deposit rates are still controlled; as a result, profits to cross-subsidize global ventures follow. The Japanese brokers compete domestically in a brokerage market where commissions, although lower than they were in the early 1980s, are still regulated. Throughout the 1980s, Japanese banks were able to take profits earned on the rising value of their shareholdings and lending against rising property values and use these to cross-subsidize other efforts. Finally, the American players have relied on a series of very profitable opportunities to cross-subsidize the trading efforts. The major investment banks enjoyed the merger boom during the 1980s. The retail commercial banks thrived on the profits earned from efficient branch networks and credit cards. The wholesale banks had the fees and lending spreads that accrued from the LBO boom of the 1980s coupled with their foreign exchange trading profits.

In this light, the carnage of the competition in the global capital markets is hardly dependent upon the dynamics within those markets at all. Rather, the battles will become more rational only when the cross-subsidies are unwound. In a way, therefore, the best competitive step for many of these firms is to attack the domestic or old franchises of their competitors as rapidly as they can. Unwinding the Swiss banking cartel would

soon reduce Credit Suisse's appetite for bailing out First Boston.
UBS would soon find Phillips and Drew's U.K. equity losses
unacceptable. Encouraging further Japanese brokerage rate cuts
would soon reduce Nomura's ability to absorb trading losses.
Slowing the mergers boom would (and has) reduced the
appetite of U.S. investment banks to compete in commodity
trading markets.

This attack on the old franchises has started to work—for different reasons—as all three of the major U.S. West Coast banks
have withdrawn from the global trading markets. Bank of
America withdrew when its core domestic banking effort was
undermined in the mid-1980s by loan losses and excess costs.
Wells Fargo withdrew at a similar time when it decided to
invest domestically to take advantage of Bank of America's
moment of weakness. Security Pacific closed its Merchant Bank
in 1990 when loan losses at home started to increase and it
could no longer afford the anchor of low earnings in the wholesale trading markets. Similarly, Morgan Grenfell in the United
Kingdom withdrew from trading in the U.K. equity and Gilts
markets when the cash flows expected from its M&A practice
were put in jeopardy by the Guinness scandal. The appetite of
the major investment banks for commodity markets was weakened when pressure from the M&A teams for more compensation put the meager returns in trading in stark focus. The actual
slowdown in mergers in 1989 and 1990 meant that the wholesale trading losses could no longer be afforded. Back in 1987,
before the October stock market break, Salomon Brothers had
signaled the beginning of this trend when it withdrew from
both the commercial paper and municipal bond markets. So the
problems in the global trading markets are underpinned by a
group of cross-subsidy scale strategies. These markets are also
plagued by scale strategies from within. These strategies further
slow the exit of excess capacity and provide individual players
with moments of success that suggest to them that they can see
the light at the end of the tunnel. In fact, the central dynamics
have not changed, and the good year they had is not sustainable.

An example of a relatively scale strategy is the way in which Nomura built its position in the Eurobond underwriting market in the late 1980s. Although its image was tarnished by scandal in 1991, at the end of the 1980s Nomura was riding high. Nomura followed the pattern we saw earlier of first using cross-market scale to afford entry into a market, and then using within-market scale to drive marginal players away. As we have seen, in the 1980s the Japanese brokers enjoyed the unique luxury among major market intermediaries of still living in a world of regulated (but declining) brokerage rates. Given the boom prices and volumes of the period, this was a wonderful position to be in. Nomura rose on a wave of commissions to become the most profitable company in Japan in 1987, ahead of such giants as Toyota and Nippon Telephone and Telegraph. From this base, Nomura was able to plan its global expansion. It also had another advantage: the unwritten Japanese guideline that only Japanese brokers should lead securities issues for Japanese companies, particularly in issues denominated in Japanese yen.

In July 1986, as reported in Institutional Investor the then president of Nomura, Yoshihisa Tabuchi, said of his firm's global ambitions: "Today Nomura makes no distinction between domestic and overseas operations. Nomura is moving rapidly to establish itself as a major force in twenty-four-hour global-linked trading."

If there was an element of hyperbole here, it was certainly true that the firm had managed to establish a significant position in some overseas markets, in particular the London-based Eurobond market. The key to their efforts up to that point had been typical cross-market scale strategies: taking domestic market profits and pouring them into hiring talent overseas to build share in foreign markets. The philosophy was referred to as *dochaku-ka*, which can be translated as "getting to know a place." The key element of this strategy was to hire locals for Nomura's offices overseas to win domestic business. The free-wheeling Eurobond market offered the most encouraging opportunities, and by the mid-1980s Nomura had established a strong position there. By buying talent, and in some cases by very aggressive pricing, Nomura established itself as the number six underwriter in 1984 and again in 1985. From being a tiny player in this market just 5 years earlier, this was impressive progress and testimony to the advantages of a cross-market scale effort. A group executive at Citibank's investment bank, said of Nomura, it can "make lots of mistakes and wouldn't even feel it."

But to go further, Nomura would have to do more, and it was here that scale within the market began to be used.

Nomura, like all the major Japanese securities houses, had one special advantage in the Eurobond market. It had the closest relationships with the key investors of the time, the Japanese institutions. As Japan's trade surplus and savings rate soured throughout the 1980s, its capital outflow into foreign assets had to increase. Nomura and the other securities firms were ready to be the conduits for those flows. Nomura happened to be the scale player and started to use this position to its advantage. It combined this with a relatively low-cost structure, particularly in Japan, where investment bankers were not paid Western-style compensation. Finally, Nomura added a further twist: equity-linked securities. As the Japanese stock market continued to climb during 1986 and 1987, convertible- or equity warrant-linked bonds became attractive ways to borrow money. The equity feature was deemed so valuable that debt could be raised at very low rates.

Putting together all these internal market scale advantages, and combining them with valuation and flexibility skills at rough parity with those of others, Nomura rose in 1987 to become the number one Eurobond underwriter, eclipsing the long-time market leader, Credit Suisse First Boston, which was forced to seek newer pastures in Euroequities. Nomura made this final climb to the top by combining its internal market strengths: strong placement scale, multiple links with Japanese corporate borrowers, and equity placement strength in Japan that enabled Nomura to scoop up a large portion of the equity-linked Eurobonds. Although the established European competitors might cry foul at some of Nomura's pricing strategies, at the end of the day its multiple internal scale advantages in the Eurobond market spoke for themselves. It had developed a real competitive advantage. Whether the vast volumes it underwrote were as profitable for the firm as the publicity suggested is unclear, but the strategy certainly fulfilled Nomura's goals of diversifying its franchises beyond Japan.

The other three major Japanese securities firms (Daiwa, Nikko, and Yamaichi Securities) did not have as spectacular a time as Nomura, although all did well in the Eurobond market for similar reasons. The successes here were in contrast to all four firms' problems in the booming M&A market. Public, friendly, or hostile, mergers were not common practice in Japan. During this period, Japanese investment bankers did not have the trial-by-fire opportunities that their U.S. counterparts experienced to hone their skills. With no natural advantages similar to their positions in the underwriting markets, the securities firms were forced to turn back to the cross-subsidy scale approach as the basis for their M&A strategy. Specifically, they took to investing in U.S. M&A boutiques, providing capital and possibly contacts, while the Americans provided the technology and most of the personnel. In 1986 Nikko linked up with the Blackstone Group, headed by Pete Peterson, who was the head of Lehman Brothers for a while before it merged with Shearson. As Nikko chairman Toshio Mori said at the time: "M&A and LBOs are somewhat new to us, and we will be able to obtain know-how and expertise, especially when we coordinate specific projects which involve the Japanese and Americans."

Also in 1986, Nomura entered the complicated world of real estate finance by buying 50 percent of the well-regarded real estate boutique firm Eastdil Realty. In 1988, Nomura then bought 20 percent of the newly founded Wasserstein Perella. Almost simultaneously, Yamaichi purchased 25 percent of Lodestar Group, another new merger boutique. At the time, much was made of the advantages that would accrue from the links. Cross-border contacts could be advantageous, and these merger firms wanted capital for building and for investing in the prevalent merchant banking craze. But underneath all this activity was a simple truth: the Japanese firms were using the scale strategy of cross-subsidy to take their domestic profits and put them to work elsewhere. They had few skills in mergers, so they decided to buy their way in. This was a perfectly respectable approach as long as the new venture developed real valuation and flexibility advantages it could use to capitalize upon the infusion of yen. Otherwise, this scale venture would lead the Japanese firms nowhere—as for some it did in the international lending markets.

The 1980s, as we saw earlier, were a period when the Japanese commercial banks expanded their international activities considerably, and in doing so employed the scale strategy. Backed by booming real estate and share prices in Japan, these banks were able to build up large, visible (and invisible) capital bases and to generate attractive earnings streams. They used this domestic asset profitability, and the profits from a good period of regulated deposit rates as well, to push aggressively into corporate lending in the United States and Europe. Partly as a result of their entry, interest rate spreads on corporate loans declined to very low levels in all major deregulated markets. Major domestic competitors quickly realized that they could not earn adequate returns on such loans and tried to deemphasize this activity in favor of fee-generating services. Alternatively, and less happily, they moved into higher-risk activities where the spreads were higher, but were still not high enough given the risks. The Japanese banks, however, kept pushing ahead, and by the end of the decade accounted for 16 percent of corporate loans in the United States. They were able to support this low-spread activity through cross-subsidies from domestic profits, and on the basis that this was a long-term investment that would eventually pay off.

Then the situation started to unravel. The Bank for International Settlements imposed higher capital guidelines on all major banks. Soon the domestic Japanese share and property markets started to decline, reducing the capital bases of the Japanese banks. They were in a squeeze, since they would have to slow their growth in assets so as not to outstrip these new constrained equity bases. At the same time, domestic profitability came under pressure as domestic deposit rates began to rise because of deregulation and tightening monetary policies. In this environment, the Japanese banks put their international assets under new scrutiny because of their low spreads and because of rising loan losses in high-spread categories like the highly leveraged transaction market. The problem was simple: these banks had not always advanced beyond the initial step in the scale strategy, the cross-subsidy stage. They had not built up real valuation and flexibility advantages. Few insider relationships had been developed, and as a result, the Japanese banks were still secondary or tertiary players in most situations. Many of their loans were the result of participations in transactions put together by the domestic banks, not of close relationships they had developed with the final borrowers. For these players, the scale strategy was not as rewarding as it should have been because of an inability to build real long-term risk/reward advantages from it.

These tales of woe should not hide the fact that the within-market scale strategies can lead to success. The success of Goldman Sachs and Merrill Lynch in the very competitive U.S. commercial paper market is testimony to the effectiveness of such an approach if carried to its logical limit.

The commercial paper market is where major corporate and financial borrowers issue promissory notes to investors to receive short-term funds. The market basically replaces short-term bank loans. Many issuers, like Exxon and J. C. Penney, are large and sophisticated enough to have their own issuing departments, which garner bids for the paper from investors of all kinds. Others, however, seek the services of an intermediary dealer to run the issuing of the paper for them. This dealer role quickly became very competitive as the market grew, so spreads for intermediaries shrank to practically nothing. In that environment, volume was essential. If revenues were only one-eighth of 1 percent of the principal balance, enormous volumes were required to cover the cost base and earn an attractive return. Goldman Sachs and Merrill Lynch used their corporate contacts, and, in the case of Merrill, the ability and willingness to buy up the operations of failing competitors, to build up scale positions that could be used to force out competitor after competitor. They were, of course, helped by the fact that the natural competitors in the market, the commercial banks, were for many years prohibited by the Glass-Steagall Act from competing. By the time these banks entered the market, it was already locked up. Even the great J. P. Morgan realized it could not enter and garner enough share to make the market in any way attractive. For Goldman and Merrill the market had acceptable economics, particularly in the context of the constant calls and contacts with the issuing companies it provided. But each company had over 25 percent of this market; by definition, few could follow or match that share.

Some markets naturally tend to scale strategies: the processing markets like mutual fund processing, custody services, and money transfer. These money and securities processing businesses involve the competitors, usually banks, earning tiny fees for processing each transaction. The winners are those that can build market share to earn enough revenue to cover the high fixed costs of the computers and clerical staff required for the business. Once the leading competitors have established their operations, they compete aggressively and reduce prices so that the inefficient, smaller players are driven out. Of course, to make good money from these businesses requires careful segmentation of the attractive customers from the unattractive, and the flexibility to introduce new products as customers' needs evolve. But without the basic scale to survive (and, indeed, to apply) the pressure of very tight pricing, a competitor cannot hope to win. So it is that BFDS and Citadel hold large shares in mutual fund trust work; State Street, Bankers Trust, Northern Trust, Boston Safe, and Chase dominate in U.S. domestic custody services; and Chase, Brown Brothers Harriman, Midland Bank, Citibank, and Barclays hold large shares in global custody services. In these businesses, scale is a prerequisite for success.

If scale can give certain financial institutions opportunities to cross-subsidize new ventures or to build withering economics within a market, lack of scale can be disastrous. Nowhere has this been more dramatically illustrated than in the relative decline of some New York money center banks.

When the United States embarked upon deregulation of financial services, including allowing interstate branching and acquisitions, the small regional and state banks were so concerned about the New York banks that they managed to convince the local legislators to enact regional interstate compacts. These allowed, for instance, banks in the Southeast to merge and branch across state lines but excluded outside banks, particularly New York banks, from entering the region. This activity took place at the beginning of the 1980s. By the end of the decade these same feared banks were in desperate shape, slicing their work forces, cutting dividends, and shrinking assets. Simply, these banks had suffered losses from ambitions that their scale, both operating and financial, could not support, and they were brought down by the consequences.

Specifically, during the 1980s, these New York money center banks were buffeted by competitive pressures and denied the advantages of scale. They were denied entry into investment banking by the Glass-Steagall Act and saw their core corporate customers turn more and more to the securities markets in place of commercial loans. They were denied the ability to expand fully into retail and small-business banking by the regional compacts. Yet they saw increasing entry into their old core corporate business by the foreign banks, most notably the Japanese. To survive and earn adequate returns on the capital bases built in the 1970s, they had to grow somewhere else, and they grew by taking on more risk—first in Latin America, then in the property market, and then in loans to highly leveraged companies. The problem with this higher-risk approach is that these banks, denied operating scale outside New York State and with finite capital resources, were unable to absorb mistakes, and yet, as history has shown, some made many. A downward spiral followed. They then lost the ability to recover as the best talent fled to the higher performers. By the end of the 1980s, the talk was not of who these banks would buy, but who might buy them or whether they would need to be merged together to create the scale they now lacked. In 1991, Chemical Bank and Manufacturers Hanover Trust announced they would merge.

Contrast the situation of these money center banks with the position of the beneficiaries of these regional compacts. They were able to generate natural scale within markets and thereby build the earnings needed for most of them to survive the losses of the property bust at the end of the 1980s. Leaving aside the laxity found in some Texas and New England institutions that would undo any firm, most of these regional banks survived the downturn because they had the innate earnings to fund the losses. North Carolina National Bank, Banc One, and First Wachovia are examples of institutions that, through merger or expansion, built up real operating scale that enabled them to develop the strength to survive downturns and take share from the weaker competitors. So supporting the segmentation, insider, technical, and inference strategies found in many of their individual businesses was an overall scale advantage that helped all these businesses. This was the opposite of the situation of some money center banks in New York. Their lack of financial and operating scale undermined each and every business. Investment was starved, costs were constantly cut, the best talent was scared away.

The experiences of these New York money center banks, of course, have parallels with the disasters of the Texas banks and the failure of Continental Illinois in 1984. The banks grew capital bases because of successful strategies in lending either to the growing energy and real estate markets in Texas or to the corporate market in the Midwest in the case of Continental. However, regulations restricting even intrastate branching in Texas and Illinois meant that these banks were never able to build up the operating scale as a foundation for their growing business. All had to rely upon fickle wholesale deposits to fund their growth, instead of the more stable retail deposits that the regional banks developed. Meanwhile the investors in these banks demanded an adequate return on the capital tied up in the banks, a base that grew with every profitable quarter. Unfortunately, these banks responded by taking more risks. Although it is unfair to argue that lack of ability to diversify and build operating scale alone led to their demise (later reviews of internal documentation and credit controls showed that other factors were at play), it is certainly true that the inability to build a stable, scale funding source contributed to the rapid demise of these firms. Forced to look outside their natural franchise for earnings and denied the stability that such a franchise could have offered, they lacked the scale to survive the shocks that hit them.

Other scale winners show how the losing New York money center banks were unable to use the scale approach to their advantage. The most telling story perhaps is that of Bank of America. At the beginning of the 1980s, Bank of America dueled with Citibank to be the largest U.S. bank in terms of assets. It was a respected international commercial bank with a farflung global branch system and a dominant position in the California retail market. Thus it could claim to be a powerhouse in both corporate and retail banking. As interstate banking barriers were unwound early in the 1980s, its threat was as much the reason for the regional compacts as was the threat of the New York money center banks. However, the bank did not perform up to its true potential, mainly because years of regulated interest rates on deposits had made the enormous branch system in California unproductive and high in cost. Deregulation of domestic interest rates applied some pressure to the bank, but then a series of loan losses, driven largely by the problems in the agricultural markets and the bank's LDC exposures, left the failure to invest in improving its core earnings very clear. The bank had to retrench to meet capital guidelines and reduce exposures to lower spread assets. The bank was vulnerable to takeover, and the chairman had to resign. The renewed focus of a new management team on the dominant retail business in California soon produced results. The bank's earnings improved because it had the operating scale required to overcome a severe set of losses. Its enormous base of retail deposits in California and Washington State proved loyal and protected the bank from the runs on deposits that finished off Continental Illinois and some of the Texas banks. By the end of the decade, Bank of America was expanding again, seeking opportunities to build its retail business by purchasing failing thrift institutions. The New York money center banks lacked this operating scale in their home markets to pull them out of trouble. Bank of America's case proved the value of scale franchises in overcoming failures in other high-risk markets.

Sumitomo Bank in Japan also used its scale to overcome problems. Sumitomo became known in the 1980s as one of the most aggressive of the Japanese major or city banks. It expanded its lending very aggressively in the home market. Sumitomo was simultaneously trying to expand its activities overseas and into the emerging investment banking markets. It purchased a stake in Goldman Sachs, although Federal Reserve rulings at the time limited the use it could make of this link.

Sumitomo also decided to expand its Tokyo retail deposit gathering and loan making capabilities. Sumitomo is based in Osaka, and in the early 1980s had a relatively weak position in the Tokyo retail market. To build the bank's position it made an opportunistic purchase of a weakening Tokyo mutual savings bank, Heiwa Sogo Bank. This savings institution had been struggling with serious loan problems since 1985, and by January 1986 it was clear that nearly 20 percent of its loan portfolio was irrecoverable. However, Heiwa Sogo did have over 100 well placed Tokyo branches and the acquisition would shoot Sumitomo into being the third placed retail bank both in Tokyo and also overall in Japan.

The Sumitomo purchase looked like a startling and courageous move. The loan portfolio of Heiwa Sogo was always known to be poor. After the transaction Sumitomo got a look at just how bad it was. Awful. In November 1986, just one month after the acquisition formerly closed, Sumitomo had to write-off 210 billion Yen ($1.3 billion) of loans. Had Sumitomo made a serious strategic blunder that would weigh down the firm for a long time, if not actually cripple it? The bank had committed significant capital to an asset that was of low and deteriorating value. But people had forgotten the bank's scale. Although the Heiwa Sogo experience was indeed painful for Sumitomo, and may have been the start of the process of retrenchment of its ambitions, it did not cripple the institution. The bank absorbed the losses and moved on. Sumitomo had the banking franchise, the corporate contacts, the earnings stream, and the capital base to survive Heiwa Sogo, and indeed eventually gain the operating improvements in its domestic markets that it had first sought. A year after the transaction closed, Sumitomo was able to show significant productivity improvements in the old Heiwa Sogo branches by applying more aggressive and disciplined techniques to raise deposits and consumer loan levels. Contrast Sumitomo's position to that of the New York money center banks who could not find a way out of the box that regulators placed them in. Sumitomo was able to earn its way out of trouble.

During the boom years of the 1980s, it became fashionable to argue that investment banks and other trading firms would need more and more capital to support higher and higher levels of trading. Many of the major investment banks sought out new sources of capital either by going public (for example, Salomon Brothers and Morgan Stanley in the United States, Warburgs and Morgan Grenfell in the United Kingdom) or by seeking infusions of capital from outside investors (for example, Salomon Brothers again, Goldman Sachs, Shearson Lehman, and PaineWebber). These higher levels of capital were used to support myriad activities, including investments in a series of high-risk activities like junk bond trading and offering bridge loans to firms undergoing leveraged recapitalizations or making major debt-financed acquisitions.

Then the troubles set in. Trading volumes and profits collapsed, and theoretical credit risks became *real* credit losses. Meanwhile, other sources of income, like M&A advisory work or plain old stockbroking for individual investors, sank to very low levels. At this point, the need for capital became clear—not to support eternal growth in good times but to weather bad times. Few could do it. First Boston had to be bailed out by Credit Suisse. American Express had to repurchase Shearson

Lehman, having only recently set a course of divesting the firm from the "blue box."

In the middle of this carnage one firm, among a small group, prospered. This was J. P. Morgan, the premier U.S. commercial cum investment bank. Morgan did so well during this period because its financial strength and conservative lending policies protected it from severe losses. As a result, Morgan emerged as the only AAA credit-rated bank in the country and one of the few AAA trading firms. This gave the bank a whole series of funding cost and reputation advantages across market after market. The advantage became clear in the trading markets.

Traders hate credit risk in their trading counterparties; they have enough problems to cope with without worrying about whether the trade they have made will fail because the other party cannot pay! So the slightest whiff of financial problems causes a trading firm to become a pariah. Its ability to do deals is severely constrained, further weakening the firm and often hastening its demise. By 1990, in the midst of the trading market downturn, the losses from bridge loans and junk bonds, and the growing real estate-related losses of the commercial banks, very few players had rock solid credit stories to tell. Except for Morgan. As a result, during this period, the bank picked up significant trading business because it had financial scale. Obviously, Morgan had been developing the trading skills and product expertise to win this business and had been consistently increasing its share. But as we have seen before, scale was the icing, not the cake. Nevertheless, throughout the trading cycles, real financial scale in terms of a strong capital base and conservative asset policies enabled Morgan to leverage the investment it had been making in the trading world.

If scale can provide real competitive advantages, it can also lead to great competitive weakness if misused or used as a prop for fundamentally unsound risk/reward strategies. A case in point is Prudential-Bache's entry into the investment banking markets. Prudential Insurance purchased Bache, the U.S. retail stockbroker, during the period when the concept of the *financial supermarket* was the rage. But the management of the then renamed Prudential-Bache apparently wanted to expand beyond just pursuing plain retail stockbroking in support of Prudential's core retail life insurance business. Seeing the attractive returns enjoyed by the investment bankers, they planned to build the firm into a significant investment banking and trading enterprise, and they had the scale of Prudential to fund them. So they began investing in global trading and stock research and developing an investment banking capability.

Performance during the mid-1980s was mediocre, but Prudential-Bache claimed it was building its position for the long term. The firm's advertising line, "Rock Solid, Market Wise," pointed up its reliance on the scale of its insurance parent. The link to Prudential Insurance was crucial for the wholesale trading and investment banking push; without this link, the effort could not have been funded. It turned out to be more crutch than link. Prudential-Bache apparently, never tested whether it was developing real segmentation, insider, technical, or inference advantages in these businesses. When the markets slowed in 1989 and 1990, these deficiencies were exposed. By the end of 1990 Prudential-Bache had to retrench, and announced a $250 million write-off as it laid off staff (for instance, two-thirds of the investment banking staff in New York) at the end of the year. Prudential-Bache had fallen into the trap of scale; it was used as an excuse for not developing risk/reward advantages.

Scale strategies, across or within markets and from financial strength, can act as powerful competitive weapons for financial institutions. They can also be used as excuses for inaction or wishful thinking. The challenge is to use them with care so that the scale can be used to crush the opposition, not the momentum and will of the company itself.

9

Change Is Good for You

In the late 1970s, I began my career in the financial world in the City of London. Eager to show that the few skills I had revealed at Cambridge could somehow be turned into magical properties in the worlds of commerce and high finance, I arrived at the merchant bank that had hired me as a new recruit with a sense of excitement but also of concern. I need not have worried; Cambridge had prepared me perfectly for the task at hand. In retrospect, the City at that time competed in the true English spirit of the "gifted amateur."

My first assignment at the bank illustrates the point. I was placed in the research department that was responsible for providing stock selection advice to the portfolio managers running large pension fund accounts. On day one, a Monday, I was told: "Dominic, next Monday you are to give a presentation to the Investment Committee on what we should do with our holdings of Bowater stock" (Bowater, a pulp and paper company at the time, was one of the many stocks I was assigned to cover and provide investment advice on). Now while this was a fascinating task for the week, it was also terrifying. At the time, I felt like the heroic figure called to the cockpit of a jetliner from the back of the plane because the entire crew had suffered simultaneous cardiac arrests (brought on by the diet of microwaved food at 30,000 feet). Using his natural wits, he guides the behemoth to a safe, if somewhat bumpy, landing at a city center airport, despite the fact that his familiarity with flying was based on close examination of 747s at Heathrow and Kennedy from the safety of the passenger observation deck. I was a similar hero; I knew *nothing* about income statements, balance sheets, or business competitive dynamics, let alone the pulp and paper industry. Yet I was to stand before the great Investment Committee in a week and guide millions of dollars toward or away from Bowater.

The gifted amateur in my mind, I set to my task with enthusiasm, poring over basic accounting texts in one hand, and previous internal and brokerage firm reports on the luckless Bowater in the other. My life was complicated by the fact that at the time, Britain was experiencing another bout of inflation. Inflation-adjusted, or current-cost, accounting was all the rage, and was deemed to be especially relevant to a capital-intensive industry (whatever that was, I said to myself at the time) such as pulp and paper. So I effectively had *two* sets of books to worry about, the original or historical cost version and the new current-cost numbers. Everyone around me was very keen that I not only understand but also *comment* on the differences in Bowater's performance revealed by these numbers. I, meanwhile, was still grappling with such basics as the difference between an income statement and a balance sheet, and wondering what was this concept called *cash flow* to which the smartest of my new colleagues kept pointing me, and what this all had to do with Bowater.

As I tried to master all this information on Wednesday I found that I had a new problem: relating it to Bowater's stock price. Given all this financial mumbo-jumbo, was the price reasonable, expensive, or a bargain? Buy or sell. Buy or sell. By Friday it was all I could think about.

The weekend was not a happy one. Would my musings on the pulp and paper industry be greeted with derision by my new colleagues? On Monday morning the fateful meeting in the large conference room began, and soon I was to speak. All eyes turned to me, mostly for the first time, as I pronounced my verdict: Bowater was a "Hold."

Of course, whatever I had said would have been disregarded by the audience. The whole affair was not intended to influence their investment decisions at all; it was simply training by fire. In the course of one traumatic week, I had imbibed more about the stock market and company accounts than I could possibly have learned in a formal training program. My employer had learned a lot about each of the new recruits: their ability to learn quickly, their reaction to pressure, their sense of humor, and their ability to present to large groups of apparently hostile executives. Over the course of the next 2 years, I went through crisis after crisis like this one. I am not sure whether I benefitted my bank or its clients significantly, but I learned so much that I became hooked on the business.

What was evident during these 2 years was the way work was then done in the City. This was the era, the end of the era, of the gifted amateur, and of "relationship" banking above all else. In retrospect, little modern management discipline was applied because it was simply not needed. Market shares moved slowly, and fixed commissions and fee rates subsidized a fair amount of loose thinking and allowed the average City lunch to be accompanied by a bottle of good wine. The brokers who tried to influence me through their research excellence would regularly take me out to lunch, 2 hours at a time, at some pleasant City watering hole to build up a personal relationship. They hoped this would also win them business.

Look at the City now, over a decade later. Perrier and tomato juice have replaced chablis; training and MBAs the gifted amateur; vast new trading floors supported by high-technology workstations the trader relying on word of mouth, gossip, and a hunch. Fees and commissions or bid/asked spreads have been reduced to the point where many in my old equity business are losing money. Many of the great brokerage firms that used to sell research to me, and wine and dine me, are gone. The game has changed, and so have the strategies required for success.

The five strategies for financial firms are guides through a world of risk and opportunity. We have already seen that they can be used in combination. For instance, a corporate banker relying on the insider strategy to make good corporate loans can also use the segmentation approach to decide which customers and projects to emphasize, and which to deemphasize because, although they may be good credits, they will take only the lowest loan rates. The five strategies, however, are not only used in combination. In any market, which strategy is appropriate may change over time. Therefore, the financial firms have to monitor their markets to decide which of the five is right for the times.

Markets around the world offer somber lessons on the need to be able to adjust strategies as competitive dynamics, external environments, or regulations change. Relying on just one strategy forever is unlikely to work. Managers must recognize that the ability to change is absolutely essential for success. The past 15 years in the equity markets have demonstrated the need to change as markets do. The upheaval started in the United States on May 1, 1975. Until then, in nearly all markets, the commissions paid to brokerage houses by their customers had been set at predetermined levels. As in all price-fixed markets, this meant that some customers subsidized others. In particular, the big institutional accounts (the pension funds, mutual funds, and insurance companies buying and selling large blocks of stock) were subsidizing the smaller institutions and the individual investors. By the mid-1970s this inequity had become too great, and deregulation of commission rates was introduced.

Immediately, rates for institutional trades began to fall. In 1974 a major institution could trade equities on the New York Stock Exchange at a commission of 26 cents per share. By 1976 that rate had declined to 18 cents. By 1985, it had dropped to about 8 cents. By 1990 commission rates had declined to around 6 to 7 cents per share for a normal trade, and to less than half that amount for index or basket trades, which made up an increasing percentage of the total shares traded. Although trading volumes had increased remarkably during that same period, with the average New York Stock Exchange trading day seeing 165 million shares traded in 1989 against 19 million in 1975, so had trading firms' costs. In sum, the major brokerage firms were facing continued economic pressure in this core business during those 15 years. The strategy that had worked in the 1970s would not work in the late 1980s.

Institutional equity brokerage in the 1970s in the United States was based on the legal insider strategy. With commission rates fixed, the key to success was becoming very close to the customer in order to win his or (very occasionally) her confidence—and trades. While quality research and sales coverage of analysts and portfolio managers was central to such an effort, it also involved a heavy dose of the relationship management I had to "suffer" in London at the time: good lunches, invitations to sporting events, even the cliché of the round of golf. New brokers on the institutional side were encouraged to develop these relationship skills and were assigned minor accounts to test these skills. The plum assignments were left to the more senior salesmen, who had both the experience and the correct gray hair to win business from the senior clients. All this is not to describe an unskilled or lazy world. Far from it. These firms were making money exactly as they needed to, by using the insider strategy, fully understanding where the best returns for the time spent would be.

Deregulation of commission rates on May 1, 1975, the infamous May Day, was to change this world. In time, as institutional commission rates declined, brokers could not afford relatively undisciplined expenses, unfocused sales efforts, and efforts spread too thinly across all clients and prospects, whatever their size. At the end of the 1970s the first wave of pressure uncovered weaknesses in some firms, and they went under or were forced to merge with larger or diversified competitors. However, just as these pressures were about to bite, the 1980s boom in the equity market arrived.

From 1982 to the summer of 1987, the institutional equity commission rates per share continued to decline—but trading volumes increased so much, and proprietary trading profits from simply holding inventories of stocks were so impressive, that the day of reckoning was deferred. In addition, the corporate finance and M&A profits of many of the leading players could be used to cross-subsidize or justify more meager returns from trading with the institutions. These trends did not simply defer the day of reckoning—they made it worse by allowing firms to build up their trading staffs despite deterioration in their fundamental economics. The extraordinary was taking place. Prices were declining, but many competitors were adding new capacity on the basis, presumably, that the market would not go down. It did.

On October 19, 1987, the steady decline that had started earlier in the late summer descended upon all these salesmen, traders, and research analysts. For a while, as investors tried to sort out what to do, trading volumes remained high enough to hide the inevitable crisis. But too many competitors were chasing declining volumes—and still the commission rates went down. It was time for a cold look at this business, especially as the revenues needed to cross-subsidize it were expected to decline as well. Everyone expected M&A volumes, and linked corporate finance underwriting volumes, to decline forthwith. In fact, the survival of the junk bond market for another 2 years and continued interest from offshore purchasers kept those fees flowing into the second half of 1989. But the insider strategy no longer sufficed any longer in the institutional equity market. The question was whether any strategy would work in this harsh environment.

The answer, for a time at least, was a segmentation strategy. Just as the fixed prices prior to deregulation had hidden different layers of customer profitability, free-floating prices now offered those who could segment the market an opportunity to understand the new segments, chase the most profitable ones, and avoid the less so. At about this time, a new breed of competitor started to become more important in the institutional market. This player, like Morgan Stanley for example, approached the market with enormous discipline and was prepared to give up unprofitable segments of customers, to break unsuccessful but formally valued insider relationships, all in the name of *profits* in place of the formally admired *revenues*.

The segmentation strategy is dependent above all upon data, preferably lots of it, to analyze and thereby uncover previously hidden opportunities. Institutional trading firms often had woeful information. They had never felt the need for it, since it was not the basis of the insider strategy. After the crash of 1987, they desperately needed it and had problems finding it. Costs could not easily be tied to each client's revenues, and yet that was essential to determine customer profitability, the basic building block for a segmentation strategy in this market. So the new winners went about trying to create the data. In this twilight period for trading, the leading players in the institutional markets were working to understand exactly how to retrieve revenue and cost data from their systems and allocate them to individual clients and products. From this data, they were able to work out where they did or did not make money, and thereby to devote their resources to clients that would pay them more than others, and avoid clients that did not cover their costs.

In 1989, as a result of this kind of analysis, Morgan Stanley started to make a number of changes in the way it covered institutions in the domestic equity marketplace. Most dramatically, a large number of smaller institutions that *only* produced commissions in the range of $25,000 a year for Morgan were told either to pay more (effectively meaning they would have to pay some other brokerage firm or firms less) or be relegated to Morgan Stanley's private client retail system. Morgan Stanley was changing from an insider strategy to a segmentation strategy—recognizing that different clients offered different opportunities and treating them accordingly. Up until 1987, this kind of segmentation had not been necessary.

Morgan Stanley's public redefinition of its strategy was followed more quietly by many other firms that came to analyze similar data and reach their own segmentation conclusions. Of course, thank goodness, not all of them adopted the same set of actions steps. Some adopted very different segmentation strategies. To some of the brokers, the function of the institution—whether it was a mutual fund company, an insurance company, or a pension fund manager—was the crucial way to differentiate one client from another. The brokers then set up groups to focus on each of these, perhaps with some size segmentation within each industry. For others, this strategy was naive; size was the most important variant. Still others focused on the way in which each client made investment decisions and traded, known in the trading world as the *behavioral characteristics* of the buyers. They then focused on those characteristics as the key drivers of the way sales skills were matched against opportunities, and of what kind of research and how much was focused on each client.

Meanwhile, commission rates continued to fall and trading volumes remained flat. Even more ominously, there were signs that some of the biggest investors were avoiding the brokerage houses altogether. For some time during the 1980s, a number of electronic trading systems or clearing houses had been trying to win market share from the established brokerage houses. The idea was very simple: if more and more of the total trading volume was in the hands of a few big investors, why not link them together directly on some sort of electronic exchange, or at least through some kind of electronic utility owned by a third party, and avoid all the commissions paid to brokers? Thus Instinet and Posit started up. By the end of the decade, they were beginning to win enough share to worry many brokerage firms. Rock-bottom commission rates, flat volume, and seepage of volume away from the old way of doing things. For some it was time for another change in strategy.

In the past, institutional brokerage firms had made money in the equity markets in two ways—from commissions earned from customers and from trading for their own accounts. This had always created some conflict, because customers were concerned that they would be given bad advice, or sold unwanted stock, to protect the trading accounts of their brokers. So the brokers walked a fine line, trying to please their customers while earning some proprietary profits. Now some of these same firms saw a very different logic. They saw their customers deserting them for the lowest price or for an electronic market. Their response was to focus on their own accounts. Trading for their own profits became crucial, and they pursued either an inference strategy or a technical strategy.

The firms relying on an inference strategy turned their large research departments, which in the past had produced reams of printed research for customers and had spent many hours courting institutional investors, inward to find, or infer investment opportunities for the firms themselves. In addition, these firms focused their trading desks on reading the markets and taking positions for themselves. Resources were focused on opportunities for the brokerage firm, not for customers.

The technical players went one step further; they felt that relying on analysis and research would not work. After all, if their customers had not benefitted from their research, why should they believe it? They hoped that computer-based analysis of trading opportunities and relationships between different securities could produce attractive arbitrage opportunities. As we saw when discussing the technical strategy, again Morgan Stanley was the most public of these firms, releasing information about its "black box" trading group in the late 1980s. This team relied upon complex analysis of the relationships between equity securities, often known as pairs trading, to develop arbitrage opportunities.

From insider, to segmentation, to inference, to technical. U.S. institutional brokerage competitors were forced to change with the markets. They were not afraid of this, for the winners realized that if they could stay one step ahead of everyone else, change was a source of competitive advantage.

The retail market was equally in flux. Anybody who has bought or sold stocks for themselves in the past few years must have sensed that the business is not stable. Just as deregulation and new technologies changed the required strategy in the wholesale equity markets, they did the same in the retail market. Again, what happened in the United States after deregulation provides a good example of the pressures at work and how competitors' strategies had to change in order to continue to win.

Retail stock brokerage in the 1970s was primarily a relationship, insider game. The famous Wall Street wire houses such as Merrill Lynch, E. F. Hutton, and PaineWebber, the large regional firms such as A. G. Edwards and Alex Brown, and the smaller local firms such as Branch Cabell in Virginia were all competing in very similar ways. They were all paid through commissions earned on trading stocks, and they got the opportunity to do this by building a relationship of trust on a person-by-person basis.

Of course, they went after building this trust somewhat differently. The wire houses spent more money on research, advertising, and training in the hope of earning more revenue per broker than the smaller firms. The regionals focused on local references and a lower-cost base to drive profits. At the center of both approaches, however, were the contacts the local broker could make through country clubs, references, old school friends, and the like. While they tried various cold calling techniques (the "dial and smile" approach), if the local broker could not build a trust-based relationship with a client, then no amount of advertising would win orders for the firm.

This central front-line skill remained very important to the business throughout this period. Meanwhile, however, serious structural changes were requiring this insider strategy to be supplemented with some new approaches. Once again, it was deregulation that caused the most dramatic changes. We have seen how the 1975 May Day deregulation of commissions caused havoc in the institutional equities field in New York; to counterbalance this at first, the full-line wire houses tried to maintain or even raise their retail commission rates. These increased rates opened up a new competitive opportunity, and thus were born the discount brokers, such as Charles Schwab, Quick & Reilly, Rose & Company and Brown & Company. They offered no-frills brokerage, at low rates. No research, just execution, but at big discounts.

They won a share of the market, or, more specifically, a seg-

ment of the market; the segmentation strategy became opera-
tive. Unfortunately for the wire houses, the segment that the
discounters won (and won in increasing amounts) was often the
most attractive one: the individuals who traded frequently and
thus were drawn to the low rates.

The retail situation was made even more complicated by the
change in monetary policy applied by Paul Volcker at the end of
the 1970s and the impact this had on short-term interest rates.
As the gap between regulated bank deposit rates and Treasury
rates increased, an opportunity emerged to attract depositors'
dollars out of the banking system into some other short-term
savings vehicle. Merrill Lynch was the first to act with their
Cash Management Account (CMA), and many other firms soon
followed. Combined with the impact of the discounters on the
market, this new product reinforced the move away from a simple insider strategy. The CMA introduced a whole new type of
segmentation into the market. Brokers could now seek to control a customer's assets, not just churn his or her stock portfolio,
and the key to long-term profitability would be to control those
assets regardless of the hot product of the day. Fees on assets
through the CMA accounts, from in-house mutual funds, and
from limited partnerships would come to be important supple-
ments to commissions on stock trades. This strategy required
careful analysis of the customer segments that valued and
would pay handsomely for these products—and could be per-
suaded not to use the discounters.

Just as in the institutional market, however, some of the
expected changes were delayed by the profits available as a
result of the market boom in the 1980s. Although the old ways
were under pressure, the need to reassess the strategic approach
was delayed by the windfalls available to many firms. Again,
October 1987 changed that situation and brought retail profitability and segment approaches under far more rigorous
scrutiny. The best players started to invest heavily in market
research to understand different types of customer behavior,
and matched that research with internal profitability analyses to
determine how to market to the most profitable customer seg-

ments. They then tried to match their costs to those priorities, cutting back on redundant or low-value spending, investing in higher-profit products, and raising prices to those segments that would pay. They invested in training new brokers or hiring away brokers from competitors when they believed it would pay off. The insider relationship approach was still required, but it was now a necessary but hardly sufficient component of a winning approach. The segmentation strategy, applied to an insider strategy base at the front line where broker met customer, differentiated the winners from the losers among the retail brokerage firms.

We have witnessed two very different businesses, the institutional equity business and the retail equity business, sell the same product, but in fundamentally different ways to very different customers. A common theme becomes clear: that the five strategies cannot be seen as static solutions to competitive problems; markets change, and so does the appropriate strategy needed to win. This is true even at the individual product level. Products go through a life cycle, and different approaches are needed to win at different stages. A good example of strategic change throughout the product life cycle is the interest rate swap market.

Interest rate swaps were one of the most dramatic and early examples of the surge of new products that was to help underpin capital markets firms' profitability in the 1980s. They appeared at the beginning of the decade, and from rather modest early activity grew to be a major trading and corporate finance market around the world. Simply, interest rate swaps enabled two companies to *swap the interest they had to pay* on their loans and bonds. For instance, if a Fortune 500 company could raise fixed-rate money from the Eurobond market at very low rates but wanted floating-rate debt, then an investment or commercial bank would seek out another (often smaller) company with little access to the capital markets that could raise floating-rate bank debt but wanted fixed-rate debt. This intermediary would then swap the obligations of the two companies, in the process offering each better terms on the type of debt it wanted than it could get alone.

The original and early swaps were *tailored* transactions, customized to meet the needs of the two parties to the swap. Pursuing an insider strategy, the early bank players scoured their corporate lending markets for companies that would agree to be counterparties and tailored the documentation for each deal. For this they received fees of about 75 basis points (1 basis point equals one-hundredth of 1 percent) of the principal amount being swapped. But this was the early period of the product life cycle for swaps. Soon new competitors emerged and more borrowers became used to the concept. Increased supply and a more educated consumer led to two key changes—declining prices and better terms. In particular, many commercial bank competitors began to keep one side of a swap rather than matching the two parties immediately. These players used their own balance sheets to be the other side of a swap and later found another borrower (or investor) that wanted this exposure.

As can be expected, the increase in volume and the declining prices and improved terms required a change in strategy. The relatively slow insider approach would no longer work. Every borrower was inundated with swap offerings, and banks had to differentiate themselves on product rather than on relationship terms alone. So the competitors began to move to a segmentation approach, just as the institutional equity brokers did at the end of the 1980s. They began to segment the overall market to find out which types of swaps earned higher fees, and which types of customers were least exposed to competitors' offerings, and concentrated on them. The opportunities for such segmentation had grown considerably. More and more borrowers around the world were now interested in swaps, and the types of swaps had enlarged considerably to include currency swaps (where bonds of different currencies were swapped) and combined interest rate and currency swaps. Fitting together the myriad combinations of currencies, borrowers (often with very different costs of borrowing in the local markets), and intermediaries prepared to hold a swap gave ample opportunities to use the segmentation strategy. The commercial banks like Citibank, with their large Treasury positions that could be used to offset swap positions, were better able than the investment banks to compete for the core simple swaps, forcing the investment banks to concentrate on the more esoteric transactions.

Still the pricing declined. By 1987 a straight U.S. dollar interest rate swap was paying only about 7 basis points. Even the most sophisticated segmenters struggled to win on those terms unless they increased volume considerably. They therefore turned the swap market into a trading market and focused on the technical strategy as the way to win. At about this time, a great deal of work to standardize the documentation of swaps came to fruition, and thus the basic mechanics required for a trading market (the trading of apples for apples) were put in place. The swap market glided smoothly into the core interest rate trading markets. The swap was transformed from a corporate finance product into a trading product.

The question now is whether the life cycle of the swap market has stabilized, or whether spreads will decline to the point where nobody can make adequate money and a scale strategy to force out the weakest will be required to win. Certainly, some of the leading players in the swap market are finding that their costs are mostly fixed and that increased transaction volumes, combined with superior position monitoring and pricing, can lead to significantly increased profits. These competitors are, therefore, moving to use their economies of scale to lower pricing further in order to drive out the less operationally leveraged competitors. Thus a scale strategy could lead to further concentrations of market share.

This transformation of a product and of the strategy required to make reasonable returns was seen in market after market during the 1980s. From the mortgage-backed security market in the United States, to the new retail fixed-rate mortgage offerings in Britain, to the equity warrant-linked borrowing in Japan, competitors who first entered these markets were able to earn very attractive spreads for some time from a customized insider strategy. This situation could not last. Competition increased, and manual processes were streamlined and automated. Educated customers applied pressure on prices. These insider strategies had to be abandoned for some variations on the segmentation strategy, often combined with the technical or inference trading strategy. Firms that could not adapt to face the risks in these new environments found their market share withering and their profitability declining. Those that could—for instance, by working out how to manage the complex prepayment risks in a mortgage-backed security portfolio in a rapid trading environment—would gain share over those that still relied on a slower, customized, insider approach.

Working with wholesale banks and investment banks during the fast-paced 1980s, an interesting conclusion emerged about how they could survive in such an environment. Traditional management theory says that organization follows strategy. First, you define where you will compete, and how you will serve customers to differentiate yourself from competitors in order to build enough market share to earn a living. Once this strategy is in place, you worry about broad organizational issues: what kind of skills, with what type of management systems, structured with what kind of reporting relationships are required by the strategy. But this would not do for the capital markets competitors in the 1980s. Strategies kept changing as new products went rapidly through their product life cycles. The trick was to seize new opportunities and adapt as they changed. There was no clear, stable strategy. In fact, organization did not follow strategy, it *was* strategy. Get the organization right, and it would find the right strategy and adapt as required. By the 1990s, as markets had cooled and the pace of change had slowed somewhat, it was possible to start reverting to the old way of thinking. But given the way products still change, as do the requirements for success, the ability to change rapidly among the five strategies will continue to be crucial.

We started this chapter in London in the 1970s, in a market still blissfully unaware of the changes that would tear up old traditions. The fate of the bank I joined on leaving Cambridge epitomizes what took place in the 1980s and what is required to win in the future. That bank prospered up to the time of Big Bang; it was generally regarded as one of the two or three top merchant banks in the City. But then it failed to handle the new securities markets properly, suffered an embarrassing episode in the corporate finance markets, and fell on tougher times. Withdrawal from the core U.K. equities brokerage markets followed, and finally the bank was sold to a European universal bank. Meanwhile, many of its peers of 10 years earlier prospered in independence, having adapted to the new world successfully.

Change is good for those who can live with it.

PROPOSITION III

FOR EVERY STRATEGY, A MANAGEMENT APPROACH

10

Avoiding Disasters, Creating Winners

The chief executive officer of a major financial institution can be very lonely. This is not because of lack either of visitors or of large meetings to attend. Very often the diary of a CEO will be scheduled down to the last few minutes with staff reports, internal meetings, visits from regulators, and a few customer calls. Add to that the civic responsibilities that seem to go with the job, and the CEO is a busy person. The loneliness comes from being often so distant from the real action. In particular, the CEO is constantly waiting for impending doom that he or she can imagine but cannot control very well. In financial institutions, major risks are taken every day by staff who are many layers removed from the CEO. All the CEO can do is to wait and hope that all will work out. If he or she becomes too paranoid about risk and clamps down on business, then performance will suffer. On the other hand, if the CEO becomes too happy-go-lucky, then each evening he or she goes home secure in the knowledge that something bad is about to happen. The CEO has a lonely life, waiting for disaster to strike.

The management challenge is to find a balance between being too restrictive or too liberal in a series of risky businesses. It is the task of simultaneously avoiding disaster while creating winners. The two aspects of the task are linked. Looking at past disasters and great successes, it is possible to outline what financial managers should focus on as they try to run the company to foster success. It is useful first to examine the best loss prevention techniques before integrating them into a complete package of management tools to be used both to avoid disaster and also to enable talented staff to go after profits.

Regulators of financial markets have enunciated a clear perspective on how to avoid disaster. The immediate reaction to disaster of major regulators in the world's financial markets is to try to make financial firms stronger. Specifically, the aim of regulatory change since the mid-1980s has been to add capital to financial firms in the hope that this will provide a cushion to future shocks. In banking, the BIS set new capital guidelines for banks around the world. In addition, regulators in many countries have been implementing their own measures to enforce these guidelines as minimums. As we have seen, financial resilience is a major component of success for many financial companies. For some scale competitors, financial strength can be the basis for competitive advantage.

In few cases, however, will financial strength overcome stupidity or market collapse. Regulators are correct to want to attract capital to industries whose cushions have been destroyed by the problems of the 1980s (for instance, the U.S. banking industry). But they should not be lulled into a false sense of security. What has been added can easily be taken away again by a rash of new losses. Regulators' focus on capital is only part of their task. They also focus on other factors. They must ensure that markets are basically rational. For instance, the anomaly in the United States that allows banks to use federally insured deposits to lend to all manner of businesses is a fundamental problem that needs to be corrected if the cycle of losses is not to be repeated. Regulators also must worry as much as the CEO does about how financial firms can make money while avoiding disaster. In reality, regulators' needs and aims are in concert with those of the companies they regulate. Companies make profits only from risk, and profits are the best source of capital. The best regulation focuses on *both* avoiding disaster *and* creating winners.

Financial firms can best avoid catastrophe in the first place by competing only in markets where they have or can develop real advantages in using risks for profit. They have to choose areas where they can compete on the basis of their risk/reward skills and then select the strategic approach that best fits the type of risk they have chosen. Choosing the right markets, and the right strategies within those markets, are the best ways to avoid major losses. However, a CEO has to be prepared to enter new markets where perhaps he or she hopes over time to build the right skills, but today recognizes that the firm still has a lot to learn. Or the firm may be faced with a competitor who undermines pricing and returns. With the best will in the world, the CEO must accept that in order to grow and because of the inherent instability of risks, losses will occur. Choosing the right risks and using the appropriate strategy is the best defense against loss, but it cannot guarantee that no losses will be incurred.

Examination of major losses reveals eight key lessons for banks, securities firms, and insurance companies seeking to avoid catastrophe: (1) avoid lemming-like behavior; (2) avoid having too many eggs in one basket; (3) maintain liquidity; (4) research new markets in great depth; (5) be wary of giving one or two individuals too much authority to take risks; (6) develop and pay heed to warning signals of trouble; (7) ensure that when profits are measured, so are the risks; and (8) do not panic when trouble hits.

The first lesson is particularly appropriate given the disasters of the late 1980s and early 1990s. It is remarkable how a large share of all the major losses around the world could have been avoided if lenders and traders had avoided a few key markets that caused so much trouble. If some banks had avoided real estate construction lending, if some securities firms had not dabbled so aggressively in junk bonds and bridge loans, and if insurance companies had avoided these two markets, a large share of the losses in the financial world at the end of the 1980s would not have occurred. The reality is, of course, that the losses in these markets happened largely because the markets themselves became hopelessly overheated. In the United States, tax advantages fueled construction activity. In Japan, there was a self-reinforcing loop between stock prices and real estate prices. In the United Kingdom, there was a speculative real estate boom created by Big Bang and easier monetary policies. In the high-yield market and in the related merchant banking and bridge loan markets, investment banks and commercial banks tripped over one another to win a share of the lucrative deals available. The up-front fees encouraged a large number of firms to enter the market, forcing down spreads and making the actual risk/reward equation unattractive. Deals that would have been priced very richly in the early 1980s were fought over by so many commercial and investment banks that all the profit was squeezed out. Some deals were done that never would have been contemplated in the early days of the LBO market.

The financial community in most countries is tight and competitive. What begins as an unique opportunity can soon turn into the latest fashion. One bank copies another. A third hires away the staff doing the new deals at the first. A fourth player hires from the first three. Then a fifth learns of the deals and enters too. Now the press has caught up, filling their columns with stories of the vast wealth to be made in these new deals; enter competitors 6 through 20. To justify the new investment in staff and technology that probably has been made by all 20, new deals are sought. Spreads and terms deteriorate. The newspaper headlines, the asset growth, and the fees are recorded today, but very often the risks lie in the future. Today's profits are followed by write-downs and catastrophe for many.

To counter this lemming-like behavior, the top management of financial firms has to think about not only which risk market to enter, and which of the five strategies to use, but also when to enter and exit the chosen market. Financial markets may well be expected to follow boom and bust cycles. But the smart competitors will recognize that even at their best, they cannot hope to win if the pricing in a market has gone awry. Nobody could make decent money in the U.S. letter of credit market in the late 1980s because a few competitors, with cost of capital advantages, had destroyed the pricing. At the same time, very few could expect to make money issuing commercial paper for large corporations in the United States, or Eurocommercial paper in the Euromarkets, because intense competition was destroying returns. Few U.S. insurers could hope to write profitable automobile insurance in those states that had distorted competition in the name of the consumer. The first rule of avoiding disaster is to recognize a lemming when you see one, and to have the courage to avoid the trends. The firm that does this will later reap the benefits of its competitors' discomfort.

The second lesson from past disasters is that financial firms must avoid concentrations of risk, or putting too many eggs in one basket. If a bank has a high percentage of its loans in one type of industry or in one region, it is taking the risk that this one exposure will go sour, bringing down the whole enterprise. Drexel Burnham Lambert was dependent on high-yield bonds. First Executive Life Insurance and First Capital Life Insurance had similar exposures. Mutual Benefit Life had concentrated exposure to real estate and junk bonds. First Options Corporation had a short list of major options traders to which it was exposed at the time of the 1987 stock market break. Their failure to cover margin calls led to a $90 million loss for First Options. Lenders to oil companies in Texas or to office builders in Arizona, and New England banks in the real estate market are all experienced of spectacular losses in the 1980s because of overexposure to one market. To avoid catastrophe, financial firms have to accept that they *must* diversify their risks.

There is a clear tension here between the need to develop special insights into a market to have a risk/reward advantage and being overexposed to one risk. Local community banks compete on the basis that they are so much closer to the customer than more distant regional or national banks that they can use the insider strategy in their local community better than anyone else can. Their problem is that in order to pursue this strategy, at their size they end up with loans only in the local community. They have all their eggs in one basket. They may be the best eggs available, but if the basket drops, their eggs will break along with everyone else's. To overcome this problem, community banks need a larger capital cushion than their bigger cousins to absorb losses. Often they do have a higher ratio of equity capital to assets than do the larger banks. They also have to make sure that they derive a large amount of nonloan income from the market, that is, from high deposit spreads and branch banking fees. In addition, community banks need to make sure that they do not have exposures to the market of too long maturity. The shorter their loan exposures, the easier it is for them to retreat for a while should the local market look weak.

Concentrations of risk can be both obvious and hidden. The obvious ones are the concentrations of industry, or region, or risk type that brought down the firms described earlier. Everyone knew they were taking the risks; the only question was whether they could survive. Problems become more difficult to manage when the risks are hidden and when previously unknown concentrations of risk suddenly appear. Lenders to commodity-producing countries tend to look at all risks separately. They believe that through careful diversification across countries and types of commodities, they will avoid severe concentrations of risk. This logic fell apart in the 1980s when these lenders found all commodities declining in price, especially when adjusted for general inflation in major OECD countries, because of the imposition of much tighter monetary policies in those countries than had existed in the 1970s. The bankers discovered that they had a severe concentration of risk to such a change in government policy. The history of LDC loan write-offs and renegotiations is littered with testimony to the failure to diversify from that risk, because it was not recognized until it was too late.

The third key lesson from catastrophic losses is to maintain liquidity. This means that financial firms have to remember that ultimately they will go bust, just like other defaulting companies, when they have no cash on hand to meet their debts. Only at this point is a company actually dead. The problem for the financial firm is that so much of its money is borrowed, in the form of deposits, that a sudden run on deposits can leave it with assets that cannot be turned into cash fast enough to meet the withdrawals of depositors. An old-fashioned run on a bank is exactly this problem. The bank may be sound—that is, its assets may still exceed its liabilities in value—but if depositors panic, it may be unable to sell enough of these assets fast enough. The haunting pictures of depositors lining up outside U.S. banks in the 1930s were enough to spur Congress to create federal insurance for bank and savings and loan deposits in an attempt to stop such panics.

Recent defaults by banks and other financial firms in the United States, however, have all been the result of panic by depositors. Bank of New England was ultimately taken over in 1991 by the FDIC because there was a run on deposits that could not be met out of liquid assets. Continental Illinois in 1984 went under because of a run on deposits that threatened to leave it with no cash. In October 1987, the securities firms that went under did so because they could not meet their bankers' margin calls. Regulators took over First Executive Life Insurance and Mutual Benefit Life Insurance in 1991 because they feared that policyholders would panic and cash in their policies, leaving the companies with no cash to honor their obligations.

Faced with this real risk of catastrophe, the best financial firms monitor their liquidity carefully. It is no use having the most valuable assets in the world if you cannot sell them when you need cash. Some firms have gone out of their way to build up less volatile funding sources. Bank of America was crippled during the mid-1980s by a series of missteps in the agricultural and energy lending markets. Its large base of consumer deposits, however, stayed faithful to the firm, giving it the liquidity it needed to pull through and become the second largest

U.S. bank in terms of market capitalization at the beginning of the 1990s.

The bank with the highest market capitalization at the time was J. P. Morgan, parent company for Morgan Guaranty Trust Company. Morgan's liquidity problem was exactly the opposite of Bank of America's. Whereas Bank of America could rely upon its California retail deposit base to stay loyal and pull it through hard times, Morgan had practically no retail deposits. Its institutional depositors, drawn from around the world, could quickly pull the plug on the firm. To counter this major liquidity risk, Morgan adopted a conservative credit posture and built a large capital base, two measures designed to calm its depositors. Proof of the success of its approach was that by 1991 it was the only remaining AAA-rated U.S. bank. To buttress its liquidity, Morgan maintained a large percentage of its assets in liquid securities that could be sold rapidly if necessary. Morgan went further by making sure that its loans were negotiated in such a way that a good portion of them could be sold as well. Obviously, the firm never wanted to have a fire sale. But if cash was needed, it would be easy to deliver it.

The fourth lesson from past catastrophes is to understand the risks of a new market or product as clearly as possible. Major problems often occur when a firm enters markets that it knows little or nothing about or when it does not fully understand the risks of a new product. In the trading world, the 1980s were a particularly rich environment for such disasters. A wave of new products entered the scene, in many cases developed by linking risks together in an entirely new way. For instance, in April 1987, Merrill Lynch lost $377 million trading interest only/principal only (IO/PO) mortgage-backed securities. Merrill decided to dominate a new offering of these complex derivatives of already complex underlying securities. The securities are created by splitting the interest payments on the mortgages from the principal and selling each separately. In April 1987, Merrill held a large portfolio of PO portions that plummeted in value as interest rates rose. Merrill found itself with very large losses and became the victim of a squeeze by other traders, which further increased its losses as it tried to unload its inventory. To some extent, Merrill was a victim of allowing one trader, Howie Rubin, to control too much of the trading in the securities. Rubin ended up trying to hide his losses on the trades by stuffing trade slips in the drawer of his desk and may not have followed all the firm's risk management procedures. Fundamentally, however, Merrill misjudged how the pricing would work, and paid the price.

In the insurance world, similar problems have occurred. In the United States, a new investment product called the *guaranteed investment contract (GIC)* became very popular in the pension market in the 1980s. In that decade, many companies changed their pension plans from those that guaranteed a pension level to those that provided a defined level of contribution each year into the pension fund but left it up to the employee to choose investments. Faced with that choice, most people were very conservative, putting their money into fixed-rate investments rather than equities. The GIC seemed the perfect vehicle for them, offering a guaranteed rate of interest for a predetermined time. The guarantee was provided by the insurance companies that dominated this market. One in particular, Equitable Life of New York, built an enormous business out of GICs. The problem was that as the competition for pension fund money increased, Equitable started to offer higher and higher yields to win more business. The only way it could do this was by investing in assets with more risk than was in fact prudent. By the end of the 1980s, the results of Equitable's approach were starting to become clear: losses mounted, and the board replaced the management. By the beginning of the 1990s, the insurer's capital position had become so weakened that it was forced to seek outside capital and in 1991 effectively to sell 40 percent of the company to the Axa Groupe, the French insurer. Years of proud mutual independence had to be relinquished so that the company could raise capital. At the root of Equitable's problems was a simple misunderstanding of the new risks they were taking on. The GIC market coupled with new junk bond and real estate investments looked like a great growth opportunity. But it was a new market, and Equitable overestimated its ability to understand and manage the risks.

The fifth lesson from past losses is that investing one or two people in a firm with too much authority to take risks can be disastrous. We have just seen how Howie Rubin's position at Merrill Lynch during the IO/PO problems allowed him to mask the trading problems for a longer period than was prudent for Merrill. As he was the expert in the market, nobody questioned his decisions until it was too late. At Morgan Grenfell in the United Kingdom, the 1986 Guinness merger work that sullied the firm's reputation was undertaken by just one or two key bankers, who were so successful and powerful within the firm that their approaches were not fully reviewed. In these cases, the fundamental problem was that the decision makers knew so much more about the risks than their managers that they could not be overruled until the problems became very obvious. Divorcing the firm from the risks it is bearing is often a red flag that disaster is just around the corner.

This problem, however, need not reside only in large companies. Smaller firms can also be exposed to the risk that a driving force, perhaps the founder, will so dominate the firm that nobody will question the risks being taken. An interesting problem of this type is faced by small community banks. These banks, using the insider strategy, often compete by establishing close contacts in the community, and the CEO and board members are usually important members of the local community. A 1988 study by the Office of the Comptroller of the Currency (OCC) showed that these community ties could backfire if social links are allowed to color credit decisions.

The OCC found that a major cause of bank failure is that neither the board nor the CEO has a clear strategic plan for determining what risks the bank will take. They also fail to put in place the controls to ensure that such a plan is actually the one that is implemented. As a result, the bank falls back on individual influence as its guide. In some cases, because the borrowers are the CEO's friends, it is often difficult for junior staff to overrule or even question the credits. The CEO, meanwhile, may be promoting the need to build goodwill in the community and to consolidate the bank's franchise with the need to protect its capital. Disaster can follow. Add outright fraud to the equation, and soon the problems associated with allowing just one or two individuals to make the key risk decisions become all too clear to depositors and regulators. An interesting question to ask in all financial firms is why the CEO needs risk-taking authority at all. If the CEO is primarily a manager of others and a salesperson, why does he or she need to have credit or underwriting authority? By divorcing the CEO from individual transactions, a clearer focus on portfolio management can often result.

The sixth lesson from past disasters is that early warning signals must be in place to identify problems before they emerge. Senior management must take heed of such warnings. The early warning systems cannot be prescribed from afar, being unique to each type of risk market. Nevertheless, a common theme appears to be that the best managers of risk invest in playing "what if" games to see how their portfolios will react to particular problems and then monitor the biggest risks. So traders in the bond markets watch every twist and turn of the monetary authorities in their country, and how they will change interest rates and thus bond prices. They also worry about liquidity in the market and about their ability to unwind their portfolios if necessary. Real estate investors watch rental rates, vacancy rates, and general levels of economic activity as harbingers of the future viability of real estate projects and investments. Life insurers review medical and health trends in the population they are insuring to catch problems early. No one warning system works for all risks, but those without any system will be the last in a market to spot trouble before it arrives, and may go on investing after it is clearly time to stop.

It is all very well to have these warning systems, but a disappointing lesson from some past failures is that even if a financial firm has the systems in place, it may not always pay them the appropriate respect. The warnings are sounded, but nobody listens. The U.S. real estate lending markets are a prime example of failure to heed this lesson. Even after office vacancy rates in major cities in Texas had started to increase, and it was evident that major new additions to available rental space would only worsen the situation, a number of Texas banks continued to fund construction projects throughout the 1980s. The same held true in New England, where the declines in the local economies at the end of the 1980s did not stop banks from funding new buildings in the hope that somewhere there would be a long-term investor to "take out" their construction loan. With no hope of finding renters to pay for the space, however, this was a delusion. The warnings sounded, but some competitors simply did not heed them.

The penultimate of the eight lessons for avoiding disaster is to measure risk and profit simultaneously, and to make sure that staff are given incentives and compensated in parallel with the overall risk/reward strategy of the firm. A fundamental problem in financial firms is that the rewards from a transaction are often gained up front when it closes, but the risks may not be played out for many years. For example, in a loan to a major corporation involved in a merger, the bank may get a fee when the deal closes, and then interest each year thereafter. The initial fee can be very large, and acts as a carrot to close the transaction. But the risks of the loan will live on for many years thereafter. The problem is compounded when compensation to individuals within the company is paid on a year-by-year basis. With the best will in the world, the performance appraisals that determine this compensation are likely to be weighed toward how successful the staff member was in the most recent year, even if "success" may actually lead to major problems a few years later.

During the 1970s and 1980s, failure to reward staff in line with the firms' economic interests twice caused problems in corporate banking. In the 1970s and early 1980s, major banks around the world focused on market share in corporate lending and rewarded their staff for booking loans that were low in risk. The more the better, for that showed that the firm had a good and growing market share. The problem was that bankers failed to take pricing fully into account. Even though the loan portfolios were usually low in risk, competition had driven down yields to the point where the business was simply not economic. The very low-spread loans took up too much precious capital for the income they generated. But staff members kept on marketing and booking the loans, because that was what they were rewarded to do. It was only in the mid-1980s that a number of banks woke up to the problem and started to pay bankers to look for loans that had a high return on assets or yield. Unfortunately, one way in which bankers could produce loans with more yield was to lend to clients with more risk. The new measures of return on assets or return on equity often did not adjust for risk properly. The second problem was created: the incentives that created the high-yielding but also high-risk loans for LBOs are clear.

This potential compensation mismatch is even more apparent in the trading world. Traders have traditionally been paid a percentage of their trading profits, but they do not have to give back a percentage of their losses. This unbalanced arrangement, while probably the only one that is feasible, can create major control problems. The trader is mostly interested in one side of the equation, and is likely to be more prone to take more risk than the firm would be. Even worse, in many markets, a trader who loses money and is fired can often find another trading job at another firm. The new firm is confident that it controls the risks, believing that "everyone loses once; that was his turn, and now it is over." The gaps between traders' interests and those of the firms at which they work create the backdrop for some of the disasters that have occurred in the trading world. Knowing that even if you lose the firm $2 million you will not have to pay a penny of it back encourages a certain calm in the face of risks.

This *agent/principal* problem is especially difficult in the insurance industry, because the lead time between closing the deal and facing any claims can be decades. So underwriters have to be especially carefully controlled if they are not to book large quantities of long-tail business that produce attractive increases in annual premiums but later cause disaster. Asbestos contamination, underground pollution, and birth defects caused by new drugs are all examples of areas where insurers have paid the price for accepting rewards today without full understanding what the losses tomorrow could be.

From all these examples, the key message from lesson seven is that the way in which risk and reward are measured and made visible is terribly important. Major problems arise when a financial firm counts success in ways that motivate the staff to do deals or write insurance coverages that are well outside the range of acceptable risks or that are priced too low. As we shall see later, the way risk is measured and made visible is crucial not only for avoiding disaster but also for creating winners.

The last of the eight lessons from disasters is that in the event of approaching catastrophe, don't panic. Panic actions can make a bad situation worse. Therefore, the trading firm that discovers that it has a large loss on some securities must think hard before dumping them into the market. If other trading houses hear of its predicament, they may force the price down before the first firm can sell. At that point, it may be wise to wait until conditions stabilize somewhat. Obviously, if the trader believes that the fundamentals will only become worse and that the firm should get rid of its holdings as quickly as it can, then this advice will not hold. But in both cases, the message is the same. The fact that the profit and loss statement is in the red instead of the black should not mean that years of training and experience are thrown out of the window.

The same applies to banks. The lender that finds a company in default of some loan covenants may not be advised to pull all the loans it has with that borrower. This might bring the company down, turning a difficult situation into a tragic one. The reality is that approaching catastrophe is not yet catastrophe. The financial firm facing apparent disaster must reassess the risk/reward situation, and act to maximize the rewards and minimize the risks in exactly the same way it does in more normal circumstances. This may call for drastic action, but in some cases it may not. Cool heads are required.

Finally, it is important to retain a sense of perspective when disaster strikes. It is quite likely that the company will survive the dread event. What is certain is that a major loss will color the way in which a company acts in a market for years to come. It will become part of the folklore of the firm. Risks will never be seen in quite the same light after a major loss, and those who have lived through a trauma of this kind will always remember it and will act differently because of it. But if a financial firm is to prosper and grow, it has to be prepared to absorb, intermediate, or advise on risk. So, in the course of a disaster, the management of a firm has to think of the future. It is important not to panic as catastrophe approaches, because the staff must be left with enough self-confidence to believe that after the danger is passed, risks can be taken again. The firm that allows such panic may find that no one will ever take a risk again. They will survive the catastrophe, only to later wither and die.

This contrast between disaster today and recovery and growth tomorrow is at the crux of the management challenge that financial firms face. Managers not only have to avoid disasters, they simultaneously have to create winners. What is needed is an organizational approach that supports both aims at once, that recognizes the eight lessons from disasters while creating an environment within a firm that supports rational growth through risk absorption, risk intermediation, or advising on risks.

Financial firms have to build their organizations on the basis that they make money from risks. *Organization* means more than just who reports to whom. It also includes how performance review and compensation systems work, how decisions are taken, what style and set of values are communicated from the top, how new staff members are trained, and all the other facets of day-to-day life that make one company different from another. Inasmuch as risk is what drives the way financial firms make money, it needs to be the theme that unifies these organizations. Managers need to build organizations that focus on and learn about risks and rewards. With such organizations, managers can be confident that the key way in which the firm can make or lose money is at the center of the way the firm is organized today, and that new or evolving risks are quickly understood by the key staff members.

There are four steps that management can take to build an organization that focuses on risk and on making money from risk: (1) determine and communicate what risks will or will not be taken; (2) make risk visible; (3) have decisions made by people who have the best skills and information; and (4) align incentives to avoid the agent/principal problem.

Although it sounds obvious, the simple step of making it very clear to everyone what risks the company will take, and what risks it will not take, is often omitted. Bankers who believe their advantage lies in getting inside credit risk let themselves take not just credit risk but also complex market and liquidity risks associated with their loans. Traders who focus on timing or inferring market risks start trading with counterparties whose credit is dubious. The best firms, however, are able to say precisely what risks they will and will not take and to orient the whole firm around the chosen risks. So some leading banks will focus on credit and liquidity risks but will not take interest rate risk. Conversely, some of the leading trading houses will not take large credit risks. Some insurance companies will not take risks relating to financial exposure of clients. Defining the risks that will or will not be taken begins the process of focusing on risk. With this start, it becomes much easier to build a rational risk/reward strategy because management has already focused the firm on a particular kind of risk. The appropriate skill building can follow.

Once this initial message has been sent, however, the largest management challenge follows: to make risk *visible* within the organization. If risk is at the heart of everything that a firm does, it follows that it is crucial to make risk clearly visible to everyone. Risk has to become a "language" that is spoken throughout a firm, so that all staff members are fluent and can instantly see when the "syntax" of a deal is wrong. In this light, financial firms must handle with great care the language they use most often—the language of traditional accounting. In most cases, traditional accounting terms are not precise enough for risk/reward decision making. In the worlds of banking and insurance, accounting is mostly based on historical measures of value. In volatile and changing markets, this is a serious deficiency. First, it makes it very difficult to balance future risk and future reward. Second, traditional accounting treats all cash flows similarly, whatever their risk. Third, traditional accounting recognizes risk only when it has become a loss, or, at the other extreme, relies upon estimates of future losses based on a banker's or insurer's best guess. Neither approach is as precise as one would like for measuring the key driver of how these companies make money. Finally, traditional accounting, even when it does recognize future risks through provisions, makes little effort to determine what type of risk it is measuring. All in all, traditional accounting terms leave much to be desired as the central tool for monitoring and communicating about risk.

Making risk visible means ensuring that the company worries about measuring and monitoring what is really important to its prosperity. Managers and staff can focus on only a limited amount of information during the day. At a company making breakfast cereal, unit sales and market share by region are probably among the key measures to be made visible. For financial firms, risk visibility is the priority. Computers today allow financial firms to measure and monitor a whole range of variables—cost trends, volumes, variances against budget, sales. All these may be useful, but for financial firms they must not overwhelm the task of making risk visible. Of the limited data managers and staff can absorb, risk and reward information must be given priority.

There are basically four stages of making risk more visible in a financial company: review, classification, quantification, and comparison of the risks. Often companies' approaches evolve through the four stages, mastering one stage before advancing to the next. Not all stages are required for all types of firms. But the largest financial firms are discovering that the final comparison stage is very important if they are to be able to manage all the conflicting risks they face and earn attractive returns.

The review stage involves bringing some light to bear upon the activities of a talented individual. We saw earlier how dangerous it is to have the key risks that a company is facing understood by only one brilliant trader or one experienced lender or underwriter. As soon as a company can make the decisions of these lone risk takers more visible through the simple process of review, it has started to understand and control risk. The institution, not just the individual, starts to learn about risk. If all risks are in the minds and under the control of individuals, then the financial firm itself does not matter; it is merely somewhere for them to hang their hats. The review process begins to create a company with skills beyond those of a few stars. With that base, not only can the firm survive their departure, it also has something to offer new recruits. The firm itself starts to have some value.

The review stage of creating visibility is simple. As its name implies, it allows others to review the work of the few key decision makers. It is appropriate in small firms, where the decisions are often made by the "gut feel" of the key officers. Review, either informally or formally by a committee, allows the day-to-day thought processes and facts to be understood by more people, raising their awareness of what the firm is really doing to make money. At this stage, however, review is still an unstructured exercise.

Classification, the second stage of making risk visible in a financial firm, applies more discipline. The review process can simply involve the evaluation of an expert's opinions—trying to see if what one person did, made sense. Classification tries to bring order to that process by putting risks into different categories. Transactions and assets are systematically broken down into the different components of risk that lie within them. For example, a fixed-rate loan funded with floating-rate deposits might have a credit risk component (the risk that the borrower will not repay) and a market risk component (the risk that the rate on the deposits will float up above the fixed rate on the loan, destroying profits). The process can go further by putting risks into different buckets to reflect their approximate severity. So, many banks now have an eight- or nine-step loan classification system that tries to describe how risky the loan is. But during classification, this process is still approximate. The classifications help focus the analysis or evaluation required, but do not by themselves provide precision.

Quantification tries to attach precise numbers to the distinctions developed in the classification stage. Through quantification, managers hope to be able to determine the likely losses associated with risks of different types and severity. The eight- or nine-step loan classifications are now supplemented with analyses of exactly how they will behave. If a portfolio has a mix of quality 1, quality 3, and quality 5 loans, the quantification step is meant to forecast losses on that portfolio. If a trader holds a particular basket of securities, the quantification approach is designed to forecast its potential losses on that portfolio. A number of trading firms have developed approaches that equate all bond trading positions with the risk of one instrument, for instance a Treasury bond, and use this measure to quantify risks in all portfolios. Obviously, in financial markets where the number of observations is large enough that competitors can pursue the segmentation or technical strategy, the quantification approach is at the heart of the way the business is managed. But in more judgment-based markets where the insider or inference approaches are required, quantifying risks is a major challenge with which firms are constantly wrestling.

Once risks are quantified, it is possible for managers to start to ask the difficult questions about what reward they are getting for the risk they are taking. They are able to quantify the reward all too easily in most cases, so the quantification of risk is very important if the right balance is to be reached between the two. Yet, this may still not be enough. Most of the quantification techniques in the market apply to individual businesses. Managers are able to compare the riskiness of one loan with that of another, or one security with another—but not a loan with a security. As the regulatory barriers that have divided financial activity into different legal forms (banks, securities firms, insurance companies) erode, it is becoming more and more important for senior managers to manage risk and reward across different businesses, and allocate capital and staff to those they believe have the best long-term risk/reward balance. In addition, using a common language for risk across different businesses means that in watching out for disaster, a CEO can see where risk is building and focus on that area. This is possible only if the measurement system is the same for all businesses, so that $10 million of risk in a lending business means the same as $10 million of risk in a trading or insurance business.

The final stage of creating visibility, comparability, is designed to provide exactly this common language of risk to be applied in all areas of a company. Undoubtedly the best example of comparability in action was that developed by the global merchant bank Bankers Trust during the 1980s called *Risk Adjusted Return On Capital* (*RAROC*). By the end of the 1980s, RAROC had become a system that required business managers and individual line officers to measure the risk of a business or a transaction and to equate that risk to the actual or prospective returns. These risk measurements were then totaled, two or three times a day for the whole firm around the world, so that top management could monitor the overall risk profile of the bank. Periodic reviews of individual businesses enabled Bankers Trust to see how the risk/reward balance was looking for that business. Constant measuring of risk and rewards meant that managers were quickly able to spot deterioration of the terms in a market. Most importantly, by 1990 RAROC had become the language of the bank, a term that all staff understood and a measure all felt comfortable using. This did not mean that it did away with arguments about the way the risks were measured or whether the results were fair (no system could hope to do this completely!), but it did mean that Bankers Trust managed its businesses down to the transaction level using a consistent measure of risk and reward across all businesses. Because the measurement was comparable, decision making was consistent from one business to another and from the corporate office down to the individual trader or banker.

RAROC did not begin with such an ambitious scope. It was inaugurated by Charlie Sanford, then head of trading and later chairman of the bank, as a tool to help manage the trading businesses. It was introduced in the early 1980s, in the era when a number of major banks were moving from measuring just gross income to measuring return on assets or return on capital. In fact, however, RAROC differed from other systems inasmuch as it did not allocate capital to businesses. The capital in RAROC has little to do with book capital or market capital notions. Instead, the RAROC capital is a number that a business or transaction *attracts* because of its riskiness. If a transaction or business is measured as risky, then it will attract more "capital" than will less risky situations. The total of all these capital measures may or may not come close to the actual book or market capital of the bank, but if it does, that is just a coincidence.

The common measurement of risk is the secret of RAROC. Specifically, Bankers Trust went back to the definition of risk we saw earlier—the volatility of potential outcomes. With this in mind, the bank started to measure the volatility of price movements of individual traded securities. It then asked a simple question: if the bank wanted to liquidate its position in a security in a mild emergency, what amount of loss could it expect? Knowing the past volatility of a security, the bank was able to calculate the most it could expect to lose (with a high degree of confidence) while trying to unwind a position. This number, the bank's highest reasonable exposure to loss in the event of liquidation, became the RAROC capital number. Obviously, securities that were very stable and liquid had little RAROC capital assigned to them; very volatile stocks or bonds had a lot of capital assigned to them. Because the measure was consistent, trading positions in different markets (for instance in different types of bonds, or in currencies versus bonds, or in bonds versus equities) could be measured on a comparable basis.

Sanford's master stroke, however, was to transfer RAROC from the trading world to the bank lending businesses. Again,

using the consistent measure of capital, Bankers Trust was able
to ask the bankers how much it could expect to lose if it wanted
to liquidate a loan. In the lending markets the liquidation
period was usually much longer than in the trading markets
(for instance, a year), but still it was possible to see how much
capital was at risk. Again, the higher-risk loans were seen to
have higher volatility in value than were the lower-risk loans,
and so attracted more RAROC capital. Now Bankers Trust had
a very powerful system, because it could measure risk consistently across its businesses. The final step was to apply a performance target to these capital measures. Businesses and
individual transactions were given a return target. They could
meet it in one of two ways: by increasing reward or by lowering
risk. Bankers Trust had formally joined risk and reward, and
done so consistently in all main areas of the bank.

A sea change in behavior ensued. Traders no longer focused
just on yields or bid/asked spreads, but were forced to look at
historic and potential volatility in a portfolio and seek out situations where the volatility seemed the lowest for the returns
available. More dramatically perhaps were the changes
wrought in Bankers Trust's banking activities. As corporate
lending spreads declined during the 1980s, the RAROC returns
for plain vanilla bank loans to major corporations began to look
less and less attractive. Returns were very low, but the loans,
however low in risk they were, still attracted some RAROC capital. The resulting ratio was well below the RAROC target.
Unable to raise spreads due to the heavy competition from
other banks (which were slower to see the problem), the
Bankers Trust bankers were forced to lower the risk.

They did this by making the loans liquid. The key steps were
redrafting the documentation on new loans, so that they could
be sold to other banks or investors, and starting a loan sale market. This lowered the RAROC capital attracted by the loans,
because the bankers could plausibly show that the loans were
now much more like securities and did not take a year to be liquidated. Given this situation, the highest plausible loss on the
loans was much lower than if they had to be held for a mini-

mum of a year. So the RAROC approach converted the bankers' traditional task from seeking to grow assets to determining when a loan could be sold. In a very real way, the RAROC approach hastened Bankers Trust's emergence as a leading global merchant bank simply because it forced all levels of the bank to focus on exactly where they had a risk/reward advantage. At the same time, it served as a crucial tool for top management. They could monitor overall trends in the level and composition of the RAROC capital and, if necessary, raise real capital if they felt the bank was taking on much more risk than before but the returns warranted it.

Making risk visible is the second step in creating an organization that focuses on risk and reward and learns about risk, and the Bankers Trust example illustrates what can be achieved by this step. But information about risk is useless without some method for taking advantage of it in a rational way. This leads to the third step for building a winning organization: determining who will make decisions about risk. The basic rule here is very simple: the decisions should be made where the best information and skills reside. The trick is to bring them together within the organization and to have the confidence to then let the individuals with the skills and information make the decisions. In winning firms, individual transaction decisions are taken where the most information and the best skills exist for that transaction, while portfolio decisions, for instance what types of risk the firm will take overall, are taken where the best overview perspective exists.

In the segmentation strategies, firms such as American Express and the leading life insurers devolve decision-making authority on the agents who are closest to the individual cases being reviewed. They then provide these agents with the best available information gleaned from the firm's large statistical databases and support their decisions with expert decision support software. In the segmentation markets, large companies are able to devolve decision making because they can bring to bear the best information and skills to the line through computer systems. They have the confidence to devolve decision making.

For overall portfolio decisions, however, these firms still look to the center. The types of credit or life insurance risk that they will take, the degree of geographical concentration they will accept, the customer segments they want to emphasize—these are all portfolio decisions that are made by senior managers. It is here that the risks and rewards of different segments can best be monitored and weighed, and so it is here that the information and the skills reside. It is then relatively easy for these firms to influence individual transaction decision making by changing the expert system's advice or by sending out new underwriting guidelines.

In insider strategies, for instance those pursued by bankers and insurers of corporations, the problem is more complex. Here very large risks are taken with each transaction, and the temptation is to bring all decision making to the center because of the fear of disaster. Unfortunately, the center may not have any better insights into the risk than the line officers. The best insider competitors recognize this and have adapted their approaches accordingly. The leading middle-market lenders have decisions about individual transactions made by the line officers who have the best information about a credit, but overall underwriting guidelines and portfolio concentrations are controlled at the center. They resist the temptation to involve a large committee in every credit decision, realizing that such a forum cannot add any value because it has no better information than the line officers.

Managers of firms using the technical and inference strategies, often living in the fast-moving trading worlds, simply cannot expect to intervene in every transaction. They have to rely on the individual trader to make transaction decisions. These transactions often place tens of millions of dollars at risk in each case, so they hope that information and skills are combined at the point of decision making. Trying to intervene in each transaction, however, would be impossible. But the managers do have a crucial role to play in setting portfolio standards and ensuring that portfolio concentrations, including concentration of risk taking in too few traders' hands, are not extreme. They set the limits that will control each trader and then allow the trader to trade within those limits. The managers ensure that the risk takers have the necessary information and skills and then manage portfolio risk.

In the scale strategy, managers at the center set the level of pain the firm is prepared to take to squeeze out lesser competitors. Then they rely on the individuals with the information and skills to manage individual transactions. Managers ensure that the hoped-for decay in the competition does occur and that the portfolio of risks being booked during the period of low pricing is not unacceptable. Then, as competitors fade, the scale competitor is able to raise pricing or win enough market share to make the low prices attractive. Managers need to monitor progress to make sure that the portfolio of risks is attractive while letting the individual risk takers make each transaction decision.

Allowing those closest to the risks with the best skills and access to information to make decisions requires managers to manage. That is, if top management is entrusting the firm's capital to risk takers, it has the responsibility to ensure that they are truly skilled. One of the most worrying sights at a financial firm's headquarters is a floor where all the senior managers have their offices—*which they never leave.* At the best firms, managers test and enhance the skills of the key risk takers by constant discussions, reviews, and encouragement. These managers know they must allow those closest to the risk with the best skills to make the risk decisions, so they get out into the thick of the action to make sure they have the right individuals in place.

This does not mean second-guessing every decision. This is a management challenge—to recruit the right people, to make sure their training and assignments build the risk skills, and then to make periodic assessments to ensure that the skills are more than adequate for the environment. Ultimately, however, there are not enough managers to check every transaction, so the task is to make sure that the company is investing in building the skills on which its success, even its survival, depends. The best firms tie advancement to achieving specific levels of accomplishment in the key risk and reward skills that drive the economics of the firm. Promotion does not come as a matter of course. Rather, promotion is a result of having achieved new skill levels and is a sign that you are ready to assume a new role. By recognizing risk and reward skills, the best firms perpetuate them.

Encouraging those closest to the risks, with the best skills, to make decisions carries with it some risk if these decision makers do not have the same objectives as the firm. This is the classic agent/principal problem reviewed earlier. The fourth component of a successful organization is to align individuals' incentives with corporate objectives. Recognizing the wisdom of allowing those with the skills and the information to make decisions, the leading firms work hard to make sure that incentives encourage staff to act like principals in deals.

This is easiest for small firms, where the risk takers may be partners or aspire to be partners and can clearly see how their livelihood is tied to the prosperity of the firm. But in large companies, the link is much less clear. For instance, often a banker or underwriter will be moved to another job before the risks they have taken on for the firm have run their course. In these situations, companies have to examine their performance assessment and compensation systems and link them to the company's aims. In situations where the risks are long-term but the payoff may occur in the first year or so, this is especially hard. To incent senior staff appropriately, long-term incentive and stock compensation is often the answer. The more the senior staff in an institution can be made to act as if they are in a partnership, where all live and die by collective risk and reward decisions, the better. For lower-level line staff, tying compensation to collective performance may be less useful. Instead it is usually linked to performance on individual transactions. Nevertheless, even though compensation may be calculated when the deal is closed it can be payable over a number of years, depending on how the risk actually plays out. In some firms, the approach is taken even further: the compensation is paid only when the risk is over. In all cases, however, the basic approach is the same. If it is through risk absorption, intermediation, and advice that the firm is to prosper, then those taking the risk decisions must have the same motivation as the firm.

The CEO of a financial firm need not be lonely. Experience from the past shows that there are clear lessons for avoiding disaster. To create winners, the CEO can turn to other well-tried principles and see if they are applicable to his or her firm. With these guidelines, disaster can be averted and winners can be created. However, if the CEO is pursuing a strategy to which the firm is fundamentally unsuited, then all these lessons will be of little use. The first rule for creating a winning risk organization is to select risk markets where the firm has a skill advantage and to apply the appropriate one of the five strategies in those markets.

11

Gaining Advantage from Information Technology

If you had visited a bank branch, bought or sold stocks, or bought insurance in the 1950s, the experience would have been largely the same as it is today. The key challenges of risk and reward management that financial firms face are relatively stable over time, and so, therefore, are the ways in which they deal with us. The bank would still have had a large number of branches all over town, and you would have found in each the familiar set of tellers, and desks or platforms to fill out new applications and deposit slips. The securities firm would have provided the same type of advice that it provides today, offering to sell or buy stocks. The insurer, like its counterparts today, would have relied on a broker or agent to convince you that you needed insurance, and only then would you have started to deal at all directly with the carrier itself. But there is one huge difference between today's offices and the offices of the 1950s: no computers.

Today's financial firms are avid users of computers, telephones, telexes, facsimile machines, and information services—

all the tools of modern information technology. The way in which these firms decide who to do business with, analyze the facts of each risk, process a loan, a stock purchase, or an insurance contract, track transactions proceeding through the firm, post them to their accounts, and then communicate with us have been transformed by information technology.

Tasks that used to be performed by armies of clerical staff are now summarily completed by pressing a few buttons and letting the mainframe computers whirr away. Analysis that would have taken a team of researchers weeks to complete on large paper spreadsheets are now performed better by one junior analyst working on a personal computer for a day. Transactions between a customer and a bank that used to involve queuing to see a teller, and then much scribbling on forms and production of carbon copies, are now completed by the customer visiting an ATM and pressing a few keys on the machine. Bills for insurance payments, which used to require individual bills prepared by the broker or agent based on instructions from the carrier, are now computer generated with coding to cancel automatically the receivable against the account. Investment banks' trading strategies that once relied upon the experience and wit of the traders to see opportunities to buy low and sell high are now often driven by computer analysis of arbitrage opportunities determined by examining years of daily price histories.

In every function of every financial institution, the proliferation of telephones, large processing computers, personal computers and workstations, and the development of specialized software to meet customers' and managers' needs have changed the way business is conducted. Surely this revolution in the productivity of many functions must have improved financial firms' profits enormously. Apparently not. As we have seen, the end of the 1980s saw faltering banks, securities firms, and insurance companies around the world. Where are the results of the information technology revolution?

Managers of financial companies have been faced with many frustrations and failed hopes during the last 20 years. But perhaps none was as overwhelming as those caused by the new information technologies in which they invested with such fervor year after year. They hoped that information technology would create a large increase in profitability. Clerical staffs would no longer be needed for processing transactions or balancing the books. Front office analysis and judgments would be improved by analytical support available from sophisticated computer modeling, aided by on-line information about markets and customers. Customer service would be improved by easy-to-use machines and more accurate processing of transactions. The telephone would enhance all aspects of communication. As a result, internal productivity would be higher because of faster communication. Once far-flung functions could be brought together. Service would be improved by allowing a much faster response to customers' complaints or requests. In retail and wholesale markets, in banking, securities, and insurance markets, the new technologies promised a new level of profitability for financial firms.

These early hopes were fed by the improvements in the underlying technologies. Most spectacularly, the traditional reliance on large mainframe computers was ended in the 1980s by the development of ever more powerful personal computers and workstations for the field officers, line bankers and traders. The cost of processing an individual piece of data declined at an extraordinary rate, bringing tasks that had once been impossibly expensive within the reach of all firms. At the same time, the major software houses developed user-friendly products that became commonplace in firm after firm. Lotus 1-2-3 and the many word processing programs were perhaps the best examples of this trend. Then the influence of Apple's MacIntosh personal computer in making such machines accessible to many more users speeded their use and raised the hopes of managers that major improvements in productivity would be possible. Meanwhile, mainframes continued to be used where still needed, but their operating costs declined and productivity increased. Software was targeted at specialized financial needs. Communications systems for both voice and data became cheaper and cheaper. New technologies were delivered every year.

But the hopes were often dashed by the results. Indeed, the new technologies often seemed to produce as many problems as benefits. Many managers were faced with a forever rising technology budget that threatened the firm's economic well-being with its hugh size and intractability. Yet users and technology staffs were perpetually frustrated. The spending kept rising, but profits rarely came with the spending. Something had gone seriously wrong.

Ironically, even when technology expenditures do not deliver improved profitability, when financial firms try to cut back on them, they find that most are essential to stay competitive. Cutting back proves to be very difficult, and yet little of the spending produces, differentiation in a market or safe profits. All too often the technology budget seems to be merely a cost of competing, with no distinctive link to profits. Therein lies the problem.

Technology is no different from any other component of a financial firm's cost base; to be valuable, it must be targeted at the special risk/reward approach of the firm. It is only when technology is used to provide a risk/reward advantage for the firm that it will produce lasting profits. The reason for this is very simple. The vendors of technology will make sure that easily copied advances are available to all competitors, so the advantage is only fleeting. The bank that achieves a cost advantage by automating a bookkeeping function will not have that advantage for long. The hardware manufacturers and software houses will sell the approach to others, and soon prices in the market will reflect the fact that all the good competitors now have lower costs. The customer benefits and society is served by the competitive economy at work, but no individual competitor raises its profits in a sustainable way. This is not to say that firms should not make such investments that are easy to copy; if they do not, they will be left behind. But managers need to recognize that much of the technology expenditure becomes a cost of competing that is necessary but not sufficient for success. That is why a large part of the technology cost base is intractable. Technology has become an integral part of the way a bank, securities firm, or insurance company works today, as necessary as the capital with which it funds itself or the staff that opens the doors each day.

Only when technology provides a valuation, flexibility, or resilience advantage tied to one of the five risk/reward strategies will a sustainable advantage accrue from the spending. The message to the top management of banks, securities firms, and insurance companies is quite clear: as far as possible, rationalize your technology expenditures to emphasize spending that supports the real risk/reward advantage and strategy you are pursuing.

Information technology supports all five strategies today. The segmentation players use technology extensively. It is crucial for them to divide their customers and transactions into statistically valid segments that they can then analyze and so determine which segments to emphasize at what price level. Without the ability to process and segment very large quantities of information as it is received, and then through expert systems to provide rapid guidance to the staff dealing day to day or hour to hour with risk and reward decisions, these businesses could not have expanded and offered the consumer the prices and services they do today. The best of them use information technology to segment the risk opportunities better, or deliver information to the line officers more rapidly and in a more usable form than their competitors, and thereby create a real competitive advantage.

Successful credit card issuers use information technology in many ways to create advantage. First, they have sophisticated, interactive, behavior-based software that continuously updates their knowledge of an individual's creditworthiness and indicates when that individual moves from one credit segment to another based on the charges and payments made. These firms are prepared to invest heavily to build proprietary databases that will distinguish their valuation of risk from that available to the average company. However, segmenting the attractive risks from the less attractive ones is only the first step. In order to make money from this advantage, the firm must again use information technology to deliver the information to the credit authorization agents who deal with exceptional or unusual requests. If a shop needs to contact the card firm directly about a charge, these telephone agents are able to look at on-line information about the cardholder and quickly determine whether the charge being questioned appears reasonable and in line with the cardholder's usual behavior. This rapid access to the valuation advantage the companies have developed not only enables them to stop fraudulent or excessive charges, it also enables them to allow large but legitimate charges by creditworthy customers and so strengthens the customer relationship. All this is dependent upon information technology.

Credit and charge card firms also use technology to build their customer base. As the credit card markets have become more competitive and saturated, it has become more expensive to bring in new cardholders. To reduce the costs of winning new accounts, the best firms use information technology to help them identify the likely target customers. They are then so confident about their credit-underwriting capabilities that they can issue preauthorized cards to the candidates they have targeted. This process can radically reduce the cost of winning new accounts compared to the old method of sending out mass mailings and asking applicants to fill out credit information forms.

Information technology can help to retain customers through quality service. This ranges from posting charges correctly, to having telephone agents who can quickly access information when someone calls with a question, to American Express' use of imaging technology to provide visual copies of each charge slip with each statement. All these service elements are dependent upon information technology, and they can materially lower the turnover in the account base. This further lowers marketing costs and builds the history within the risk databases year by year, further lowering underwriting losses. So, in the credit card business, the best competitors use information technology to support their core risk/reward advantages, and therefore are getting good returns from that expenditure. These firms also spend heavily on information technologies to fulfill accounting needs and lower transaction processing costs. But these investments, while necessary to stay in the game, do not create an advantage. It is only when the technologies are applied to the key segmentation approach that their costs are far exceeded by the benefits of the competitive advantage that is achieved.

The same formula is at work in other segmentation strategies. The branch banking business is highly dependent upon achieving great convenience for the customer at reasonable cost. A bank will strive to collect a disproportionate share of deposits for the number of branches it has to support. To achieve this advantage, winning banks must understand commuting and business flows better than every other bank, and must position their branches and ATMs to create the impression that their service is available everywhere that their potential customers want to be. In order to understand these patterns, branch banking firms use sophisticated modeling techniques first to define the broad parameters of where they need to be, and then to place their outlets as precisely as possible. The same analysis is pursued when two retail banks merge: the consolidation of branch networks presents opportunities to eliminate duplicate costs and increase market share. The new merged network is often cheaper to run than the two separate networks because unnecessary overlaps can be eliminated. In addition, the newly merged banks will analyze demographic flows in the market and where their most profitable customers live and work, and will position their new network to capture the most attractive present and potential business at the lowest cost. This analysis is highly dependent upon the use of information technology.

Once inside a branch, we find that we are subject to information technology in ways that clearly differentiate the strong from the weak players. Whether we are attractive customers to the bank depends not only on whether we keep large deposit balances there, but also on how many products of the bank we use. Cross-selling, therefore, becomes a crucial skill for banks to master. In this context, information technology plays an important role. By supporting their branch bankers with on-line information about each customer and with expert systems that identify high-probability cross-selling opportunities, banks have been able to increase the average number of bank products each customer uses. As customers inquire about a particular product or make a purchase, the bank officer is able to introduce them to other opportunities that the software suggests they are likely to find attractive. By investing in the most advanced technology and taking the time to educate the branch staff on how to use it, the best firms have created a real advantage with technology that enables them to outperform the average competitor. Again, they have also invested heavily in other technology that is necessary just to stay even, but the extra edge comes from technology aimed at supporting the key strategy they are pursuing.

Other segmentation competitors also use information technology extensively for competitive advantage. Insurance companies use it to analyze large quantities of demographic data and to identify attractive and unattractive segments. Securities firms and brokers use it to target their efforts to customers who will pay the full price and away from those who will take all the research and service but turn to a lower-priced, lower-service firm for trading. A less obvious example of the use of information technology in the segmentation game is provided by Fidelity Investments' FAST telephone service. Through this service, Fidelity investors are able to call a computer system to get routine information about their fund balances, the prices of funds, and their yields; it is necessary to talk to a telephone agent only when, they want to execute a transaction. Not only does this service keep Fidelity's staff small, it also improves the service that customers receive, enabling the firm to keep customers and build profitability significantly. Of course, Fidelity also uses all the other segmentation approaches of cross-selling based on the investment needs and activities of its customers. They also invest in technologies like transaction processing that provide little direct competitive advantage, apart from increasing scale pressures on competitors by lowering costs and prices, but are a necessary part of the business.

The insider competitors also use information technology.

However, because the insider strategy is focused on fewer and larger risks than the segmentation strategy, its dependence on large computing facilities is usually much less. The insider strategy relies upon developing unique insights into the risks of individual situations. Fundamentally, the insider approach is a judgment-driven strategy, but it often uses sophisticated modeling techniques to analyze data and value the risks better than the competitors who do not have these capabilities. In the LBO field, as well as getting so close to the company that they can make advantaged judgments about the management and its forecasts, firms such as KKR model the cash flows to determine at what level they are prepared to bid. The same is true of venture capital firms considering investments in a new venture. They supplement their insider judgments with the best fact-based analysis.

Less obviously, the insider competitors use information technology to win new business and to hone their capabilities. The major M&A and corporate finance houses are investing in two types of databases to support the decision making of their front-line bankers. The first kind collects all types of information about clients and prospects and provides it to the bankers in a synthesized, easily accessible form. This enables them to call a client, secure in the knowledge that they are up-to-date with what is going on in its market, in its dealings with all other financial firms, and in all correspondence and telephone contacts between the client and the firm. This is actually an electronic client file, but its easy access provides an advantage over firms that employ many types of poorly used and documented paper files.

The second type of database collects information about different types of transactions and their key characteristics. So a banker on the road could get, via a modem, information about transactions the firm and competitors have done around the world, and the key factors that have to be in place for the transaction to work. The real power of these two approaches comes, of course, when they are combined so that the bankers can scan their customer and prospect lists and identify targets that meet the criteria for a type of issue or transaction that is particularly hot at the time. So, although the insider strategy may be less dependent upon information technology (beyond the essential telephone and fax) than is the segmentation strategy to perform its core tasks, the smartest insiders recognize that, when focused on their key risk and reward decisions, information technology can help identify opportunities and support better judgments.

Technical competitors, who are processing and analyzing large quantities of data, are highly dependent upon information technologies. Indeed, without them, the technical approaches would generally not be possible. Finding the price discrepancies that underpin many technical strategies is often dependent upon analyzing years of price histories to identify patterns, and then capturing them in the market when they appear. For both steps, information technology is crucial. It is no surprise to find the trading floors of major financial firms stuffed with expensive gadgetry. Indeed, many firms have been forced to move from old buildings to (expensive) new quarters just to house the computers and wiring, and the air conditioning to cool them, that are essential for these strategies. The trick here is to be disciplined in recognizing what is really necessary to support the proposed technical advantage of the firm, and to resist the temptation to invest in every gadget and technology element that the hardware, software and telecommunications vendors proffer.

The inference strategy is more like its cousin, the insider strategy, in its need for information technology. Fundamentally judgment based, it needs to be able to assemble all available information as quickly as possible, and then undertake as much analysis as possible to narrow the margin for error within which the ultimate inference judgment will be made. In this context, information technology can improve the flow of information within investment research departments. The best research departments have developed wide area networks (WANs) to share information and ideas between offices in, say, New York, London, Paris, and Tokyo. The information then flows to traders and investors. But the scale and nature of this investment, and the need to provide on-line, instantaneous access to data, are much less than they are for the technical and segmentation strategies. Again, the focus of management's attention on information technology should be on how it can best be used to improve the risk and reward decisions the inference practitioners are making. Little other investment in technology will bring competitive advantage.

Scale strategies often use information technology, although once again, much of the spending does not produce a distinctive advantage. Scale strategies are driven by either financial or operating resilience that enables a firm to outlast and then beat existing and potential competitors. Information technology may be integral to the way the scale players run their finances and operations day by day, but it creates a competitive advantage within the scale strategy only if it is integral to the financial or operating resilience of the firm. For instance, in many processing businesses, like mortgage servicing, custody, and mutual fund record keeping, scale players use their large computer processing facilities to advantage because smaller competitors cannot justify the costs of replicating this investment given the levels to which the scale competitors have driven down prices.

Firms like Bear Stearns in the United States have made this information technology scale advantage a crux of their strategy. Bear Stearns has become one of the leading third-party securities clearing houses. They offer second- or third-tier brokerage firms the advantages of scale-based pricing and have ended up replacing these firms' in-house capabilities. American Express, through its First Data Resources subsidiary, has become one of the largest credit card processing firms by offering banks with relatively small credit card portfolios a cheaper way of building a credit card business than having to replicate all the back office services in-house. The costs of replicating the information technology are a major part of these costs. In the global custody business, just a few firms are coming to dominate the provision of services centrally to global fund managers because of the complexity and cost of building, updating, and maintaining the software and processing systems that are the backbone of the custody business. In the mutual fund business, again only the largest players seem to be able to support the investment in trustee and other processing and tracking services in-house, and most smaller competitors have tended to outsource this task to competitors who have real scale advantages.

If the manner in which the five strategies apply information technology varies, managers pursuing any of these strategies are starting to see some common patterns in the way that they need to view their investments in information technology. In particular, they are focusing on which component of the technologies they should really worry about. At their simplest, these technologies can be seen to have three major components. The first is not a piece of hardware or software at all. It is the *link* between the business that needs technology and the technology itself. Ensuring that what is delivered actually supports the business, and that it does so in a way that the users find easy to understand and use, is a crucial part of the technology strategy of a firm. Businesses are in a state of constant change, so the technology has to be flexible enough to accommodate these changes. This means linking the developers, maintainers, and users of the technology as closely as possible. It also requires viewing technology as an equal partner with the nontechnological parts of the business. If it makes economic sense to redesign the way people work to take advantage of a new technology, then so be it. The second component of the technology, after the link between technology and the real world, is the software. The applications that support the business are crucial to the value of the technology investment. Finally, there is the visible infrastructure that supports the applications—the hardware, operating systems, and communications networks that process and link the data flowing through the applications. The most advanced firms are looking at these three components of technology and asking where they must invest to achieve a risk/reward advantage, and where it is acceptable to outsource the technology that creates no advantage.

Except for the scale competitors, more and more firms are

questioning the value of continuing to invest in the major hardware, operating systems, and communications networks. Especially for small to middle-sized competitors, it is becoming clear that these utility functions provide little advantage in-house. Specialized scale players can in fact offer these same services at lower cost and higher quality. So today, many medium-sized banks are actively seeking to outsource their data center activities to scale players such as IBM and EDS. Regarding the second technology component, the software, many firms have already turned to packaged, rather than proprietary, software for their major repetitive tasks (for instance, Hogan Systems' deposit and loan systems for commercial banks). Some are even trying to outsource the maintenance of their proprietary software. We saw earlier how smaller brokerage houses are turning to scale competitors for many of the technology-dependent processing activities, believing that these are not crucial to achieving a risk/reward advantage. Indeed, the challenge many firms now face is to adapt the way they do business to the characteristics of their packaged software or their data center services to achieve the full cost advantage of using a scale provider. If they ask for too customized a package or service, much of the cost advantage is lost.

Financial firms are looking hard at the value they receive from the investment in hardware, operating systems, and even communications systems (after all, they have long outsourced much communications activity to the telephone companies). But they are also focusing increasingly on where they believe information technology creates an advantage for them. Their attention is captured by the link they can make between specialized applications and the risk/reward decision makers to achieve an advantage from technology. By freeing the technology staff from day-to-day concern with the major processing systems and applications, they believe they can achieve greater productivity and advantage. So the segmentation strategists are investing most heavily in proprietary software that provides unique insights into the risk behavior of various segments of the market. They are then ensuring that the delivery of this data to the ultimate business users is as swift and comprehensible as possible. The insider strategists are focused on the unique analytics and market databases they can make available to the bankers and underwriters on the road. The technical strategists invest most heavily in the analytical software that will identify the fleeting pricing discrepancies upon which they often feed, downplaying in-house utility processing. The inference players are focused mainly on the analytical support that information technology provides to their judgments. Most are happy to have others undertake the more repetitive tasks. It is left to the scale players to worry about the major processing hardware and operating systems, because they are the ones who have focused on the operating and investment risks in this area as their field of competition. Since they are the only major group of competitors to focus on this area, most of the scale information technologies can be expected to shift to them over time.

Looking ahead, many managers not competing in scale markets would like to concentrate only on the "front-end" technologies (the applications and links with the users that they believe will make all the difference). But they do not have the luxury of forgetting altogether about the underlying operating systems and hardware. They run the risk of creating very expensive technology unless they set some standards that application builders will follow. The need for some measure of control has grown in parallel with the increased availability of powerful workstations and personal computers. As technology has become more decentralized, the opportunities for duplication and redundancy have increased. Management has to ensure that the revenues to be gained by meeting every marginal need of users outweigh the costs incurred today, and in the future, to meet those needs. The business that requires its software to be run on a computer and an operating system that are different from those used by every other business within the firm must be able to prove that the revenue increases or risk decreases that come with the unique technology outweigh the initial investment and the ongoing unique maintenance and support costs. In addition, cross-product issues need to be considered, and these can often be complicated by hardware issues. In the segmentation strategy, would sharing of customers' files across products create new marketing or risk analysis opportunities? In the trading world, would sharing of customers' credit lines and credit netting between businesses open up new revenue opportunities? If sharing of data across products is required, then the issues of compatibility and communication between the technologies of different businesses become even more important.

All too often, as users have gained more direct access to technology in recent years, they have demanded the machines with which they feel most immediately comfortable, even if these are not used elsewhere in the firm. Sadly, in many cases, the ability to quantify the costs of this choice is poor. Top management has found it easier to satisfy the businesses than to support the arguments of the technology staffs. Expensive technology has resulted.

The corollary of this problem is that as technologies advance, investments become outmoded and cause disadvantages, not advantages. The 1980s witnessed a wave of investment in IBM PCs and the DOS operating system developed by Microsoft. Yet, at the beginning of the 1990s, many financial firms were starting to question whether that investment would last throughout the decade. First IBM's OS/2 operating system, and then the very powerful UNIX operating system, challenged the status of DOS as the core for workstations in the 1990s and beyond. Companies that use the newer operating systems can write complex software more easily and offer businesses requiring powerful distributed processing a clear advantage. The question managers face is whether to bow to their technologists' advice and start to shift to UNIX or OS/2 and unravel years of investment in PCs and DOS. The cost will be extremely high, but so could the advantage. The task is to pinpoint the risk/reward advantage of the new approach and to limit new investment to those areas where a competitive advantage will accrue. So even if managers would like to focus just on writing software and ensuring that risk decision makers use it, they cannot escape the technology infrastructure issues completely.

All these issues are related to the fundamental point about the successful use of technology by financial firms. Technology cannot be seen as a separate discipline from the rest of the business. As we have seen, if it is to add value to the corporation, it will be because it supports or amplifies the core risk/reward proposition of the firm. At the same time, technology can be very expensive, so business managers have a responsibility to understand it as well as they do the other major supports for their efforts—for instance, their staff and their capital needs. With this understanding, they will be able to join with the technology specialists in balancing the pros and cons associated with each technology choice. In sum, information technology can be crucial to many risk/reward strategies, so it must be managed in conjunction with the other components of those strategies.

12

The Games of Inches: Pricing, Costs, and Capital

When all the analysts and experts gather around to decide whether a financial firm has succeeded or failed, they will almost certainly use a few simple economic criteria. How has the stock price done? Has the company created shareholder value or not? How are profits, up or down? What is the company's return on equity, adjusted for the riskiness of its business? The most elegant mission statements, the slickest annual reports, and the sponsorship of high-profile sports events will all come to nought if over time the firm's economic performance is poor.

We have seen that in order to achieve strong economic returns, financial firms must accept that they are somewhat different from other types of companies. The key to their economic success is to focus on risk and how to profit from risk. Building on three core risk/reward skills (valuation, flexibility, and resilience), these firms can select from among five key strategies (segmentation, insider, technical, inference, and scale) they can pursue to win in most situations. Careful selection of markets in which the firm has a potential risk/reward skill advantage, followed by use of the appropriate strategy for the situation, will underpin success. Most economic underperformance over time will come from poor selection of markets and mediocre execution of strategies for those markets.

Then there are the *games of inches*. Once the strategy is set in a market where the firm has a risk/reward skill advantage, the day-to-day execution of the strategy involves managing pricing, costs, and the use of capital. It is these levers that will ultimately determine whether the firm produces the profit and loss statement that the analysts want to see, and does so with an economy of capital use that sets the stock price on the right trajectory. The five strategies set the firm in the right direction. But day-to-day management of the key performance levers determines whether it takes full advantage of this correct strategic direction.

The 1980s saw massive dislocations in pricing approaches, cost configurations, and capital structures of companies across a wide range of industries. This extreme process, however, was largely a one-time dislocation. Capital markets were deregulated (opening up new financing opportunities). Industries were globalized, deregulated, and exposed to new technologies that created new competitive pressures. Years of uneconomic operating and financing practices were swept away in a tumult of restructurings, mergers, and bankruptcies. From this period, many have drawn the wrong conclusion that the way to deal with the key economic levers of a company is through revolution. A blank sheet of paper, revolutionary discipline emerged that was appropriate given what had to be done to so many inefficient and outmoded companies. However, this revolutionary outlook on the key profit levers is in most cases wrong. The approach is one of crisis and dislocation rather than of steadily advancing strength and success. Pricing, costs, and capital usage must be continuously upgraded and improved so that the major dislocation is avoided. Evolutionary change is the most appropriate way in which to advance a company's fortunes. The best performers address the three levers that way. They have a constant discipline of reexamining pricing opportunities to ensure that nothing is being "left on the table." They have a rigorous attitude to costs, spending liberally to support value-creating opportunities but controlling other spending. They think of capital as a cost too, one that must be rationed toward major positive cash flow activities and drained from areas with no hope of producing cash. These processes are continuous and disciplined. As a result, the best firms are constantly fine-tuning the execution of the five strategies to extract the most value from them while preparing for the next move in the market requiring a change in strategic approach.

Careful attention to pricing offers opportunities over and above what many believe is possible. The best firms are able to extract the last cent, penny, or yen of value that they are delivering to the market. They do so by focusing on value delivered as the true barometer of price; more exactly, they focus on *perceived* value. They understand that the way to price is first to understand how their current and potential customers value their products and services, and then to price to the limit of their valuation. To do this successfully requires a clear understanding of customer sensitivity to various pricing options. A small example of how this principle works was driven home to me in London in the early 1980s.

At that time the London evening newspapers sold for 5 pence each—a convenient price, as it could be covered by one coin, the 5 pence piece. As inflation advanced, however, it became necessary for the newspapers to increase the price. Once they moved from 5 pence, they suddenly discovered they had a major opportunity. The next coin in the U.K. coinage was the 10 pence piece; paying any price between 10 and 5 pence involved the average customer in a major inconvenience to find or receive small change. As the evening newspaper was almost invariably purchased on the street or in an Underground station, nearly all purchases involved fumbling for money. In the next few years, the newspaper companies took advantage of this fact to increase the price of the papers rapidly, well above the rate of inflation in order to reach the convenient 10 pence price as quickly possible. They had discovered that at these low price levels customers were much more concerned about inconvenience than they were with the doubling of the price in a relatively short time.

This same principle of understanding what the customer really values and pricing accordingly can yield real profit gains for financial companies too. This approach has very little to do with the way in which many firms price—based on their internal costs. Clearly understanding costs and aligning them with available revenues is a crucial discipline, but it is irrelevant to the customer. Costs should be the derivative after a company has determined the full revenue opportunity that is available in a market. Once the opportunity is clear, a company can decide whether it has the ability to make a profit at all in that environment. If it cannot, then the answer about costs is clear: the company should not be in the business at all!

At the other extreme, should the company discover a market where the customer is prepared to pay many multiples of required costs, and other competitors cannot reeducate the customer about lower-priced options, then management should consider capturing the maximum perceived value even if it is well above the costs required to serve that market. Of course, most companies find themselves in markets where the revenue-cost equation is between these extremes, but costs should still be derivatives of the opportunities. By focusing on the maximum possible price for the service or product, the company is addressing what the customer will pay for the service. The company will therefore stay abreast of market changes and opportunities, and will constantly be forced to adjust its cost base to the realities of the market. If, instead, the company is driven by its own costs in setting prices, with little regard for what the market will swallow, over time it will lose market share and become disconnected from the market opportunities that emerge.

Value-driven pricing is crucial in all five strategies. Segmentation winners are masters of value-driven pricing; indeed, it is at the core of what they are trying to achieve. These firms understand that segments of their usually large customer bases behave very differently from one another in terms of their risk of losses. They also show very different price sensitivities. So the segmenters work hard to understand what the customers do or do not value and price accordingly. We saw earlier, for instance, how American Express developed the Platinum Card on the basis that there was a sufficiently large, prestige-driven segment of the retail customer base to support a card priced at some five times the nearest competing card. American Express's internal costs are nowhere near the price that they charge for the Platinum card, but they understand the customer opportunity very well and price accordingly.

In the mortgage market, a number of players have discovered a similar segment pricing opportunity. While many mortgage purchasers are extremely price sensitive, there is a segment that is more concerned about fast service than about saving one-quarter or one-half of 1 percent on the mortgage rate. These firms focus on finding those customers and serving their needs. They offer rapid turnaround on mortgage applications, but in return are able to extract higher interest rates that more than compensate for the cost of such service.

In the mutual fund and investment trust business, firms have been able to discover hidden pricing opportunities based on customers' inability in many cases to understand pricing options. The pricing here is so complex that many of these companies are able to sell on the basis of performance alone. Thus they earn revenues through a number of trailing fees and loads that few investors bother to look for in the small print of the prospectus—a document, in fact, that very few read at all. Similar factors are at work in retail life insurance, where the calculations on investment-oriented products like whole or universal life insurance are so opaque to most of us that it is very difficult to compare offerings or to determine how much profit the insurers are making.

The fact that customers are often indifferent to charges they rarely see or simply do not understand has been exploited further by the banking, securities, and insurance industries. Bank after bank has learned to raise fees for services that customers use very infrequently or cannot shop for with ease. In the U.S., the fees for certified checks have been raised to $15–25, levels unheard of in the early 1980s. Yet this has caused very few customers to shift their accounts. When they need a certified check, it is usually for some major event like buying a house or a car, and so although the fee is annoying, it is a small percentage of the total cost of the transaction. Add to this picture the infrequency with which most customers use the certified check service, and the bother and cost of switching from one bank to another, and it is easy to see why banks have been able to garner the new revenues at little cost in terms of customer attrition. A similar approach has been taken by the major retail brokerage firms, which have learned to focus on fees that are borne by unprofitable or marginally profitable customers but hardly affect the key high-volume customers. In insurance, carriers have been able to emphasize revenues in the retail property and casualty market from existing customers rather than constantly trying to win new business. They know that when you or I buy a house or a car, we initially seek out the best insurance rate we can get. But the next year, when renewal time arrives, we are much less price sensitive. In many cases, we are probably unaware of the amount we paid in the first place and are unlikely to shop around again. So the opportunity exists to raise rates on renewals more aggressively than on initial contracts. Smart firms take advantage of this customer indifference as far as they can.

In the insider strategy, the best example of value-driven pricing is the way in which the major M&A houses maintain very high advisory fee levels. Sometimes these fees run into the tens of millions of dollars for their work, which is often completed in a few days or weeks. Top-notch M&A firms have been able to charge such high fees for two reasons. First, their insider strategy is difficult to copy, so the number of credible new entrants into their business is relatively limited, creating constraints on supply and thus an upward bias to pricing. Second, these firms rely upon two arguments that play on their clients' sensitivities. They equate all their fees to the capital values they are advising on, arguing "What is a $10 million fee compared to getting another $5 a share (which is worth $250 million) for the sale of your company?" They then add their knowledge of their clients' severe nervousness. For most CEOs, a merger in which they hold the reins is a pivotal event, so they are, of course, quality conscious and relatively price insensitive. Understanding these factors, the M&A teams have extracted very large fees for their advice.

There are even value-based pricing opportunities in the technical strategy. Stronger credit-rated companies are able to achieve premium rates for trading in OTC transactions where the credit quality of counterparties is an important part of the overall risk. An AAA-rated bank engaging in technical strategies may be able to earn incremental returns over those available to an A-rated bank, because the number of transactions it is offered combined with the price it can get on one side of an arbitrage or swap are better than what is available to an A-rated player. Their technical skills may be similar, but the AAA-rated competitor is able to use its pricing leverage to augment returns. In the inference strategy, a similar pricing opportunity exists. Investors and traders are relying upon their judgments about future events to determine their trading and investing approaches, but they are as price sensitive as the technical firms. In transactions involving the use of OTC investments, the inference player with a strong credit rating will try to extract the best possible price from the other party to increase potential returns.

In the scale strategy, pricing can be the real opportunity that the best scale players target. By steadily squeezing out other firms, the scale competitor effectively limits the supply to the market. This creates a real pricing advantage to be exploited once competitors have been neutralized. In the property and casualty markets, as the pricing cycle moves in line with capacity, the insurance companies that survive the period of low or soft prices are swift to raise prices once a number of competitors have withdrawn. Of course, this rapid runup in prices encourages additions of new capacity, which starts the pricing cycle all over again. But in the scale approach, the firm must be a scale player in order to take advantage of the good times at all—and often the way this is done is through rapid pricing adjustments.

The best firms constantly work to find pricing opportunities. They do not suddenly decide, under the pressure of declining returns, that now is the time to raise prices. Instead they work hard to understand how price fits into the overall package they are offering, and how they can garner as much of the value they are creating as possible. Pricing is a core function in the way they run the firm, not an afterthought or something that is simply in line with what all the competitors are doing. Since the way to win in financial markets is to understand where the risk/reward line lies in each market, they concentrate on both the risk and the reward (the price for the risk) simultaneously.

The second of the games of inches is cost management. Just as we have seen in pricing, the best firms approach cost management as a core activity to be pursued in line with the risk/reward objectives of the firm. Unfortunately, cost management is often mistakenly translated into cost control or cost reduction and becomes a knee-jerk process in times of crisis. Faced with falling returns, firms suddenly find themselves forced into rigid cost reduction programs, often characterized by a phrase such as "5 percent across the board" or "15 percent head count reduction target." These numbers probably have little to do with maximizing the returns from the risk opportunities at hand. You often find the dismal scene of major financial firms going through wrenching staff and investment reductions in a hurry, a process that obviously undermines their ability to win in their risk and reward markets. In some cases, they are trading short-term survival for long-term success. Very few winning strategies result from frantic cost cutting. This is not to argue, however, that for those firms that have let their costs get out of line, restructuring programs are not valid. It is simply to note that the approaches adopted in these cases are often rather primitive.

Firms often become involved in situations where a major adjustment or restructuring of the cost base is required. Many financial markets are cyclical, and regulatory change has often made the competitive balance quite unstable. Changing technologies, both financial "technologies" and the advent of new computer technologies, have also undermined many strategies. Given the competitive environment, it is to be expected that some companies will be forced to retrench and perhaps try a more focused market approach in place of an earlier broad vision. However, there are ways to restructure that work and others that do not.

The focus again, as in pricing, is on value. A losing firm soon finds that much of what it is doing has little or no value internally or externally. Rather than adopting an across-the-board cost reduction program, the best cost restructurers take a value-driven approach to the activities of the firm. They reduce or stop activities of low or no value. They realize that by reducing activity, they will make costs decline as well. The across-the-board approaches miss the simple truth that unless activities are reduced, costs will not go away (leaving aside a breakthrough in productivity, which is not to be counted on in a situation like this). Diligent review of all activities in a company, both major and minor, and establishing the real value of the end products of all this activity to the internal and external customers who receive them, is the best way of undertaking such a restructuring.

So the sales department, the human resources department, the auditing function, and the data center are all subject to tailored reviews of their activities and end products to ascertain what is really of value, and what is less relevant in the new world that has caused the cost restructuring in the first place. These restructurings work best if they include both the big picture (Can we merge these two departments? Do we need this function at all? Could we outsource this?) and microdetail (How many reviews does this report need? How many copies need we print? On what quality paper?) simultaneously. From this combined effort the best, most rational results seem to emerge. Importantly, the restructured entity is now focused on how the firm intends to create value. That is, it is focused on its risk/reward strategy. If the strategy of the past has not worked and something new is needed, the activity value approach is designed to redesign the cost base to support the creation of a new winner, not simply the shrinkage of a loser.

Nevertheless, restructurings, however rational, are not the preferred way to compete or to manage costs. The goal is to think of costs as something to be managed, not cut in panic. The best firms focus their efforts on constantly adjusting costs to match risk/reward opportunities. So, cost management is a game of inches, of constant improvement that month by month turns the screw on those that are less diligent. If the risk/reward strategy of the firm is fundamentally unsound, cost management will not make up the difference. But it can make a competent risk/reward firm a real winner. When combined with excellence in risk/reward management, it can create a firm that constantly outperforms all competitors.

Continuous cost management of this type can be seen in all five of the risk/reward strategies. Just as risk/reward management has become specialized by type of risk, cost management approaches differ, depending upon which costs really are key to the strategy. Winners have developed specialized techniques to manage the key costs in their businesses.

The segmentation competitors not only seek to discover the risk segments they can cover with the best returns for the risk they take on, they also constantly attempt to lower their costs of winning and servicing this business. Branch banking companies continuously try to reduce their teller costs and to force more business through the ATM networks so that they can staff their branches even more leanly. Credit card companies strive to automate every aspect of their processing to lower staff costs and expensive errors, while simultaneously experimenting with new distribution approaches to lower the cost of finding new cardholders. Life insurers experiment with new, lower-cost ways of originating clients.

The life insurance experiments were most dramatically illustrated in Europe in the late 1980s, when a whole series of link-ups took place between banks and life insurance companies. In Germany, after Deutsche Bank had announced it would create its own insurance sales force, Dresdner Bank and Allianz began to collaborate on the distribution of their respective products. In France, major life insurers and banks have begun to work together. In the United Kingdom, Lloyds Bank purchased a majority stake in Abbey Life, while Trustee Savings Bank continued to build its own insurance operation. The only reason major companies in the United States and Japan have not followed this route is that, for all practical purposes, it is illegal in those countries, although legislation in the United States may be changing the situation there. The success of the Trustee Savings Bank's effort in the United Kingdom illustrates why these firms are eager to cross product lines this way.

The major costs in delivering life insurance products to the market are marketing and sales costs. This is because no one seeks out life insurance. It is a product that is sold, not bought. At the best of times, customers do not like to think about their own deaths, but then to be required to pay for the privilege is just too much! So, life insurers pursue their customers; everyone has probably endured insurance sales calls. It will come as no surprise to anybody, therefore, to discover that the return on these calls is very low. The average salesperson may close only one sale a week. As a result, this dedicated sales approach is very expensive. Companies have tried less direct approaches, for instance including insurance brochures in bank mailings, but have run into the problem that life insurance has to be sold on a one-on-one basis. The answer to the cost problem is to make the sales force more productive, not to abolish it.

That is exactly what Trustee Savings Bank has done. It has a dedicated insurance sales force, like any good insurance company. But it arms this sales force with leads provided by the branches of the bank. The branch managers are compensated partially on the basis of their performance in supporting the insurance effort, and therefore help the insurance teams by providing good leads and often by introducing clients to the insurance team. The results have been astonishing: by some measures, Trustee Savings Bank's insurance team is some four times more productive than those of other insurance companies! This opens up the cost opportunity for Trustee Savings

Bank. It can offer its sales force lower commissions per sale and yet pay them better than competitors, simply because it can show a track record of more closings per week. A similar insurance strategy was followed by Westpac Bank in Australia, with similar success. In this market, both firms are segmentation competitors that have developed a cost advantage. As others copy their formula, this advantage will slowly dissipate, but for now, it is very important. In the long term, however, their risk/reward skills in selecting and serving segments will determine whether they can sustain their success.

Insider competitors also are very concerned about costs. Admittedly, many have to spend lavishly to win the confidence of their clients, through lengthy dinners or extensive research projects to show their clients that they know their markets and needs very well. Behind this expenditure, however, lies a sharp pencil calculating the returns. One way to deal with out-of-pocket and project expenses is to have clients pay for them directly. The best M&A firms track these expenses very closely and, whenever possible, bill clients for them as part of the project's cost.

For general expenses, however, few firms pursuing the insider approach have such an opportunity. In most insider strategies, the main costs are the compensation and benefits given to the experienced professionals whom the company trusts to make the insider judgments. The leading M&A and corporate finance houses have recognized this and adopted techniques to manage these costs very tightly. They recognize that they must adopt the disciplines used by law or consulting firms. These firms work hard to match the skills and costs of their staff to the task at hand. They make sure that if somebody is promoted or paid more, it is because they are fulfilling a higher-value role for clients. Staff who cannot make the transition to a new role are asked to leave, allowing more talented junior staff to take their place. At the same time, these firms watch their overall organizational leverage or gearing (i.e., the ratio of partners to associates), and hire and fire to keep the ratio in line. If they see a bulge in a particular year's hiring, they know that they may have to lose a number of these people a few years later if the ratios of people with different skill levels are to be properly balanced. Where people are the costs, careful planning for the future to control organizational ratios is crucial.

The M&A and corporate finance firms that have adopted these approaches have taken them one step closer to law or consulting firm practices by introducing time sheets. Corporate finance staff members at Kidder Peabody and Morgan Stanley track their activities on time sheets so that managers can see who is busy and who is not. For businesses dependent upon people, such careful tracking is the equivalent of the just-in-time inventory practices introduced into manufacturing, and just as revolutionary. Firms pursuing insider strategies, using expensive staff, are being forced to manage their people much more tightly than in the past. Those who get it right are identifying major savings.

In the technical and inference strategies, so often seen in the trading and investment markets, costs have become more and more of an issue as margins have declined and competition intensified. The best firms approach cost management as a continuous challenge. In the front office, they manage total compensation costs by reviewing traders' and salespeople's productivity (for instance, the number of sales per day, profitability of a salesperson's clients to the firm, profits per trader), and by adjusting both the number of staff and their compensation accordingly. They also scrutinize the costs they incur in giving these traders and salespeople the information they need. Companies like Reuters, Telerate, Datastream, and Quotron have become enormous due to the trading and investing worlds' need for up-to-the minute information about news, market prices, and trading volumes. The trading and investing firms have spent large amounts of money each year buying these data feeds, and in the boom times of the mid-1980s probably did not control their purchasing as carefully as they should have. After the market declines of the late 1980s, these costs came under greater scrutiny. Now the best firms find ways to get bulk discounts or even to unbundle the packages of services the vendors offer and buy only the pieces they actually want.

Moving to the back office, trading and investing firms continuously try to automate their trade processing activities by increasing the use of standard settlement instructions with counterparties or by introducing direct dealer input to cut out many manual steps. More radically, they even try to outsource processing altogether, finding a low-cost scale competitor to provide these functions. It is this rigorous attention to the entire business, from the trading floor to the activities used to process and clear the trades, that differentiates the cost management of the best trading and investing firms from that of the weaker players. Again, however, superb cost management will not cover serious risk/reward management deficiencies in selecting markets or stocks to invest in or trade.

Scale competitors are constantly reviewing their costs, as for some this is often the first wedge in their overall approach to breaking into a market. Very often, in fact, scale competitors appear to be *too* aggressive in controlling costs. For instance, property and casualty insurers that aggressively lower claims administration costs are probably underestimating the savings that can accrue from diligent claims administration and adjustment. By increasing investment in analyzing and challenge inflated claim, the firm can realize very large net cost savings. The phrase "penny wise, pound foolish" can be applied to some efforts to lower the costs of core risk management functions. In the marketing and processing areas, however, the scale competitors continuously lower their costs by adopting new technologies or by adjusting their marketing force to reflect the real opportunities. Since they expect to incur large losses sporadically, they cannot burden their capital with extra operating costs. Again, however, tight cost management will not make up for a lack of real risk/reward management skills.

A special cost management problem arises for many financial firms whatever strategy they are pursuing because their costs are shared across different lines of business. Computer data centers may support many businesses or products. Expensive communications networks may be used by many different areas. Real estate costs are shared by many departments. A central financial department is used to support all businesses. In practice, this means that if top management wants to exit or reduce the size of one business, it will find that many of the costs it may have allocated to that business will not really go away. If a business has been allocated one-tenth of the data center costs and half a floor of real estate costs, these data center costs will still be incurred, as before, to serve everyone else, and half of a floor of the building probably cannot be leased out to another firm (especially in the early 1990s if that floor is in a building in the overbuilt northeastern United States or in London).

Often over one-half of a financial firm's costs are not incurred by only one major product or business. These costs are shared across products. This large shared cost base creates special management challenges. First, managers must recognize that the costs will be shared when the original investment is made, and therefore will be difficult to reduce very quickly. Therefore, managers must be sure that the businesses they will support are viable for the long term. The best also create a panel of users of these costs to oversee their budgeting and control from year to year. Since no single business is responsible for incurring these costs, a group of users works with the support cost manager to control them. In practice, this is a tricky management challenge that many firms underemphasize. As a result, users do not understand these costs and often believe they are overcharged for the use of the shared facilities. Major frictions emerge within the company.

So, all five strategies require careful cost management—not knee-jerk cost cuts, but a year-by-year effort to redesign the way things are done so that when a CEO looks at a business after 5 years, the operation has really changed—but almost imperceptively in the process. Cost management becomes a way of life, but it is not an uncomfortable way of life. Cost-efficient companies do not have to be "cheap"; they just know where to spend money and where not to spend it. Most important, they keep adjusting this judgment day by day as the market dictates.

The final game of inches is the way in which financial companies manage the capital that underpins their balance sheets. This is the base that investors have leased to them to use for profit. The point here is simple. Just as the best financial companies recognize that they must adjust their costs to fit the opportunities before them, they also recognize that their capital must be equally flexible. If capital, like operating costs, is being employed in an unproductive area, then the task is to withdraw it and employ it elsewhere. If management cannot find anywhere to use it profitably, it is a good bet that investors would probably like their capital back.

To succeed in managing capital obviously requires great flexibility, a risk/reward core skill. Companies must be able to unlock capital from a business with poor returns, and this usually means curtailing or even stopping the business' activities altogether. However, to be able to apply such flexibility to capital management, firms need some signals to tell whether the capital is well employed or not. They need to measure the capital used, just as they measure operating costs.

Today, there are two general ways in which this is done. The first takes a calculation of the firm's cost of capital or cost of equity and applies it to the historic, and maybe prospective, performance of each business, loan, or transaction. Businesses or transactions that can exceed the hurdle rate are provided with as much capital as they can use at those levels of return. Underperformers are reduced quite naturally by not being offered more capital. The more sophisticated firms have adjusted these hurdle rates to reflect the riskiness of the business or transaction being measured. Stable businesses may have a lower hurdle than less stable businesses.

The second approach relies more on looking to the future and treats each business within a company as a project investment to be measured purely on a cash flow basis. Using projections, this value-based planning approach measures cash out (the initial capitalization of the business, capital investments over the years, operating costs) against cash in (revenues, asset sales, the value of the business as a going concern). After discounting all these flows at the risk-adjusted cost of capital, managers can see if any value is being created by all this activity. If it is, then capital is applied; if not, then capital is denied.

Poor returns on capital need not mean, however, that the business must be closed down. Just as prices and costs can be managed, so can capital. By restructuring a business so that it consumes or needs less capital, many firms have been able to turn unattractive activities into winners. This process has become best known through the securitization phenomenon of the 1980s. At its simplest, securitization involves financing an asset with the cheapest and smallest amount of capital.

For many financial firms, securitization has forced them to recognize that their capital is both constrained and relatively expensive. It is constrained because it is needed to absorb or intermediate a whole range of risks, and should be applied carefully to those areas where the best returns are possible. It is expensive because investors recognize the risks these financial firms are absorbing or intermediating and expect the companies to offer them a good return for their money. It is also expensive because, in most cases, the profits on the capital are taxed, whereas pension funds and some other investors can invest on a tax-free basis. As their profitability has come under pressure, many banks, for instance, have come to originate assets like mortgages but to package them in uniform, easily tradable securities like GNMAs. Investors with more capital and lower hurdle rates (that is, with cheaper or tax-free capital) purchase the securities and trade them like any other bonds.

The securitization process began with mortgages and has grown into an enormous activity in the United States, where two federal agencies, the Federal National Mortgage Association (Fannie Mae) and the Federal Home Loan Mortgage Corporation (Freddie Mac), provide credit guarantees between the originating banks and mortgage companies and the final investors. In 1990 some 40 percent of all mortgages originated in the United States were sold on to the public markets with their guarantees. The banks and thrifts have been able to stay in the mortgage business by recognizing that in the provision of capital for this business they were no longer the low-cost competitors. So they managed their capital accordingly, retaining customers like you or me who are largely unaware of what happens to the mortgage once we have signed it.

The logic of the approach to mortgages in the United States has spread to other countries to some degree. Salomon Brothers has exported the approach to the United Kingdom by offering fixed-rate mortgages for the first time in that market. They do this by placing the paper with investors interested in fixed-rate assets rather than on the balance sheets of building societies that need floating-rate assets to match their floating-rate deposits.

The success with mortgages has encouraged banks to seek out other assets that can be securitized, freeing up capital for activities where the returns are greater. Credit card receivables, again structured to protect the public market investors from most credit risks, have found a place in the public markets. The issuing banks retain a large interest rate spread between the rate they charge the cardholder and the rate at which they sell the securitized paper to the investor. This spread is more than enough to cover credit losses and operating costs and still generate a profit. The banks have been able to build a very profitable business to a much larger size than their balance sheets alone would have allowed and to earn more income, boosting the return on capital. The theme in all these transactions is to divide what had once been a single event into its risk components, and then find the institution that will accept each part of the risk at the lowest cost. At its extreme, some securitized financings have involved many financial firms taking on different parts of the risk to produce the lowest overall cost for the deal. Two or three firms might absorb different elements of the credit risk in which they specialize; another might absorb the interest rate risk on the floating rate debt; finally one more might absorb commodity risk in the loan. Then the straight fixed rate debt, devoid of so many risks, is sold to investors with the lowest internal investment hurdle rates.*

This capital management approach has not been limited to the retail assets on banks' and trading firms' balance sheets. In their wholesale activities, too, these firms have learned to manage the use of their capital to maximize returns. The theme is to retain your capital for assets or exposures for which you can get paid adequate returns, and to pass on the lower-yielding assets to investors or other financial firms that will be interested in them because they have lower costs of capital.

In the early 1980s, major U.S. banks like Bankers Trust, Citibank, and Chase Manhattan developed techniques to sell loans to other banks when lending spreads in the large corporate markets declined rapidly. This was more than the well-established process of syndicating a loan before it closed among a large number of banks. It involved selling the loan after it was closed. The fronting bank retained the crucial relationship with the client while using the lower-cost capital of other banks to take a large share of the assets. This secondary loan-trading market became a major way in which the capital-constrained U.S. banks funded their activities in the low-margin corporate banking markets in the 1980s. Again, they were managing their capital to treat it like any cost—something to be continuously fine-tuned to produce the best results.

Trading firms adopted the same approach, laying off their commitments to underwrite securities as quickly as they could after the deal had closed. At the same time, these underwriters wanted to control the relationship with the issuing companies more and more tightly. The *bought deal* in the underwriting market, where one firm purchased an entire issue from a company without first assembling an underwriting syndicate, came of age. The major securities houses in the United States, in the Euromarkets, and later in Japan that adopted this approach sealed the crucial relationship with the issuer by excluding all

---

*For a full explanation of the securitization process, see Jim Rosenthal, and Juan Ocampo, *Securitization of Credit*. John Wiley, New York, 1988.

other firms from their bid—but then had to move swiftly to lay off the position elsewhere in the market if they did not want to tie up too much of their capital.

Obviously these capital management approaches, and their many cousins and near cousins that are used by major firms, are only generic tools that managers must apply with care to each situation. But for financial firms pursuing any one of the five financial strategies, they are very important. They provide a score card that investors in the company can use to determine which risk/reward strategy is working and which is not. Just as pricing and cost management disciplines are crucial for any of the strategies, so is the discipline of capital management. None of these three games of inches will make up for inadequate risk/reward skills, but without them, even the best-thought-out approach will fail due to inadequate revenues, bloated costs, or inadequate returns on capital. These games of inches do not make a financial strategy, but they can destroy it if not managed with care.

Financial firms are indeed different from other types of companies. Whereas industrial or consumer products companies seek to avoid or lay off risk, financial firms must seek out risk and learn how to absorb, intermediate, or advise about the risk in a way that enables them to earn attractive returns. This unique characteristic of financial firms means they must focus on developing advantages in the management of risk/reward opportunities if they are to prosper. Without superior risk and reward strategies, a financial firm will not long deliver superior results. But this unique nature of financial firms does not mean that they are released from the basic need for wise day-to-day business management. The games of inches are as important to them as they are to other companies—but by themselves, they are not enough. What makes financial firms different is that they are, and should be, deliberately risk-seeking businesses. That is their unique challenge and opportunity—how to survive and win by seeking out risk.

Index

311

E - 2